T0185565

Pro Java ME MMAPI

Mobile Media API for Java Micro Edition

■■■

Vikram Goyal

Apress®

Pro Java ME MMAPI: Mobile Media API for Java Micro Edition

ISBN-13: 978-1-4842-2094-8

ISBN-10: 1-59059-639-0

DOI 10.1007/978-1-4302-0157-1

Lead Editor: Steve Anglin
Technical Reviewer: Robert Virkus
Editorial Board: Steve Anglin, Ewan Buckingham, Gary Cornell, Jason Gilmore, Jonathan Gennick, Jonathan Hassell, James Huddleston, Chris Mills, Matthew Moodie, Dominic Shakeshaft, Jim Sumser, Keir Thomas, Matt Wade
Project Manager: Sofia Marchant
Copy Edit Manager: Nicole LeClerc
Copy Editor: Julie McNamee
Assistant Production Director: Kari Brooks-Copony
Production Editor: Laura Esterman
Compositor and Artist: Kinetic Publishing Services, LLC
Proofreader: Nancy Riddiough
Indexer: Carol Burbo
Cover Designer: Kurt Krames
Manufacturing Director: Tom Debolski

Distributed to the book trade worldwide by Springer-Verlag New York, Inc., 233 Spring Street, 6th Floor, New York, NY 10013. Phone 1-800-SPRINGER, fax 201-348-4505, e-mail orders-ny@springer-sbm.com, or visit http://www.springeronline.com.

For information on translations, please contact Apress directly at 2560 Ninth Street, Suite 219, Berkeley, CA 94710. Phone 510-549-5930, fax 510-549-5939, e-mail info@apress.com, or visit http://www.apress.com.

The source code for this book is available to readers at http://www.apress.com in the Source Code section.

In loving memory of my Papa, who would go to the ends of the Earth to find that one particular book. This one is for you.

Contents at a Glance

Contents

About the Author

VIKRAM GOYAL is a software developer living in Brisbane, Australia. Vikram writes on Java development issues for the mobile environment at *http://today.java.net/pub/au/179.* You can contact him at *vikram@mmapibook.com.*

About the Technical Reviewer

ROBERT VIRKUS is the architect and lead programmer for the open source project J2ME Polish. He is an internationally recognized J2ME expert and is a member of Mobile Solution Group, Bremen, Germany.

After studying law and computer science in Bremen, Germany, and Sheffield, England, Robert began working in the mobile industry in 1999. He followed WAP and J2ME from their very beginnings and developed large-scale mobile betting applications.

In 2004, he founded Enough Software, the company behind J2ME Polish.

In his spare time, Robert enjoys the company of his friends and his dog, Benny. Other spare-time favorites are going to concerts of soul, ska, and punk-rock bands, and playing around with old computers such as Atari 400, Commodore 8296, and MCS Alpha 1.

Acknowledgments

Even though you see my name at the front of this book, it's the result of a collective effort on the part of several individuals. All these individuals need to be honored and acknowledged because without them, you would not be holding this book in your hands.

In order of my acquaintance with them, I would like to start with **Gary Cornell**, Apress Publisher and **Steve Anglin**, Java Editor at Apress for having the vision to build a comprehensive library of wireless Java books. **Tina Nielsen** as the Publisher's Assistant was quick with the contracts ensuring a speedy startup on the writing process. **Sofia Marchant**, the Project Manager for this book, was like a conductor who ensured that the various harmonies blended together perfectly to produce a book on time. **Robert Virkus**, the Technical Editor, was very forthcoming with his analysis of the text and code, and the final book is a better copy because of his efforts. **Julie McNamee**, who I hope reads and corrects this before it gets to you, worked tirelessly as the Copy Editor ensuring that I meant what I wrote. **Laura Esterman**, as the Production Editor, had an eagle eye that did not let even the tiniest of errors pass through via the production process.

There are, of course, other people involved in the production of this book, whom I never met, and a big Thank You to all of them for a job well done.

Finally a note about the loved ones: My mum and dad worked very hard to bring me up, and I can never thank them enough for their persistence and hard work.

My wife, Shellie, has suffered because of the hours I have spent in "the office" and deserves a reward for her patience. More than that, she supports me to be all I can and even puts up with my interference of her routine when I take away her mobile phone (to test the applications). To miss all the holidays and breaks and not complain is a feat in itself. I look forward to spending more time with her and to the upcoming addition to our family.

CHAPTER 1

Introducing Mobile Media API (MMAPI)

Embedding multimedia capabilities in a MIDlet is the next step in the evolution of MIDlets. Sun recognized early that audio and video are the future and introduced the Mobile Media API (MMAPI) via Java Specification Requests (JSR) 135 (*http://www.jcp.org/en/jsr/detail?id=135*).

The biggest requirement of the MMAPI specification was to ensure compatibility with small footprint devices while creating a specification that would be scalable for future—possibly more capable—devices. To this end, MMAPI has succeeded tremendously.

This chapter introduces you to MMAPI and explains several factors that make it a successful specification. You'll learn how this API fits in the overall scheme for MIDlet creation with the Mobile Information Device Profile (MIDP) 2.0. The chapter concludes with information on the current list of devices that support this API.

What Is Mobile Media API (MMAPI)?

MMAPI is the optional API that developers use to embed advanced multimedia capabilities in any Java-enabled device. If you've been using the audio capabilities in MIDP 2.0, you've already been using a subset of MMAPI. This subset is a forward compatible version of MMAPI created for limited-capability devices.

MMAPI allows you to create applications for Java-enabled devices that can discover and use the multimedia capabilities of the device that they are running on. You can play different formats of audio and video files from the network, a record store, or a Java Archive (JAR) file; have advanced control over the playback of these files; capture audio and video and take snapshots; play MIDI files; generate and play back tones; stream radio over the network; and do a whole lot more.

To encourage device manufactures to use this API in their Java-enabled devices, MMAPI was designed specifically to be protocol and format agnostic. In other words, this API does not come with assumptions about the supported protocol for accessing multimedia content, nor does it makes assumptions about the formats that it would be able to play. Thus, different device manufactures implement this API in their own way and make it available with the protocols and formats that their devices can support. This characteristic makes MMAPI a high-level interface and allows it to be compatible with any Java configuration.

Most devices, however, support some basic protocols and formats; for example, most allow you to access media over HTTP and play the WAV file format for audio and MP3 for video.

If a device supports a particular media format, MMAPI may mandate some control over the functionality of that format to create control uniformity across different devices. Other formats may require entirely different controls that may or may not be mandatory. Chapter 2 provides more information about mandatory controls for different formats in the "Feature Sets Implementations" section.

MMAPI Features and Requirements

MMAPI was designed for Java-enabled mobile devices, but the design is intentionally general enough that any Java-enabled device can benefit from it. This forced a set of rules on the API designers that they had to adhere to:

- **Low footprint API**: Because the main target of this API is Java-enabled mobile phones, which are severely constrained for available memory, the API must be able to support media playback in the available memory. Typically, because the Java-enabled mobile phones run on the Connected Limited Device Configuration (CLDC), the memory available ranges between 128KB and 512KB. This is the memory available for the virtual machine, the core libraries, your MIDlets, *and* MMAPI. MMAPI's place with MIDP is covered in the "How Does MMAPI Fit with MIDP 2.0?" section later in this chapter.
- **Ability to support multiple media types**: By defining the core API as a set of interfaces, MMAPI is protocol and format agnostic. Device manufactures supply their own implementation of MMAPI and implement interfaces that support the multimedia capabilities of their devices. This allows a wide range of protocols and formats to be supported based on the device, without any hard wiring of protocols and formats built-in the API itself. This makes MMAPI immensely scalable as new formats are discovered and supported by device manufacturers.
- **Support for basic controls**: Although the previous requirement states that MMAPI is protocol and format agnostic, some support for basic controls is guaranteed to be present. This creates uniform procedures for managing media, whatever format or protocol it may take. For example, all media can be played, started, or stopped.
- **Support for device capabilities discovery**: Similar to the previous requirement, all devices can be queried to discover their capabilities. This allows you to find out which protocols or formats the device supports.
- **Support for basic audio and tone generation**: Because MMAPI uses CLDC as the base minimum supported configuration, it requires some support for audio playback and tone generation. Note that the API mandates support for audio playback but doesn't restrict it to any particular format or protocol, in keeping with the ability to support multiple media types requirement. Device manufacturers are free to choose which format or playback they will support. Tone generation is important in Java-enabled mobile phones, and therefore, the API provides simple ways to play tones as well.

These requirements have led to an API interface that is truly extensible and capable of supporting a range of multimedia formats and protocols on an array of devices.

How Do I Get MMAPI?

If you have used the Java Wireless Toolkit (*http://java.sun.com/products/sjwtoolkit/download-2_3.html*) to develop your MIDlets, you already have MMAPI installed. The Toolkit comes with a reference implementation (RI) of this API installed as an optional package. Of course, MIDP 2.0 contains a subset of this API, so if you are only going to use a limited subset of MMAPI, you don't need this RI.

Most development environments (such as Netbeans and Eclipse) that support mobile application development include a version of this Toolkit, so MMAPI is included as an optional package.

Of course, the RI supplied with the Toolkit may not be your target platform (in all likelihood, it *won't* be your target platform because it contains only virtual devices). For example, you may be developing applications for the mobile devices supplied by Nokia. In which case, you need to download the implementation of MMAPI supplied by Nokia for its devices. This implementation will come bundled with the Toolkit supplied by Nokia (*http://forum.nokia.com/main/0,,034-2,00.html*). Similarly, different device manufacturers, and not just mobile device manufacturers, will supply their own implementations bundled in with their overall Java Wireless Toolkit.

In short, to start developing multimedia applications for Java-enabled devices using MMAPI, you need the Java Wireless Toolkit supplied by the device manufacturers. The last section in this chapter points you to some popular Toolkits. In this book, I will develop multimedia MIDlets using the Sun supplied Java Wireless Toolkit 2.3 and the Motorola SDK V5.2 (*http://www.motocoder.com*). In Chapters 8 and 9, I will also use the BenQ (formerly Siemens) CX 75 emulator (*http://www.benqmobile.com/developer*). The Sun Wireless Toolkit will be integrated in the Netbeans Integrated Development Environment (IDE) (*http://www.netbeans.org*), which will be the main development environment for the examples in this book. The Motorola device emulators will be used to test the MIDlets before deploying them on an actual Motorola device (the Motorola C975), and Chapters 8 and 9 will use the BenQ CX 75 emulator before testing them on the BenQ M75 device.

How Does MMAPI Fit with MIDP 2.0?

MMAPI is an optional package for the Java Micro Edition (ME) platform. MIDP 2.0 is a profile for the development of MIDlets, or applications for Java-enabled mobile devices, such as mobile phones and PDAs. MMAPI can be used with not just MIDP 2.0, but with any Java ME profile and configuration, provided an implementation is available for the device you are developing for. Refer to *Beginning J2ME: From Novice to Professional*, Third Edition, by Jonathan Knudsen and Sing Li (Apress, 2005) for a review of configurations, profiles, and development of MIDlets.

As you may already know, MMAPI is not the only optional package available for developing applications for the Java ME platform. Other prominent packages include the Web Services API (JSR 172), the Mobile 3D Graphics API (JSR 184), and the Location API (JSR 179). All of these optional packages, like the MMAPI package, are applicable to all available configurations, such as CLDC and Connected Device Configuration (CDC). On the other hand, an optional package such as the Wireless Messaging API (JSRs 120/205) is only relevant to the CLDC-based MID profile (MIDP).

MMAPI differs from the other optional packages because a scaled down version of it is present in MIDP 2.0 under the `javax.microedition.media` and `javax.microedition.media.control` packages. No other optional package makes an appearance in MIDP 2.0. So if you are developing applications that only require basic audio control, you don't need the full MMAPI installed or available. You would still be using MMAPI, just not the optional and bigger part of it. Your application will run on all devices that support MIDP 2.0, as MIDP 1.0 does not have the scaled version.

■ Note Some devices support the MMAPI in MIDP 1.0 as an optional library, for example, Nokia 3650, Nokia 7650, and Sony Ericsson 610. Applications that use the features of the optional package will only run on devices that have both MIDP 2.0 and the optional MMAPI package installed. The next section includes a comprehensive list of all such devices at the time of the book going to print.

Figure 1-1 gives a bird's eye view of how MMAPI, along with the other optional packages, fits in the development of applications for Java-enabled devices. Because this book concentrates on applications developed using MIDP, which are called MIDlets, I'll use that term when talking about such applications.

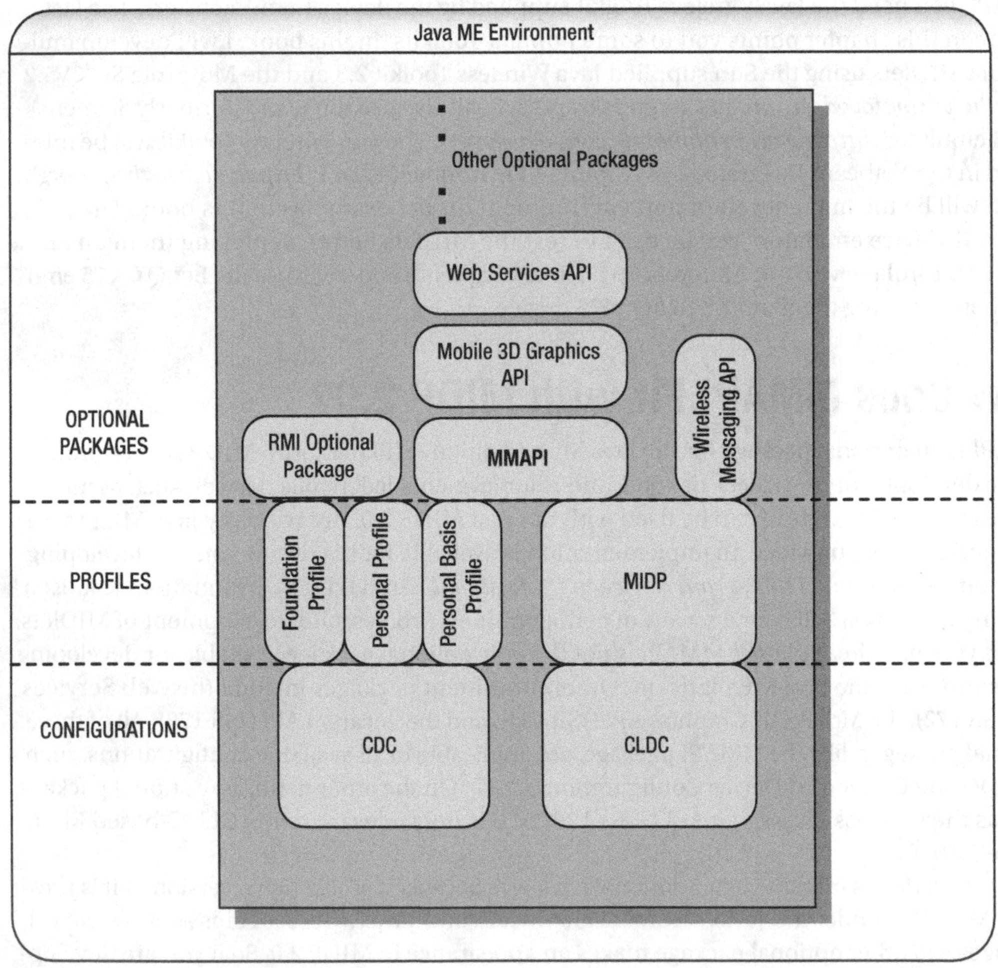

Figure 1-1. *Java ME development environment showing MMAPI as an optional package*

Who Supports MMAPI?

The specification for MMAPI was developed using the Java Community Process (JCP) (*http://www.jcp.org*) by a consortium of organizations, including device manufacturers, network operators, and multimedia companies, besides Sun Microsystems. This specification is numbered 135 and can be accessed at *http://www.jcp.org/en/jsr/detail?id=135.* The initial expert group for the development of this specification was composed of Sun, Nokia, and Beatnik.

Afterwards, several other organizations chipped in and lent their support for the development of this specification. A final release with a version number of 1.0 occurred on June 27th, 2002. A maintenance release (version 1.1) incorporating security enhancements and minor modifications was released a year later on June 26th, 2003, and is the version used for the examples in this book. Recently, JSR 234 has been released that identifies advanced supplements for this MMAPI.

As part of the development of this specification, Sun released a reference implementation of this API and a technology compatibility kit (TCK) that can be used to certify that an implementation of this API is compatible with the specification. This is par for any specification developed using the JCP. As stated earlier, this RI is bundled with the Java ME Wireless Toolkit supplied by Sun. Different device manufacturers supply their own implementations compatible with the TCK.

All devices that support MIDP 2.0 automatically support the scaled-down version of MMAPI. Many devices support the full version as an optional package. Table 1-1 gives a comprehensive list of devices that support MMAPI as an optional package.

Table 1-1. *Devices That Support MMAPI As an Optional Package*

Device Manufacturer	Supported Devices	Wireless Toolkit
Alcatel	One Touch 756	*http://www.my-onetouch.com*
BenQ	AX75 (MIDP 1.0), C70, C75, CF75/76, CL75, CX70/EMOTY, CX75, M75, S75, SL75, SXG75	*http://www.benq.com/developer*
Motorola	C975, E1000, A1000, A630, A780, A845, C380, C650, E398, E680, SLVR, T725, V180, V220, V3, V300, V303, V360, V400, V500, V525, V550, V551, V600, V620, V635, V8, V80, V980, i730	*http://www.motocoder.com*
Nokia	All Series 40, Series 60, and Series 80 based devices	*http://forum.nokia.com/main.html*
Samsung	E310, E380, E710, D400, P705, D410, 170X192 Series, E810, E310	*http://uk.samsungmobile.com/club/developers_club/cl_de_sdk_01.jsp*
Sony-Ericsson	W900, Z600, T610, T616, T618, V600, W800, K608, W550, W600, z520, D750, Z800, K600, K750, K300, K500, K700, J300, V800, Z500, S700, Z1010	*http://developer.sonyericsson.com*

Summary

This chapter introduced MMAPI, an optional package for the development of MIDlets that have embedded audio/video capabilities.

MMAPI provides these capabilities by defining a specification that is protocol and format agnostic, thereby increasing general acceptance and uptake. This has made MMAPI very popular and more and more devices support it.

With this introduction to MMAPI's features and requirements complete, the next chapter addresses the MMAPI architecture, which is key to understanding and using MMAPI.

CHAPTER 2

MMAPI Architecture

The MMAPI specification was created to cater to the widest range of multimedia options, and this is reflected in its architecture. It supports the most basic audio functions in a constrained device and at the same time provides ways to handle advanced multimedia data on more capable devices. MMAPI supports data from various sources and in various formats. MMAPI's protocol and format agnostic characteristic is achieved by a well-designed, high-level interface.

This chapter explains how the MMAPI specification achieves this aim of platform and format neutrality. You'll become familiar with the details of its architecture and the high-level objects that make it a successful specification. You'll see how the subset of MMAPI present in MIDP 2.0 differs from the overall specification. Finally, the chapter covers several small details of the MMAPI architecture, such as feature sets and security scenarios, to help you better understand and use MMAPI.

Understanding Players and DataSources

MIDlets can receive multimedia data from a variety of sources: located in a MIDlet's JAR file; come over the network via several different protocols (HTTP, RTP); sourced from the device's record store on which the MIDlet is running; and even come from user input via an audio or video capture device. In short, not only can this data be sourced from different locations, but also these locations can be accessed using any number of present or future protocols. At a conceptual level, MMAPI can handle all such locations and protocols without getting tied down to a specific protocol or location.

After data has been sourced, MMAPI should be able to process this data and make it available for rendering on the device. Processing multimedia data is inherently complex and requires the API to not only understand the data but decode it as well. Rendering the data and providing controls to manipulate it further complicates the process. Because MMAPI is a high-level interface, it doesn't mandate any specific data-processing functionality, besides a very low level of audio handling.

To achieve this neutrality with regard to sources of multimedia data and processing, MMAPI encapsulates these concepts into two high-level objects: `Player` and `DataSource`. Whereas `Player` is an interface that deals with processing and playing multimedia data, `DataSource` is an abstract class that encapsulates the task of data location and retrieval while maintaining protocol independence. The `Player` interface is defined in the `javax.microedition.media` package, and `DataSource` is defined in the `javax.microedition.media.protocol` package.

Player and DataSource work together to provide multimedia capability in a device. A Player instance parses data supplied to it from a DataSource instance. The Player may then render this data on the device and provide controls to manipulate it. For example, an audio Player can provide volume controls to increase or decrease the playback volume.

DataSource Basics

The DataSource class provides access to multimedia files by locating and opening a connection to them. You may not need to use this class directly, unless you are going to create a DataSource for a custom protocol or location. The MMAPI implementation provided by the device that you are targeting your MIDlet to will provide enough DataSource instances to satisfy most requirements.

Each DataSource is composed of one or more streams, known as a SourceStream (an interface in the javax.microedition.media.protocol package). A SourceStream is used to abstract a single stream of media data. Conceptually, multimedia data may be composed of several streams. For example, video files may be broken down into separate streams, one for audio and one for video. Thus, each individual stream can be acted on, independently of the other stream, thereby giving greater control than is possible otherwise. Most DataSource instances are composed of a single SourceStream.

A SourceStream also has the advantage of being randomly seekable, because it provides the seek(long where) method. This is an important consideration for multimedia data because it allows you to render this data from an arbitrary position. Of course, a particular stream may not support random seek operations, and this is reflected by the getSeekType() method. This method returns one of three integer constants, shown in Table 2-1.

Table 2-1. *Constants to Test a* SourceStream *for Seekability*

Constant	Description
NOT_SEEKABLE	The specified stream is not seekable.
SEEKABLE_TO_START	The specified stream can only be sought to its beginning.
RANDOM_ACCESSIBLE	A true seekable stream, this constant indicates that the specified stream can be randomly accessed anywhere.

A SourceStream has one more advantage. For multimedia data that supports it, a SourceStream can be used to read the logical transfer size of the data. For example, video data is normally composed of individual frames, so the logical transfer size of the data would be the size of one such frame. This allows you to create an in-memory buffer of the right size, equivalent to or greater than the size of the frame, to read data, thereby creating an efficient data read process. SourceStream instances that support this concept return a positive integer value for the method getTransferSize() and return -1 if they don't support it.

A DataSource instance is created by providing the location of the media to its constructor: DataSource(String locator). The locator parameter is specified in a Uniform Resource Identifier (URI) (*http://www.ietf.org/rfc/rfc2396.txt*) syntax—<scheme>:<scheme-specific-part>—which delineates the delivery protocol, the location of the media file, and its name. You are already familiar with HTTP for accessing files, which provides an easy example:

```
http://www.mmapibook.com/resources/media/audio/chapter2/siren.wav
```

where http refers to the protocol, http://www.mmapibook.com/resources/media/audio/chapter2 to the location, and siren.wav to the name of the file. Appendix B gives an overview of this syntax.

Player Basics

The Player interface is your handle to playing and managing your multimedia data. It provides methods to render, control, and synchronize the data with other players, and listen to player events such as starting, stopping, and pausing the data.

All media types, except for simple tones, require a Player instance for playback and control. A media type is mapped to a Player instance that can handle its playback by evaluating the extension of the file that contains the multimedia data and mapping it to a MIME type. For example, if you wanted to play an audio file with the wav extension, a Player instance that can handle the MIME type audio/x-wav is created. Similarly, a file with an mp4 extension results in the creation of a Player instance that can play video/mp4. In the next section, you'll learn about the Manager class that does this mapping between MIME types and Player instances.

Player instances are independent of the media type that they are playing and only depend on the implementation provided by the device manufacturer. This allows you to use generic methods to manipulate this data. So to start the playback of *any* multimedia data, you use the start() method, which starts playback as soon as possible. To pause, you use the stop() method, which pauses the playback. To close the data and release any resources associated with it, you use the close() method, and so on. Chapter 4 will introduce you to all the methods that you can use to control media playback.

If you are creating a multimedia MIDlet that is responsible for simultaneously playing multiple Player instances, you will run into synchronization issues, for example, making sure that video playback starts simultaneously with a separate audio track. In such cases, synchronizing different Player instances can be a problem without a timing reference. Each Player instance has a way to measure time using the TimeBase interface. This interface provides a constantly ticking source of time, and each Player instance has a default TimeBase instance built in. You can access this default instance by using the method getTimeBase(); you can override this default instance with your own implementation by using the setTimeBase(TimeBase base) method. To synchronize two Player instances so that they use the same TimeBase, you can use player2.setTimeBase(player1.getTimeBase()) code. To reset a Player instance's TimeBase, you can pass a null value to the setTimeBase(TimeBase base) method.

Player instances generate events during different stages of their working. By implementing the PlayerListener interface, you can receive notifications of these asynchronous events. This interface defines several common events, but you can create your own proprietary events as well. Chapter 4 discusses the event management of Player instances in detail.

Understanding the Manager Class

The Manager class in the javax.microedition.media package provides developers access to Player instances. These Player instances, as you already know, source their data from DataSource instances. In a nutshell, a Manager class is a bridge between a DataSource and a corresponding Player instance. Figure 2-1 shows this relationship.

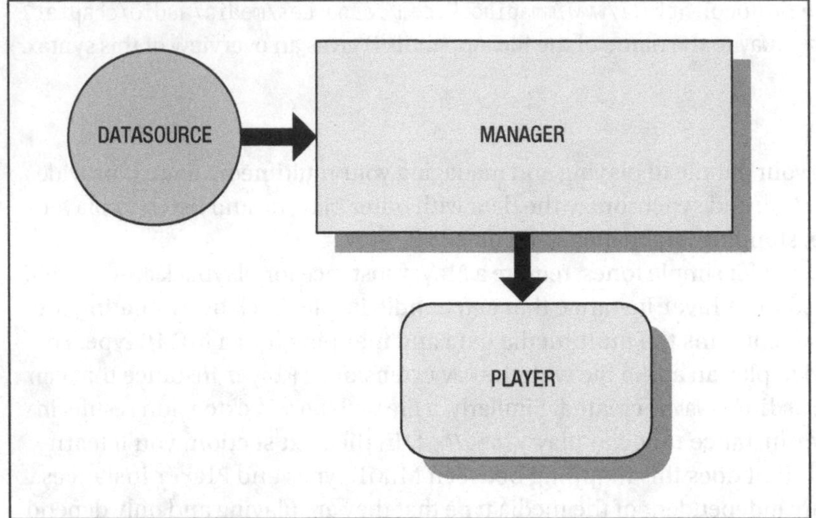

Figure 2-1. *The* Manager *class is the bridge between a* DataSource *and a* Player.

Creating Player Instances

Using methods of the Manager class is the only way to create Player instances in MMAPI. To this end, this class provides three such methods. Not surprisingly, all the methods are called createPlayer() and are static. The methods differ in the way the location of the multimedia data is provided to them.

As expected, createPlayer(DataSource source) is one of these methods. You create an instance of a DataSource using the DataSource(String locator) constructor and pass this to the createPlayer() method. The other two methods eventually call this method internally to create the Player instance.

You are more likely to use the createPlayer(String locator) method because it is more convenient than the previous method. Instead of having to create a DataSource, you only specify the location of the multimedia data using the locator parameter. The method internally translates it into a DataSource and creates a Player that is suitable for handling the multimedia content.

The third method, createPlayer(InputStream is, String type), provides a slightly different way of creating players. It allows you to create an InputStream on the data and specify the content type of the data yourself, because the MIME type of the data cannot be determined with file extensions. This method has a further disadvantage because by using an InputStream instead of a SourceStream, it disallows random seek operations within the multimedia data. Player instances created with this method are not likely to support such operations.

Creating Player Instances for MIDI and Tone Sounds

Some Player instances do not require a physical file or location. For example, when you create a MIDlet that will play tones or Musical Instrument Digital Interface (MIDI) sounds, you need to tell the device to use its built-in MIDI synthesizer to play these sounds based on a supplied MIDI or tone sequence. The Manager class provides constants for creating Player instances based on these requirements. Table 2-2 gives details of these constants.

Table 2-2. *MIDI and Tone* Player *Constants*

Constant Name	Constant Value	Content Type	Usage
MIDI_DEVICE_LOCATOR	device://midi	audio/midi	Manager.createPlayer (Manager.MIDI_DEVICE_LOCATOR)
TONE_DEVICE_LOCATOR	device://tone	audio/x-tone-seq	Manager.createPlayer (Manager.TONE_DEVICE_LOCATOR)

You can still create MIDI and tone Player instances by specifying physical locations for them. For example, to create a MIDI Player based on a physical file, the extension of the file should be either mid or kar. Similarly, for a tone Player instance the extension of the file should be jts.

Because most simple devices support tone generation, the Manager class goes one step further by providing a static method to play single tones: playTone(int note, int duration, int volume). This provides a handy method that plays a single note for the specified duration and at the specified volume. Chapter 6 covers tone playing in detail.

Supported Protocols and Content Types

With MMAPI development for disparate devices, it becomes imperative to know beforehand what protocols are supported and what multimedia content can be rendered by the target device. The Manager class provides two methods that can help you understand the capabilities of a target MMAPI implementation.

The static getSupportedContentTypes(String protocol) method provides a list of all supported content types for a particular protocol. If you pass a null parameter to this method, it will give you a list of all content types supported by this device's MMAPI implementation. The static getSupportedProtocols(String contentType) method does the opposite; given a content type, it tells you all the protocols over which it can be accessed. If you pass a null parameter to this method, it will give you a list of all protocols supported by the device's MMAPI implementation.

Table 2-3 lists the output of running these methods on three different environments.

Table 2-3. *Supported Protocols and Content Types on Different MMAPI Implementations*

Method	Sun Java Wireless Toolkit 2.3	Motorola C975 Emulator	Motorola C975 Actual Device
getSupported ContentTypes (null)	audio/x-tone-seq, audio/x-wav, audio/midi, audio/sp-midi, image/gif, video/mpeg, video/vnd.sun.rgb565	audio/x-wav audio/x-tone-seq audio/midi video/mng video/x-rgb	audio/amr, audio/x-amr, audio/amr-wb audio/x-amr-wb, audio/mp4, audio/x-mp4, audio/3gp, audio/mp3, audio/x-mp3, audio/mpeg3, audio/x-mpeg3, audio/mpeg, audio/x-mpeg, audio/mpg, audio/x-mpg, audio/wav, audio/x-wav, audio/au, audio/x-au, audio/basic, audio/asf, audio/x-ms-wma, audio/x-pn-realaudio, audio/midi, audio/x-midi, audio/mid, audio/x-mid, audio/sp-midi, audio/mobile-xmf, audio/imelody, audio/ x-imelody, audio/imy, audio/x-imy, text/ x-imelody, audio/ x-tone-seq, video/mp4, video/x-mp4, video/3gp, video/asf, video/x-ms-asf, video/x-ms-wmv, video/x-pn-realvideo, video/vnd.rn-realvideo, application/x-pn-realmedia, application/ vnd.rn-realmedia, image/gif, audio, video, camera
getSupported Protocols(null)	device, http, file, capture	http, https, device, capture	file, rtsp, http, https, device, capture
getSupported ContentTypes ("capture")	audio/x-wav video/vnd.sun.rgb565	audio/x-wav video/x-rgb	audio, video, camera
getSupported Protocols ("audio/x-wav")	http, file, capture	http, https, capture	file, rtsp, http, https

As you can see from Table 2-3, the supported protocols and content types vary greatly depending on the target device or emulator. Even though the emulator for Motorola C975 should support the same protocols and content types as the actual device, the difference is huge, especially for the supported content types. Actual device configurations vary greatly from their supposed emulators, and this is a typical result. Your MIDlets should always be tested on actual devices before bringing them into a production environment.

Understanding Controls

MMAPI defines Control objects that provide fine-grained control over the functionality of a Player. For example, if you have created a Player object to play an audio file, you will want to control its volume. Rather than provide volume control as a method in the Player interface, the interface VolumeControl is used. Volume is a type of control that is applicable to audio files, indeed to almost all multimedia files, but there may be several such individual controls that are exposed by individual media types. For example, FramePositioningControl is a control that is exposed by video players to control precise positioning of individual frames. The Control interface in javax.microedition.media package is used to abstract this concept.

MMAPI defines some standard controls in the javax.microedition.media.control package, but you are free to create your own controls by implementing the Control interface. The controls in the javax.microedition.media.control package are all defined as interfaces, and it is left for actual MMAPI implementations to provide concrete classes for them. Table 2-4 lists these controls and provides a brief explanation of each control.

Table 2-4. *Standard MMAPI Controls*

Control Interface	Description
FramePositioningControl	A control for video data that allows access to individual frames.
GUIControl	A control for data that requires a display, such as video.
MetaDataControl	Used to determine the metadata information stored within a media stream, such as title, copyright, author, and so on.
MIDIControl	A fully functional control that enables access to a device's MIDI player.
PitchControl	Used to control the pitch (frequency) of audio data.
RateControl	Used to control the playback rate of a Player.
RecordControl	Allows you to control the recording of data from a capture device, such as video from a camera or audio from a sound recorder.
StopTimeControl	A control that allows you to set a preset time when you want the Player to stop playing.
TempoControl	Similar to RateControl, this control allows you to change the tempo (speed) of playback for an audio Player, typically, a MIDI Player.
ToneControl	A fully functional control that allows you to play monotonic tone sequences.
VideoControl	Extends GUIControl and controls the display of video.
VolumeControl	The simplest control that allows you to control the volume of audio in a Player.

To get a list of controls that a Player instance exposes, use the method getControls() on the Player instance. To get to an actual control, use the method getControl(String controlType) and pass to it the name of the control interface. For example, to access the VolumeControl on a Player, you can use the method getControl("VolumeControl"). These methods are not defined in the Player interface, but the Controllable interface that the Player interface implements. As a point of interest, both SourceStream interface and the DataSource abstract class implement the Controllable interface, which gives you access to type-specific controls, if available.

As you may expect, some Player instances may expose multiple controls. For example, a Player created to handle video data will expose both a VideoControl and a VolumeControl at the very least. An audio player may expose a VolumeControl, a RateControl, a PitchControl, and a ToneControl. Some Player instances may support no controls, in which case, getControls() returns a zero length array (and not a null value).

After you have access to a control, you have access to the behavior of that control (and control of the underlying multimedia data). Each control is different in terms of its behavior and exposes methods that manipulate this behavior. For example, FramePositioningControl has a method called seek(int frameNumber) that when invoked on a video Player, renders the specified frame in the video on to the display. The method skip(int framesToSkip) skips the given number of frames from the current video position. Similarly, other controls define their own methods that best allow you to manipulate the underlying multimedia data. Detailed descriptions of the controls listed in Table 2-4 are scattered throughout this book.

The MIDP 2.0 Subset

MMAPI is an optional package, which means that device manufacturers may choose not to include an implementation for it in their devices. However, if the profile on a device is MIDP 2.0, then the device includes a subset of MMAPI. This subset was created to provide a base common MMAPI implementation for the MID 2.0 profile.

This subset was created to solve two problems: (1) resource constrained devices do not have enough processing power to display video-based multimedia data, and (2) even if these devices were powerful enough, they would be constrained in terms of the size of a MMAPI implementation. To support extensive processing and multiple multimedia data formats, the size of a MMAPI implementation can be large.

To solve these problems, the MIDP 2.0 subset of MMAPI ignores some of the requirements of the complete set. Although still a forward compatible version of MMAPI, it ignores some of the controls and provides a scaled-down version of the Manager class. Table 2-5 lists how the MIDP 2.0 subset differs from the complete MMAPI implementation

Table 2-5. *MIDP 2.0 MMAPI Subset Features*

Feature	Description
Audio only	The subset only supports audio-based data. Thus, no video-based controls, such as VideoControl, GUIControl, or FramePositioningControl, are present, and any content type that is video-based is ignored.
No MIDI support	Even in audio, only simple tones and sampled audio is supported, ignoring MIDI. Thus MIDIControl is absent and only ToneControl and VolumeControl is provided.
No support for synchronization	The subset is missing the TimeBase interface, and the Player interface is without the setTimeBase() and getTimeBase() methods. Thus, multiple Player instances cannot be synchronized to play back simultaneously.
No support for recording	Even for audio data, recording and capturing are not enabled, and thus RecordControl is absent.
No support for controlling the rate of audio playback	TempoControl and RateControl are absent.

Feature	Description
Controlling audio frequency is not supported	`PitchControl` is absent.
Other missing controls	`StopTimeControl` and `MetaDataControl` are also not supported.
No support for custom protocols	The `javax.microedition.media.protocol` package is excluded. The `Manager` class, therefore, does not include the `createPlayer(DataSource source)` method.

These features make the subset a lightweight implementation that meets the design goals of MIDP 2.0, including support for low footprint audio playback functionality in MIDlets, support for tone generation, and consistent media playback options. At the same time, the subset maintains upward compatibility with the MMAPI specification and is a true subset.

Feature Set Implementations

With intrinsic support for such a diverse range of features, protocols, and file formats, MMAPI is a truly flexible specification. It doesn't mandate support for any formats but allows device manufacturers to build in support for formats that they deem fit. However, with this flexibility, application development becomes a bit more difficult. You can query for a device implementation to give you a list of supported protocols and formats, but are you guaranteed that it will behave how you expect it to?

To alleviate this concern and to bring about some uniformity in the way multimedia data is controlled, MMAPI specification defines feature sets. A *feature set* is a grouping of multimedia data that has some common features. The API defines required and expected behavior for each feature set if the feature set is implemented by a device manufacturer's implementation. This way, if you are developing applications that target a particular feature set, you are guaranteed that it will behave by exposing controls that are similar across different manufacturers.

The simplest feature set is called *sampled audio*. As far as MMAPI is concerned, sampled audio refers to any audio data that is digital in its format, ignoring its origin. If a device supports sampled audio, it *should* implement the `VolumeControl` and `StopTimeControl` interfaces. Note the emphasis on should, which implies that this is a recommended practice, which barring any adverse circumstance, must be implemented. The MIDP 2.0 MMAPI subset is good example. Because it supports sampled audio, it should implement both `VolumeControl` and `StopTimeControl`; however, it only implements `VolumeControl` and ignores `StopTimeControl`.

MIDI is the next feature set. If a device's MMAPI implementation declares that it supports the MIDI feature set, which means that it allows you to play external audio files with extensions of `mid` or `kar`, it *should* implement `VolumeControl`, `MIDIControl`, `TempoControl`, `PitchControl`, and `StopTimeControl`. Again, notice the emphasis on should. Although there's no guarantee that the device will support all these controls, there's a good chance that it will.

The *Tone Sequence* feature set is the first set that mandates a "must" requirement. If a device allows you to play tone sequences, it *must* implement the `ToneControl` interface. If the device doesn't implement this interface, then it does not conform to the MMAPI specification. The Tone Sequence feature set is applicable to `Player` instances that are created using the `Manager.createPlayer(Manager.TONE_DEVICE_LOCATOR)` method.

Similar to the Tone Sequence set, the *Interactive MIDI* feature set is applicable to `Player` instances that are created using the `Manager.createPlayer(Manager.MIDI_DEVICE_LOCATOR)` method, which allows you to create MIDlets that directly manipulate the device's MIDI player. This feature set *must* implement the MIDIControl interface.

Finally, the *video* feature set applies to all video data. If video is supported by a device's MMAPI implementation, it *must* allow you to control the video with the VideoControl interface. The implementation *should* also support FramePositioningControl, the StopTimeControl, and the VolumeControl, but it doesn't have to. If it doesn't support the last three controls, but supports VideoControl, it is still an MMAPI-compliant implementation.

Security Architecture

As you now know, MMAPI does not work in isolation; it is an add-on or optional package that works on top of a profile. In this book, we are concerned with exploring MMAPI for the profile for small devices, MIDP 2.0; however, as explained in Chapter 1, MMAPI can be run on any compatible profile and configuration.

The capability to acquire and render multimedia data on any profile or configuration, even with an optional package such as MMAPI, creates a few problems with the security architecture of the device in question. The device must be able to control certain aspects of the multimedia process, such as recording using a camera and microphone for devices that have them. Similarly, the network and device's file system should be accessed only by a permission-based model.

Keeping these issues in mind, MMAPI allows control over the methods that are security sensitive. However, the specification does not dictate a particular architecture, and leaves it to specific implementations to work out the exact details, much like the interfaces that it describes for Player and Control objects.

Methods that are security conscious throw a SecurityException if permission to run that method has not been granted. Table 2-6 lists all these methods, the classes/interfaces they reside in, and the permissions required to make them run.

Table 2-6. *Security Conscious Methods*

Method Name	Method Class/ Interface	Permission Required
setRecordLocation(String locator)	RecordControl	javax.microedition.media.control. RecordControl
setRecordStream (OutputStream stream)	RecordControl	javax.microedition.media.control. RecordControl
getSnapshot(String type)	VideoControl	javax.microedition.media.control. VideoControl.getSnapshot
createPlayer(String locator)	Manager	
createPlayer(InputStream is, String type)	Manager	
createPlayer(DataSource source)	Manager	
realize()	Player	
prefetch()	Player	
start()	Player	
start()	DataSource	
connect()	DataSource	

Permissions are granted by the profile that MMAPI is running in. This is, in turn, either inherently built in the profile—for example, if recording is not supported at all then permissions will be false irrespective of any other conditions—or requested from the user running an application on the device to explicitly enable them.

As you may expect, the first three methods in Table 2-6 relate to privacy issues. An application must not start recording, even if the underlying device can record, without an explicit permission from the user of the application. The rest of the methods are related with general security issues of network access for data retrieval and depend on the protection domain that the MIDlet is running in. If data has to be retrieved over HTTP, then the user must be asked if transmission over the network is permitted, as it may result in charges billed to the user.

For HTTP/HTTPS access, the required permissions are `javax.microedition.io.Connector.http` and `javax.microedition.io.Connector.https`, respectively. Permissions are specified in the descriptor file (the Java Application Descriptor or JAD file) for the MIDlet and can be granted to a signed MIDlet. Refer to *Beginning J2ME* by Knudsen and Li (Apress, 2005) for an understanding of the process required for enabling permissions in Java ME. Chapter 5 also contains a detailed example of this process.

Summary

The MMAPI architecture was purposefully built to be extensible and not cater to a particular format or protocol. `DataSources`, `Players`, and `Controls` make the MMAPI a very flexible API that gives freedom to its implementers to support any media types, and at the same time, be true to the contract specified between the MMAPI interfaces.

This chapter explained this contract by specifying the MMAPI architecture. You saw the way the interfaces interact with each other and how device manufacturers can implement them. Using three different MMAPI implementations, you saw the different contents and protocols that they supported and how they still provided support for the basic MMAPI/MIDP 2.0 subset. Finally, you understood the security issues involved in using the libraries and classes of MMAPI.

The next chapter will leave the theory of MMAPI behind for a moment to introduce your very first media player using MMAPI.

CHAPTER 3

Getting Started with MMAPI

By now, you know that MMAPI is an optional API for building multimedia-enabled MIDlets. You also know that creating a MMAPI application requires knowledge of not just the MMAPI architecture, but also the MIDlet architecture, which you should be well conversant with. MMAPI MIDlets don't require any modifications to the way MIDlets are created, and basic architectural knowledge of the API is enough to get you started creating the simplest of multimedia MIDlets. You have already learned about the architecture in Chapter 2, and in this chapter, you'll use this knowledge to create two simple MMAPI MIDlets.

The first MIDlet is an example of the simplest MMAPI MIDlet that can be created. It plays an audio file and shows basic interaction between the `Manager` class and the `Player` interface. The second MIDlet is much more advanced and shows the interplay between the `Manager` class and the `Player` and the `Control` interfaces.

Both MIDlets will give you grounding in MMAPI MIDlet creation. Consider them as the Hello World MIDlets of the MMAPI world.

A Simple Multimedia Player

The simplest MMAPI MIDlet that can be built allows you to easily play a multimedia file from within your MIDlet without worrying about controls, feature sets, or security architecture. If all you're doing is adding some sampled audio (or any other media) in a game, MMAPI allows you to do so in two lines of code. Listing 3-1 shows this code within a complete MIDlet.

Listing 3-1. *A Simple MMAPI MIDlet*

```
package com.apress.chapter3;

import javax.microedition.midlet.MIDlet;

import javax.microedition.media.Manager;
import javax.microedition.media.Player;

public class SimplePlayer extends MIDlet {

  public void startApp() {
```

```
    try {

      Player player =
        Manager.createPlayer(
          getClass().getResourceAsStream("/media/audio/chapter3/baby.wav"),
          "audio/x-wav");

      player.start();

    } catch(Exception e) {
      e.printStackTrace();
    }
  }

  public void pauseApp() {
  }

  public void destroyApp(boolean unconditional) {
  }
}
```

To keep things simple at this stage, the media file is played by creating an `InputStream` on a wav file, which is embedded in the MIDlet's JAR. This media file is kept in the folder `media/audio/chapter3` and is called `baby.wav` (which is the sound of a baby crying).

Of course, you don't need to play an audio file only. You can substitute the wav file with a video file, provided the emulator supports the format of the video file. The video will not show anywhere, because this listing doesn't provide a mechanism to show the video. You can substitute the wav file for a midi, tone, or any other supported audio format. The point is that playing multimedia files using the MMAPI is as simple as creating a `Player` instance using the `Manager` class and calling method `start()` on it.

Let's analyze the two lines that make up the core of this MIDlet.

```
Player player = Manager.createPlayer(
 getClass().getResourceAsStream("/media/audio/chapter3/baby.wav"),    "audio/x-wav");
```

A `Player` instance is created here using the `Manager` class's `createPlayer(InputStream is, String contentType)` method. Simpler still would have been to use the `createPlayer(String locator)` method, which would let the `Manager` class figure out the content type of the audio file. However, using this method would have required specifying a protocol to access the file. Because the file is stored in the MIDlet's JAR file, there is no protocol to access it directly. If the multimedia file had been stored on the Internet or the emulator/device's local file system, you could have used either `http://<url-to-file>` or `file:///<file-location>` (if the optional `FileConnection` API [JSR 75] is supported by the device), respectively. However, to access files over these protocols would require explicit permission from the user or a signed MIDlet requesting these permissions, and therefore, this example would not remain simple anymore.

Note Some devices support the `resource` protocol for accessing files stored in a JAR file. In such devices, you can use `resource://media/audio/chapter3/baby.wav` or similar to create a locator for a media file. However, because this support is not universal, use it only if you are confident that the target device(s) will understand it.

The second line of code,

```
player.start();
```

is where the `Player` instance gets to start playing the media file. A lot of things happen behind the scenes when you call this method, but effectively, the media file will play back as soon as possible when this method is called. The method returns as soon as the media has started playing. The `start()` method is also used to resume playback of a media file that was previously paused (or had stopped because it had reached its end), with playback starting at the point where the media was paused.

Both the lines of code described previously throw several exceptions. Although Listing 3-1 ignores the individual exceptions, you can catch them and deal with them individually. Table 3-1 shows a list of these exceptions and information on which method throws what exception.

Table 3-1. *Exceptions Thrown Playing a Media File Using MMAPI*

Exception	Thrown By	Description

`IllegalArgumentException`	`createPlayer(String InputStream, String type)`
	`createPlayer(String locator)`
	`createPlayer(DataSource source)`
		Thrown if the `InputStream`, locator, or `DataSource` is null.

`MediaException`	`createPlayer()`—all three variants	Thrown if a `Player` instance cannot be created for the given stream and type, `DataSource`, or locator, possibly because the protocol and/or the format is not supported.
`IOException`	`createPlayer()`—all three variants	Thrown if connection to the source of the media file encounters a problem, such as network congestion, corrupt file, and so on.
`SecurityException`	`createPlayer()`—all three variants	Thrown if permission to create a `Player` instance has not been granted to the calling MIDlet.
`IllegalStateException`	`start()`	Thrown if the `Player` instance cannot be started because it has been closed. More about `Player` states appears in Chapter 4.

Continued

Table 3-1. *Continued*

Exception	Thrown By	Description
`MediaException`	`start()`	A catchall exception that is thrown if the `Player` instance can't be started because of any number of reasons.
`SecurityException`	`start()`	The calling MIDlet may have permission to create the `Player` instance but not to start it, in which case, it throws this exception.

After a `Player` instance has been started, it can be paused, closed, restarted, played repeatedly, and controlled by instances of the `Control` interface. A `Player` also fires information about various events that can be listened to and appropriate activities performed based on these events. Chapter 4 will cover handling `Player` events and the lifecycle of a `Player` instance. For now, let's create a slightly advanced `Player` instance that can be paused, restarted, played in a loop, and closed.

Creating a Functional Player

Listing 3-1 created a very basic `Player` instance. In this section, you'll learn to create a slightly more advanced and functional `Player` that allows you to select a media file to play from a list and gives you control over the volume.

Before we get into the actual code, let's look at Figure 3-1, which shows the finished MIDlet, called `AudioPlayer`, in operation using the Sun Java Wireless Toolkit 2.3 DefaultColorPhone emulator, the Motorola C975 emulator, and the Motorola C975 actual device.

Figure 3-1. *AudioMIDlet shows list of audio files on Sun's DefaultColorPhone emulator, Motorola C975 emulator, and Motorola C975 device.*

The MIDlet shows a list of three audio files that the user can select and play. Figure 3-2 shows the resulting screens when the user selects one of these files.

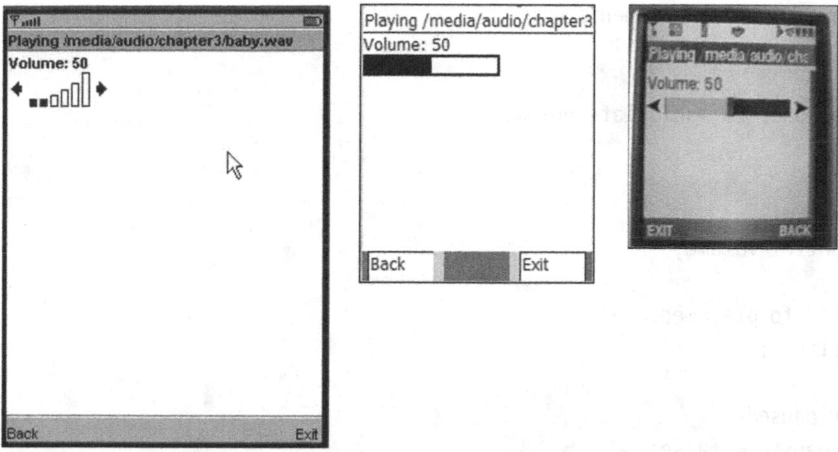

Figure 3-2. *Playing* `baby.wav` *in Sun's DefaultColorPhone emulator,* `applause.wav` *in Motorola C975 emulator, and* `laughter.wav` *in Motorola C975 device*

When a file is selected from the list, a new screen shows the actual file name and location, plays this file, and allows the user to control the volume of the playback. This volume control is rendered on the screen using a `Gauge` item. The user can use this gauge to increase or decrease the volume, and the actual volume level is reflected on the screen. The user can also choose to go back to the audio list or exit from the MIDlet. The audio file is played twice unless the user exits or goes back to the list before that.

Writing the Code

The code for this MIDlet is divided into two files: `AudioPlayer` and `AudioPlayerCanvas`. `AudioPlayerCanvas` is responsible for the canvas that the user sees when an audio file is being played and allows the user to increase or decrease the volume. More importantly, it manages the playing of the audio files and their lifecycle when they are paused or stopped. `AudioPlayerCanvas` is shown in Listing 3-2.

Listing 3-2. `AudioPlayerCanvas`*—an Interface for Playing Audio Files*

```
package com.apress.chapter3;

import javax.microedition.lcdui.*;
import javax.microedition.media.*;
import javax.microedition.media.control.*;

public class AudioPlayerCanvas implements ItemStateListener {

  // the parent MIDlet
  private AudioPlayer parent;
```

```
  // form that contains canvas elements
  private Form form;

  // gauge to allow user to manipulate volume
  private Gauge gauge;

  // the volume control
  private VolumeControl volume;

  // the player used to play media
  private Player player;

  // is the player paused?
  private boolean paused = false;

  public AudioPlayerCanvas(AudioPlayer parent) {

    this.parent = parent;

    // create form and add elements and listeners
    form = new Form("");
    gauge = new Gauge("Volume: 50", true, 100, 50);
    form.append(gauge);
    form.addCommand(parent.exitCommand);
    form.addCommand(parent.backCommand);
    form.setCommandListener(parent);

    // a change in volume gauge will be handled by this class
    form.setItemStateListener(this);
  }

  public void playMedia(String locator) {

    try {

      // create the player for the specified string locator
      player = Manager.createPlayer(
        getClass().getResourceAsStream(locator), "audio/x-wav");

      // realize it
      player.realize();

      // get the volume control
      volume = (VolumeControl)player.getControl("VolumeControl");

      // initialize it to 50
      volume.setLevel(50);
```

```
      // initialize the gauge
      gauge.setValue(volume.getLevel());
      gauge.setLabel("Volume: " + volume.getLevel());

      // play it twice
      player.setLoopCount(2);

      // start the player
      player.start();

      // set the title of the form
      form.setTitle("Playing " + locator);

    } catch(Exception e) {
      e.printStackTrace();
    }

  }

  public void pauseMedia() {

    // if the player needs to be paused, either due to an incoming call,
    // or due to user actions
    if(player != null) {
      try {
        player.stop();
        paused = true;
      } catch(Exception e) {}
    }
  }

  public void restartMedia() {

    // restarting after player was paused
    if(player != null) {
      try {
        player.start();
        paused = false;
      } catch(Exception e) {}
    }
  }

  public boolean isPlayerPaused() {
    return paused;
  }

  public Form getForm() {
    return this.form;
```

```
  }

  public void itemStateChanged(Item item) {

    // there is only one item on the form, the gauge, and any change in its
    // value means the user wants to increase or decrease the playback volume
    volume.setLevel(gauge.getValue());
    gauge.setLabel("Volume: " + volume.getLevel());
  }

  public void cleanUp() {

    // clean up, either due to user action or AMS call
    if(player != null) {
      player.close();
      player = null;
    }
  }
}
```

AudioPlayerCanvas creates a Form that displays the volume control and allows the user to interact with it. It attaches a Gauge to this Form for the volume control and adds the back and exit commands to the Form. These commands are created in the parent, which is the main MIDlet class AudioPlayer, shown in Listing 3-3. However, the canvas takes care of any changes to the Gauge (and consequently to the volume of a Player instance) by implementing the itemStateChanged(Item item) method.

A Player instance is created when the parent MIDlet calls the playMedia(String locator) method on this canvas. This method attempts to create a Player instance by using the createPlayer(InputStream is, String contentType) method, guessing the content to be of type audio/x-wav. The next step after a successful player creation is the realization of the player, which is done by calling player.realize(). You'll learn more about realization in Chapter 4, but suffice to say at this point that after a Player instance has been realized, it can expose any controls that may be associated with it. Thus, you couldn't have accessed the VolumeControl associated with the player without actually realizing the player. This VolumeControl is used to initialize the Gauge besides allowing the user to control the volume in the itemStateChanged (Item item) method.

By calling player.setLoopCount(2), the player plays the audio file twice. By default, this value is set to 1, and if you wanted to play the file indefinitely, you could set this value to -1. Setting this value to 0 will result in an IllegalArgumentException. The loop count must be set before the start() method is called or rather when the Player instance is in a paused state; otherwise, an IllegalStateException will be thrown.

The Player instance is paused in the pauseMedia() method, which calls the stop() method to pause the media at the current media time. The next time the player is started, or rather, restarted, it will resume from the same media time. This occurs when the restartMedia() method is called, where the audio file's playback is restarted by a call to the start() method on the Player instance. Although this example does not allow the user to pause or restart the playback explicitly by way of commands, this behavior can be easily simulated by an incoming phone call when this MIDlet is being run.

The final noteworthy method is the `cleanUp()` method that closes each `Player` instance after it is no longer required. This method is called any time the user issues the `exit` or `back` commands. Calling `close()` on a `Player` instance releases any resources held by the player (including the audio file and the audio device, such as a speaker). After a `Player` instance has been closed, it can no longer be used.

In a nutshell, the `Player` instance is created when the `playMedia()` method is called with the location of the media file. This instance, if successfully created, is then realized, which allows it to expose the `VolumeControl`. This control is initialized and shown on a canvas to the user to interact with. Finally, the `Player` instance is started by calling the `start()` method. The `Player` instance is paused and restarted in the `pauseMedia()` and `restartMedia()` methods, respectively. The `cleanUp()` method closes the `Player` instance.

The actual MIDlet code is written in the `AudioPlayer` class. Listing 3-3 shows the code for this class.

Listing 3-3. `AudioPlayer MIDlet` *Creates* `AudioPlayerCanvas`

```
package com.apress.chapter3;

import javax.microedition.midlet.*;
import javax.microedition.lcdui.*;

public class AudioPlayer extends MIDlet implements CommandListener {

  // the list of media names
  private String[] audioDisplayList =
    {"Baby Crying", "Applause", "Laughter"};

  // the list of media locations
  private String[] audioList        =
    {"/media/audio/chapter3/baby.wav",
     "/media/audio/chapter3/applause.wav",
     "/media/audio/chapter3/laughter.wav"};

  protected Display display;
  private AudioPlayerCanvas canvas;
  private List list;

  protected Command exitCommand;
  protected Command backCommand;

  public AudioPlayer() {

    // initialize the list and add the exit command
    list = new List(
      "Pick an Audio file", List.IMPLICIT, audioDisplayList, null);
    exitCommand = new Command("Exit", Command.EXIT, 1);
    list.addCommand(exitCommand);
    list.setCommandListener(this);
```

```
  // the back command
  backCommand = new Command("Back", Command.BACK, 1);

  // create the canvas
  canvas = new AudioPlayerCanvas(this);

  // and initialize the display
  display = Display.getDisplay(this);
}

public void startApp() {

  // if startApp() is called after MIDlet has been paused
  if(canvas.isPlayerPaused()) {

    // restart the player
    canvas.restartMedia();
    display.setCurrent(canvas.getForm());
  } else {

    // else display the audio list
    display.setCurrent(list);
  }
}

public void pauseApp() {
  // pauses the playing of the player, if any
  canvas.pauseMedia();
}

public void destroyApp(boolean unconditional) {
  // cleans up and closes player, if any
  canvas.cleanUp();
}

public void commandAction(Command command, Displayable disp) {

  // exiting the MIDlet
  if(command == exitCommand) {
    canvas.cleanUp(); // clean up, if any
    notifyDestroyed(); // let AMS know clean up is done
    return;
  } else if(command == backCommand) { // back to the list
    canvas.cleanUp();
    display.setCurrent(list);
    return;
  }
```

```
      // the implicit list handling
      if(disp == list) {

        // play the current selected file
        canvas.playMedia(audioList[list.getSelectedIndex()]);

        // display the canvas's form
        display.setCurrent(canvas.getForm());
      }
    }
  }
```

The AudioPlayer constructor creates a List of audio files, adds the exitCommand to it, and initializes the current display for the MIDlet. It also creates the player canvas of Listing 3-2 (earlier in this chapter). When the MIDlet is started using the startApp() method, the method checks whether the player canvas was playing any media. If the player canvas was startApp() the method restarts the media. If nothing was being played, and presumably this would be the case the first time the MIDlet is run, the list of audio files is displayed for the user to select from.

After the user selects a file from the list, the implicit list handling takes over and selects the location of the actual audio file from the String array audioList. It then proceeds to call the playMedia() method on this location and sets the Form instance created by the canvas as the main display.

If the user issues either the back or exit commands, the canvas is told to clean up by calling the cleanUp() method before acting appropriately. The same is true when the Application Management Software (AMS) calls the destroyApp() method; cleanup is done before quitting by calling the cleanUp() method. When the MIDlet needs to be paused by the AMS by invoking the pauseApp() method, the pauseMedia() method is called.

Improving AudioPlayerCanvas: Caching Player Instances

One problem is obvious with the AudioPlayerCanvas class: It creates new instances of the Player interface each time a request to play an audio file is received, even if the audio file has been played before. This happens in the playMedia() method. Creating objects is an expensive task, especially multimedia objects such as Player instances. Performance can be improved by caching Player instances that do not need to change. For examples like this, where the media file and its location do not change and especially media stored in the MIDlet's JAR file, caching Player instances is an obvious choice.

However, caching Player instances is not an easy task. In Chapter 4, you'll learn about the various states of a Player instance. If an instance is cached, it must be cached so that the next time it is played, it starts in the right state. Also, when an instance is started, it acquires resources on the device. For example, audio files acquire access to the audio device (speakers, in-memory buffers, and so on) on a multimedia device. These resources must be released before the instance is cached so that other instances can acquire exclusive access.

Let's modify the commandAction() method from the AudioPlayer MIDlet in Listing 3-3 to find out the time taken to play one of the audio files (baby.wav). The following snippet shows the changes in bold.

```
long t1 = System.currentTimeMillis();

// play the current selected file
canvas.playMedia(audioList[list.getSelectedIndex()]);

long t2 = System.currentTimeMillis();

canvas.getForm().setTitle("Time taken: " + (t2-t1) + " ms");
```

The title of the canvas's form is changed to reflect the time taken to start playing a listing in milliseconds. Table 3-2 now shows the time taken to play the file `baby.wav` three times over the different devices: Sun's DefaultColorPhone emulator, Motorola C975 emulator, and the actual Motorola C975 device.

Table 3-2. *Time Taken to Start Playback of* `baby.wav` *Across Three Devices*

Device	1st Attempt	2nd Attempt	3rd Attempt
Sun's DefaultColorPhone	180ms	40ms	40ms
Motorola C975 emulator	100ms	10ms	10ms
Motorola C975 device	236ms	218ms	207ms

The values shown are reflective only and will be different on different machines and environments.

The fact that the emulators take a long time for the first attempt and much less time for the next two suggests that the emulators are performing some sort of caching themselves. The actual device doesn't seem to be doing any caching, and the times are pretty consistent for the device. However, the emulators aren't really performing any caching of `Player` instances, and the long startup delay suggests latency in acquiring audio device on the emulator's computer platform.

Let's now modify `AudioPlayerCanvas` to `CachedAudioPlayerCanvas` so that it caches `Player` instances and plays the cached instances when called upon (and creates them when called for the first time). Similarly, `AudioPlayer` will be modified to `CachingAudioPlayer` to use this new canvas class. Listing 3-4 shows `CachedAudioPlayerCanvas`.

Listing 3-4. `CachedAudioPlayerCanvas` *Caches* `Player` *Instances*

```
package com.apress.chapter3;

import java.util.*;
import javax.microedition.lcdui.*;
import javax.microedition.media.*;
import javax.microedition.media.control.*;

public class CachedAudioPlayerCanvas implements ItemStateListener {

  // the parent MIDlet
  private CachingAudioPlayer parent;
```

```
// form that contains canvas elements
private Form form;

// gauge to allow user to manipulate volume
private Gauge gauge;

// the volume control
private VolumeControl volume;

// the player used to play media
private Player player;

// is the player paused?
private boolean paused = false;

private Hashtable players;

public CachedAudioPlayerCanvas (CachingAudioPlayer parent) {

  this.parent = parent;

  // create form and add elements and listeners
  form = new Form("");
  gauge = new Gauge("Volume: 50", true, 100, 50);
  form.append(gauge);
  form.addCommand(parent.exitCommand);
  form.addCommand(parent.backCommand);
  form.setCommandListener(parent);

  // a change in volume gauge will be handled by this class
  form.setItemStateListener(this);

  players = new Hashtable();
}

public void playMedia(String locator) {

  try {

    // first look for an existing instance
    player = (Player)players.get(locator);

    if(player == null) {

      // create the player for the specified string locator
      player = Manager.createPlayer(
        getClass().getResourceAsStream(locator), "audio/x-wav");
```

```
        // fetch it
        player.prefetch();

        // put this instance in the Hashtable
        players.put(locator, player);
      }

      // get the volume control
      volume = (VolumeControl)player.getControl("VolumeControl");

      // initialize it to 50
      volume.setLevel(50);

      // initialize the gauge
      gauge.setValue(volume.getLevel());
      gauge.setLabel("Volume: " + volume.getLevel());

      // play it twice
      player.setLoopCount(2);

      // start the player
      player.start();

      // set the title of the form
      form.setTitle("Playing " + locator);

    } catch(Exception e) {
      e.printStackTrace();
    }
  }

  public void pauseMedia() {

    // if the player needs to be paused, either due to an incoming call,
    // or due to user actions
    if(player != null) {
      try {
        player.stop();
        paused = true;
      } catch(Exception e) {}
    }
  }

  public void restartMedia() {

    // restarting after player was paused
```

```
    if(player != null) {
      try {
        player.start();
        paused = false;
      } catch(Exception e) {}
    }
  }

  public boolean isPlayerPaused() {
    return paused;
  }

  public Form getForm() {
    return this.form;
  }

  public void itemStateChanged(Item item) {

    // there is only one item on the form, the gauge, and any change in its
    // value means the user wants to increase or decrease the playback volume
    volume.setLevel(gauge.getValue());
    gauge.setLabel("Volume: " + volume.getLevel());
  }

  public void cleanUp() {

    // clean up, either due to user action or AMS call
    if(player != null) {

      try {
        player.setMediaTime(0);
      } catch(Exception e) {}

      player.deallocate();
      player = null;
    }
  }

  public void closeAll() {
    // iterate through the player instances and close all
    for(Enumeration e = players.elements(); e.hasMoreElements();) {
      Player p = (Player)e.nextElement();
      p.close();
    }
  }
}
```

The major changes between AudioPlayerCanvas and CachedAudioPlayerCanvas are shown in bold. A Hashtable is used to cache Player instances, and the locator String is used as the key. When a request to play a particular audio file is made, the Hashtable is searched and an instance is used if found. Note that a VolumeControl is still constructed fresh for each instance.

Instead of using the realize() method, prefetch() is used when creating a Player instance for the first time. The purpose of these methods and the distinction between them will be explained in Chapter 4. Note that using prefetch() instead of realize() allows quicker startup time for media playback.

Similarly, the cleanUp() method is modified to use deallocate() rather than close(). Further, the media time is set to 0 to allow the media to be played back from the starting point of the file each time it is started. This is done by using the method setMediaTime(), which is like a fast-forward and rewind method for moving through the media. Player instances that don't support seek operations like this will throw a MediaException. In this case, calling this method is really only necessary for the Sun emulator, which does not reset the media time on deallocation.

Finally, a new method called closeAll() is added to allow the CachingAudioPlayer MIDlet to shut down all the Player instances before it is itself shut down.

Listing 3-5 shows the modified CachingAudioPlayer. Once again, the changes from Listing 3-3 are highlighted in bold.

Listing 3-5. CachingAudioPlayer *Uses the New* CachedAudioPlayerCanvas

```
package com.apress.chapter3;

import javax.microedition.midlet.*;
import javax.microedition.lcdui.*;

public class CachingAudioPlayer extends MIDlet implements CommandListener {

  // the list of media names
  private String[] audioDisplayList =
    {"Baby Crying", "Applause", "Laughter"};

  // the list of media locations
  private String[] audioList        =
    {"/media/audio/chapter3/baby.wav",
     "/media/audio/chapter3/applause.wav",
     "/media/audio/chapter3/laughter.wav"};

  protected Display display;
  private CachedAudioPlayerCanvas canvas;
  private List list;

  protected Command exitCommand;
  protected Command backCommand;

  public CachingAudioPlayer() {
```

```
    // initialize the list and add the exit command
    list = new List(
      "Pick an Audio file", List.IMPLICIT, audioDisplayList, null);
    exitCommand = new Command("Exit", Command.EXIT, 1);
    list.addCommand(exitCommand);
    list.setCommandListener(this);

    // the back command
    backCommand = new Command("Back", Command.BACK, 1);

    // create the canvas
    canvas = new CachedAudioPlayerCanvas(this);

    // and initialize the display
    display = Display.getDisplay(this);
  }

  public void startApp() {

    // if startApp() is called after MIDlet has been paused
    if(canvas.isPlayerPaused()) {

      // restart the player
      canvas.restartMedia();
      display.setCurrent(canvas.getForm());
    } else {

      // else display the audio list
      display.setCurrent(list);
    }
  }

  public void pauseApp() {
    //pauses the playing of the player, if any
    canvas.pauseMedia();
  }

  public void destroyApp(boolean unconditional) {
    // closes all players before shutdown
    canvas.closeAll();
  }

  public void commandAction(Command command, Displayable disp) {
```

```
    // exiting the MIDlet
    if(command == exitCommand) {
      canvas.closeAll(); // close all players
      notifyDestroyed(); // let AMS know clean up is done
      return;
    } else if(command == backCommand) { // back to the list
      canvas.cleanUp();
      display.setCurrent(list);
      return;
    }

    // the implicit list handling
    if(disp == list) {

      long t1 = System.currentTimeMillis();

      // play the current selected file
      canvas.playMedia(audioList[list.getSelectedIndex()]);

      long t2 = System.currentTimeMillis();

      canvas.getForm().setTitle("Time taken: " + (t2-t1) + " ms");

      // display the canvas's form
      display.setCurrent(canvas.getForm());
    }
  }
}
```

Using the new version of these files, Table 3-3 shows the times taken to play `baby.wav` over the three different emulators/devices.

Table 3-3. *Time Taken to Play Back* `baby.wav` *with Caching of* `Player` *Instances*

Device	1st Attempt	2nd Attempt	3rd Attempt
Sun's DefaultColorPhone	180ms	30ms	30ms
Motorola C975 emulator	100ms	0ms	0ms
Motorola C975 device	202ms	14ms	14ms

Comparing Table 3-3 with Table 3-2 should show the obvious performance improvement that caching has brought about. The real gain is on the actual device, which is where it matters the most. The time to playback has been reduced to a consistent 14ms after an initial startup time of 202ms. The performance on the emulators is encouraging as well with reduction in playback time by about 10ms each over the noncached version.

Summary

Creating MMAPI-based multimedia MIDlets requires knowledge of not just MMAPI, but an understanding of the MIDlet creation process as well. The understanding required is nominal, as MMAPI MIDlets are no different from other MIDlets in terms of their architecture and process.

This chapter gave you a hands-on introduction to MMAPI by creating a simple media player. You enhanced the media player MIDlet by caching, and saw how the enhancement improved the performance of the original player.

The next chapter, on media player lifecycle and events, will explain what happens behind the scenes when the media player is used to play media files. You'll also see the various events that occur during a media player's lifecycle and how to respond and take advantage of this knowledge.

CHAPTER 4

Media Player Lifecycle and Events

As a MIDlet transitions between different states during its lifecycle, so does a Player instance that has a lifecycle of its own. A Player instance has many more states that it transitions between. These states are well defined, and transitions between them raise events that interested parties can listen to and respond accordingly.

In this chapter, you'll learn about these different states, the lifecycle of a Player instance, and how a Player instance transitions between these states. Finally, you'll learn how events generated during these transitions can be captured by interested listeners and acted upon.

Overview

A Player instance goes through five different states during its lifetime. The capability for an instance to go through these many states gives developers greater control over the working of an instance. These states are UNREALIZED, REALIZED, PREFETCHED, STARTED, and CLOSED.

A Player instance is guaranteed to go through all these states if started; that is, the instance is not just created but playback (or recording as the case may be) is initiated. Moving between states is not necessarily linear and can happen either due to programmatic control or some external or internal events. Movement from the CLOSED state to any other state is not possible.

Movement between different states results in events being fired for any listeners to act on. These events are delivered asynchronously and in the order that they are generated. The whole event delivery mechanism is extensible, which allows you to define application-specific events. Several system-level events are already defined that will satisfy most cases.

Exploring the Different Player States

MMAPI allows you to programmatically move between different states (except moving away from the CLOSED state). This gives you greater control over the way you manage the lifecycle of a Player instance, increases responsiveness, and allows manageability of these instances. This section explores these different states and the methods that allow you to gain this control.

In a nutshell, a Player instance starts life in the UNREALIZED state. It moves from this state to the REALIZED state when the user calls the realize() method. The REALIZED state gives way to the PREFETCHED state when the `prefetch()` method is called. Calling `start()` moves the instance to the STARTED state, and calling `close()` leads to the CLOSED state. This simple transition path is displayed in Figure 4-1.

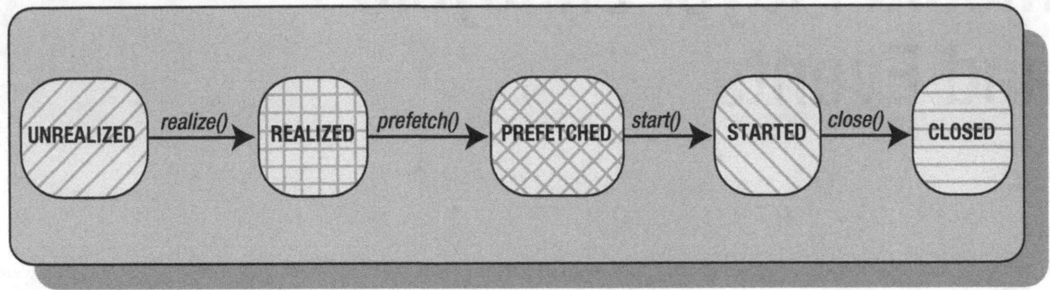

Figure 4-1. *A simple linear transition path for a* `Player` *instance*

Figure 4-1 shows the most *likely* transition path for a `Player` instance. Except for the CLOSED state, transitions can occur between the other states by calling special methods. These methods are covered shortly when the individual states are discussed.

Calling any of these methods to make a transition between different states is synchronous in nature. The methods don't return till the transition is complete. However, if any of these methods cannot make the transition, a `MediaException` is thrown to indicate so.

You can determine the current state of a `Player` instance by using the method `getState()`. This returns one of five constants defined in the `Player` interface corresponding to the five states shown in Figure 4-1. These constants are `UNREALIZED`, `REALIZED`, `PREFETCHED`, `STARTED`, and `CLOSED`.

Let's examine each of these states individually to see what they mean and how movement between them is not always so linear.

■ **Note** Most of these state transition methods are implemented in Java, as opposed to the code for parsing and decoding multimedia data, which is implemented in the native language of the device on which the MIDlet is running. Parsing and decoding are memory-intensive operations and implementing them in Java would sacrifice performance. Media transition methods, on the other hand, are not CPU-intensive and can be safely implemented in Java, as most of them are. Some parts of these methods may be implemented in native language to take advantage of device-specific performance features.

UNREALIZED

A `Player` instance starts life in an UNREALIZED state. When you use the `Manager` class to create a `Player` instance using any of the three `createPlayer()` methods, it creates a barely usable instance in the UNREALIZED state. An UNREALIZED `Player` is of no use because it doesn't have enough information to start functioning. It needs to acquire resources, such as audio and recording hardware on the device; set up in memory buffers for acquiring the media content; and communicate with the location of the media data. All these processes are performed in other states.

A Player instance moves away from the UNREALIZED state when the realize() method is called, which if successful, moves it to the REALIZED state. If unsuccessful, a MediaException is thrown, and the instance remains in the UNREALIZED state. If the realize() method blocks for a long time because it is a synchronous method, you can attempt to call the deallocate() method on the Player instance, which tries to keep the method in the UNREALIZED state. You'll learn more about this in the upcoming "REALIZED" section.

Not many actions can be performed on an UNREALIZED Player instance. For example, you cannot retrieve any controls from this instance using the getControl() or the getControls() methods, because the instance doesn't have enough information to generate the controls. You cannot change the playback time of the media, provided that it allows you to change the media time in the first place, with the setMediaTime() method. You cannot even retrieve or change the instance's TimeBase for synchronization using the getTimeBase() or setTimeBase() methods. A call to any of these methods in the UNREALIZED state results in an IllegalStateException.

The only useful operation that you can do with an UNREALIZED instance, besides realizing or closing it, is to set the number of times the instance should loop using the setLoopCount() method. You can also retrieve the likely duration of the media, which almost always returns –1, indicating an unknown time (TIME_UKNOWN constant in the Player interface).

The Player interface has a static integer constant to represent this state, UNREALIZED.

Figure 4-2 summarizes the UNREALIZED state and its transitions.

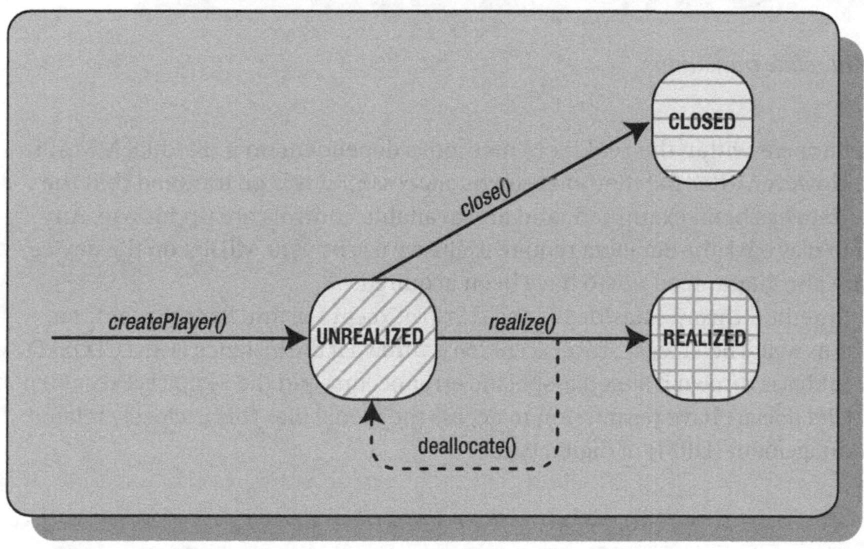

Figure 4-2. *UNREALIZED state transitions*

REALIZED

A Player instance moves from the UNREALIZED to the REALIZED state when the realize() method is called. The realize() method can be time consuming because it actually retrieves the media data. If the UNREALIZED state represents that the instance has connected to its media location, in a REALIZED state, it has in all probability retrieved this data (except for data that is streaming in nature).

After it has been REALIZED, a `Player` instance cannot go back to the UNREALIZED state. As you learned in the last section, a `realize()` method that is taking too long to return can be preempted by calling the `deallocate()` method, which keeps the instance in the UNREALIZED state. But from a REALIZED state itself, an instance can only go to the PREFETCHED or the CLOSED states. Figure 4-3 shows the REALIZED state transitions.

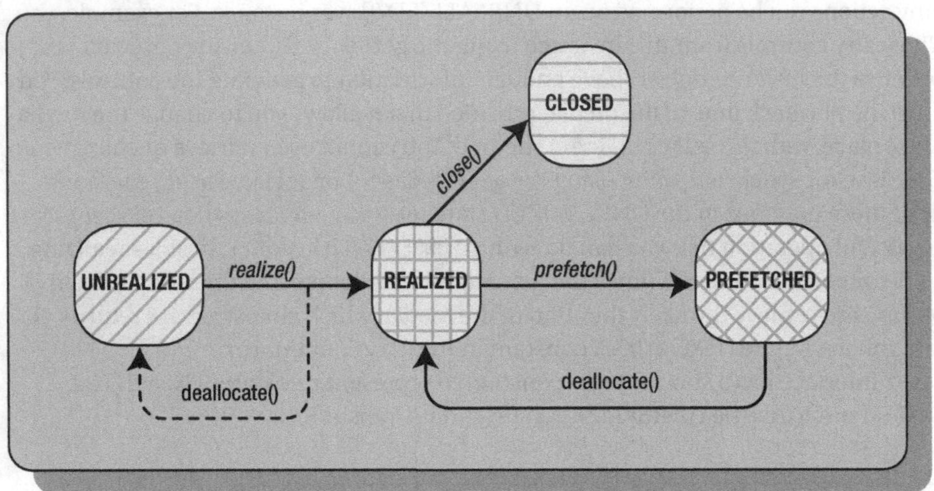

Figure 4-3. *REALIZED state transitions*

What actually happens within the `realize()` method is dependent on individual MMAPI implementations. However, after the method returns successfully, it is guaranteed that the underlying media data has been examined, and any available controls are up for use. Any resources required to play back the data that require exclusive use by your MIDlet on the device that it is running are also guaranteed *not* to have been acquired.

The `realize()` method throws, besides `IllegalStateException` and `MediaException`, a `SecurityException` as well. The `IllegalStateException` is thrown if the instance is in a CLOSED state; the `MediaException` is thrown if a media-specific error occurs; and the `SecurityException` is thrown if the MIDlet doesn't have permission to access the media file. This is closely related to Digital Rights Management (DRM) of digital data.

Note DRM is an industry term that refers to a service or technology to control access to digital data.

Because MMAPI is used to access some of the most popular digital data, such as music and video, it allows implementations to plug in a DRM technology to control this access. This allows very simple control over the media data. For example, `SecurityException` is thrown by the realize() method if the DRM indicates that the right of the user to use the media data has expired (because it could only be used within a specific timeframe, it could only be played once, or for any other DRM-based reason). The realize() method implementation calls the DRM technology built in to the device to make this call.

Ideally, a call like this happens when the Player instance is created. DRM kicks in when createPlayer() is called on a Manager class, and you'll receive a SecurityException for trying to create an instance on an expired or inaccessible content. (You'll also receive a SecurityException for protocol-specific restrictions built in to the user's device, such as accessing the network when no permission to access the network has been given.) However, you might want to replay content without needing to create another Player instance on the same media data (as you saw in Chapter 3 when you cached Player instances). In those cases, realize() checks to make sure that DRM rules haven't been breached; if they have been, realize() throws a SecurityException.

The Player interface has a static integer constant that represents this state, REALIZED.

PREFETCHED

In the PREFETCHED state, a Player instance is in the best possible state to get started with the playback (or recording in case of a player for capturing data) of media. The instance has decoded the data and acquired access to any exclusive resources required for playback (or recording). A Player instance that hasn't been prefetched cannot be started.

Player instances move into the PREFETCHED state when the user calls the prefetch() method on a REALIZED instance. Calling deallocate() does the reverse, that is, moves a PREFETCHED instance to the REALIZED state, thereby releasing any exclusive resources acquired to move into the PREFETCHED state.

Note that calling prefetch() doesn't necessarily mean that all the media data would have been decoded and ready for playback (or recording). It just means that most of the processing has been done and the media can be played back (or recorded) with the minimum possible latency. To accentuate this point, if an instance is already in the PREFETCHED state, and you use the prefetch() method, the instance will try and minimize the latency even further. However, the reduction in startup times is not guaranteed, and different implementations of MMAPI will differ in what they exactly do if prefetch() is called twice. If you do call prefetch() on an already PREFETCHED instance, it is guaranteed not to throw any errors.

An IllegalStateException is thrown if you call this method on a CLOSED instance. A MediaException is also thrown if an error occurs when processing or decoding the media data. However, this same exception is thrown if an exclusive resource cannot be acquired. For example, if a Player instance requires exclusive access to the audio hardware on a device, and this is not available because it is being used by some other instance, a MediaException will be thrown to indicate this. Although there's no way to differentiate between the two reasons for MediaException, in the case of the latter reason, you can call prefetch() again and if exclusive access is now possible, the instance will move to the PREFETCHED state.

Similar to the realize() method, calling the prefetch() method may throw a SecurityException if the Player instance has insufficient permissions to either decode media data or acquire exclusive resources.

Figure 4-4 shows the possible state transitions in the PREFETCHED state.

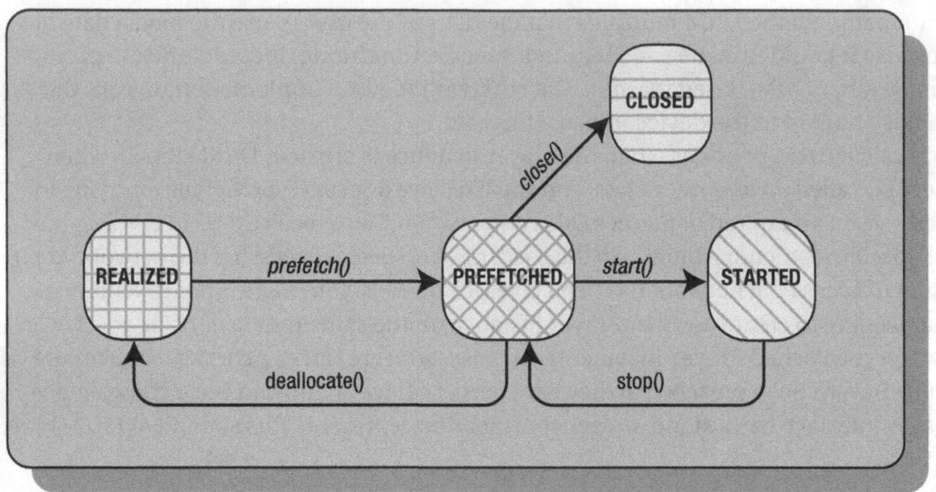

Figure 4-4. *PREFETCHED state transitions*

As you can see, there is no direct transition path for an `UNREALIZED` instance to go to the PREFETCHED state. This is why, if you call `prefetch()` on an `UNREALIZED` instance, it implies a call to the `realize()` method first. However, a transition from the PREFETCHED state to the REALIZED state can occur by using the `deallocate()` method. By doing so, you allow your instance to give up the exclusive resources acquired by your instance for other instances (or other MIDlets, applications, or AMS) to use.

An instance can arrive in the PREFETCHED state from the STARTED state as well. This transition can occur in several ways as explained in detail in the next section.

The `Player` interface has a static integer constant that represents this state, `PREFETCHED`.

STARTED

A `Player` instance in the STARTED state is playing back (or recording, streaming, and so on) actual media. This is the most useful state that an instance can be in. This state is achieved by calling the `start()` method on a `PREFETCHED` instance. However, note that calling the `start()` method doesn't guarantee that the instance will actually move immediately into the STARTED state. By calling the `start()` method, you are telling the instance to move into the STARTED state as soon as possible. Only when the `start()` method returns successfully is the instance considered to be in this state.

Of course, the instance may not be able to successfully move into the STARTED state when this method is called. Besides a `SecurityException`, thrown if there is not enough permission to start the media, a `MediaException` may be thrown if an error occurs when processing the media for playback (or recording). When any of these exceptions is thrown, the instance remains in the PREFETCHED state. As expected, an `IllegalStateException` is thrown if you try calling `start()` on an instance that is in the CLOSED state.

STARTED is the only state that has an automatic transition based on the state of the media playback (or recording). If you call start() on a Player instance, it automatically moves to the PREFETCHED state if the end of media playback is reached; that is, there is nothing left to play. STARTED also automatically moves to the PREFETCHED state if a preset stop time is reached. Preset stop times are set using the StopTimeControl.

Media that has a very short playback time moves to the PREFETCHED state almost immediately. For example, consider that you are trying to play an audio file and want to initiate some action when its Player instance is in the STARTED state. When you call the start() method, the instance temporarily moves to this state, but before you can react to the STARTED event, the playback would be over for a very short audio file, and the instance would have moved back to the PREFETCHED state. Thus, there are no guarantees for successfully acting on a STARTED instance because of this automatic transition.

Besides these automatic transitions, a Player instance also moves back to the PREFETCHED state when the stop() method is called in the STARTED state and the method returns successfully. The effect of the stop() method is to pause the instance at the current media time. (Note that there is *no* corresponding STOPPED state for the STARTED state. When stopped, an instance is in the PREFETCHED state.) Similar to the start() method, the stop() method also throws the IllegalStateException and MediaException. The first exception is thrown if this method is called on a CLOSED instance, whereas the second is thrown if the instance cannot be stopped.

If you call the start() method again, after you have stopped a previously started instance, it resumes at the media time that it was stopped at, effectively restarting paused media. This can, of course, be overridden by using the method setMediaTime(), which allows you to restart the playback from whenever you want it to. As expected, this will not work for media that is being recorded, and may or may not be supported for streaming data. In cases where this is not supported, calling setMediaTime() will throw a MediaException.

After a Player instance is in the STARTED state, calling either setTimeBase() or setLoopCount()throws an IllegalStateException. This makes sense. A Player's TimeBase allows it to synchronize itself with other instances via the internal clock. After the instance has already started, this clock will be out of sync if changed midstream. Similarly, changing the number of times the instance must play back in the STARTED state will cause confusion over this count.

If you call the start() method on an UNREALIZED instance, it implies a call to the realize() and prefetch() methods, in that order. If you call it on a REALIZED instance, it implies a call to the prefetch() method first. In short, no direct transition occurs between the UNREALIZED state and the STARTED state on the one hand, and the REALIZED and STARTED state on the other, with the start() method taking care of these transitions for you. This is why listings in Chapter 3 were able to get away with calling the start() method only. However, calling the start() method on a PREFETCHED instance is always better than calling on UNREALIZED or REALIZED, because it reduces the overall startup time. You should only call the start() method after you've brought the instance to the PREFETCHED state, rather than letting the start() method bring it to that state.

Figure 4-5 shows the state transitions for the STARTED state.

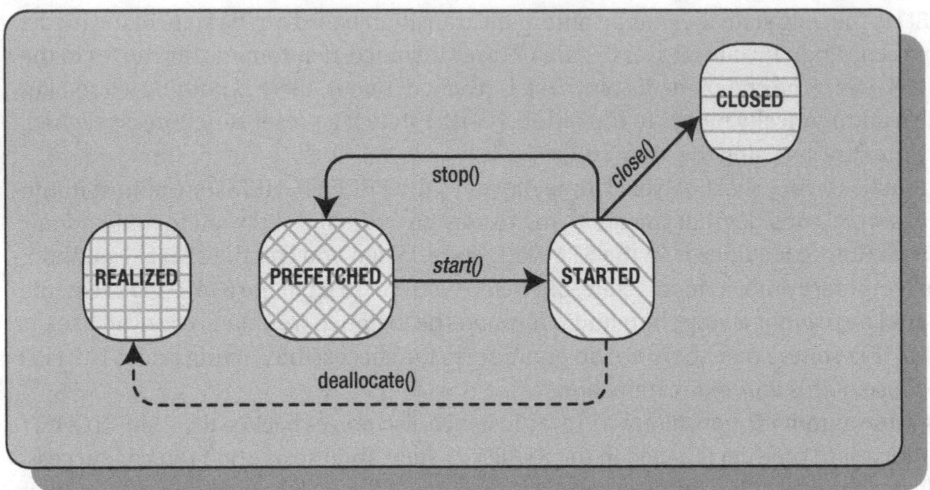

Figure 4-5. *STARTED state transitions*

You can call the `deallocate()` method on a `STARTED` instance, which internally implies a call to the `stop()` method first, and thus, the state of the instance transitions from STARTED to PREFETCHED to REALIZED, if both methods return successfully.

The `Player` interface has a static integer constant that represents this state, `STARTED`.

CLOSED

A `Player` instance in the CLOSED state is no longer usable. No methods can be called on it in this state with the exception of the `getState()` method. All other states transition to this state when the `close()` method is called, but there are no automatic transitions. If you call `close()` in the CLOSED state, no exception is thrown and the call is ignored. In fact, this method does not throw any exceptions; if any errors occur, the method returns silently and moves the instance to the CLOSED state anyway. All resources held by the instance are released, including any connections, exclusive device resources, and internal buffers.

■ Note Although the MMAPI specification does not say so, calling `close()` during different states causes different actions to be performed. Because the specification is silent on this issue, different implementations implement the actions in their own way. However, most implementations try to call the `deallocate()` method before performing any closeup actions. Recall that the `deallocate()` method can be called in all states (except, of course, the CLOSED state, whereas in the REALIZED state, the `deallocate()` call is ignored). Calling the `deallocate()` method in the STARTED state causes the `stop()` method to be called first. Thus, in all probability, if you call `close()` on a `STARTED Player` instance, it will go through the following cleanup methods: `close()` ➤ `stop()` ➤ `deallocate()`.

The `Player` interface has a static integer constant that represents this state, `CLOSED`.

Responding to Player Events

Each state transition and many other events generate a regular stream of notifications for any listener objects interested in a Player instance. This event delivery mechanism is implemented using an asynchronous model that is similar to most Java event delivery mechanisms.

The key class in this mechanism is the PlayerListener interface. Any class may implement this interface, register this implementation with the target Player instance, and start receiving notifications as the instance goes through its lifecycle. Several events are defined within this interface that cover a comprehensive list of Player events. You can create your own events as well and listen and react to them.

The PlayerListener interface defines only one method that implementations must implement. This method—playerUpdate(Player player, String event, Object eventData)—is invoked when an event takes place. To register an implementation with a Player instance, you use the method addPlayerListener(PlayerListener listener); to remove the instance, you use removePlayerListener(PlayerListener listener). Multiple listeners can be attached to a single instance, and multiple instances can send their events to the same listener. Because the playerUpdate() method receives the instance as an argument, it knows how to differentiate between the different instances.

As a simple example, let's modify Listing 3-1 from Chapter 3 to receive notifications from the simple Player instance that was created in that listing. The new code will display the events on the device screen as they are received. Listing 4-1 shows this modified code in the MIDlet called EchoEventsMIDlet.

Listing 4-1. EchoEventsMIDlet *Echoes Player Events Onscreen*

```
package com.apress.chapter4;

import javax.microedition.media.*;
import javax.microedition.lcdui.*;
import javax.microedition.midlet.*;

public class EchoEventsMIDlet extends MIDlet implements PlayerListener {

  private StringItem stringItem;

  public void startApp() {

    try {

      Form form = new Form("Player State");
      stringItem = new StringItem("", null)
      form.append(stringItem);
      Display.getDisplay(this).setCurrent(form);

      Player player = Manager.createPlayer(
        getClass().getResourceAsStream(
        "/media/audio/chapter4/baby.wav"), "audio/x-wav");
      player.addPlayerListener(this);
```

```
      player.start();

    } catch(Exception e) {
      e.printStackTrace();
    }
  }

  public void pauseApp() {
  }

  public void destroyApp(boolean unconditional) {
  }

  public void playerUpdate(Player player, String event, Object eventData) {
    stringItem.setText(event);
    System.err.println(event);
  }
}
```

The EchoEventsMIDlet acts as the listener for the Player instance that it creates by implementing PlayerListener and adding the playerUpdate() method. When created, the Player instance registers this MIDlet by using the method addPlayerListener(this). Any event that is now generated by the corresponding event is delivered to the playerUpdate() method.

The other change in this MIDlet from Listing 3-1 is to create a Form object with a single StringItem on it to promptly display onscreen and print the current event received by the playerUpdate() method to the error output stream.

Running this MIDlet returns mostly consistent results because the Sun Java Wireless Toolkit's DefaultColorPhone emulator fires an extra volumeChanged event.

■ Note You may not notice the volumeChanged event on the DefaultColorPhone emulator because it may happen too fast depending on the time it takes for the media file to enter the STARTED state. Check the error output stream. The volumeChanged event is fired when the Player instance enters the PREFETCHED state (on the Sun MMAPI implementation).

The Motorola emulator and actual C975 device do not fire this volumeChanged event. The events that are fired and received by all three environments are the started and the endofmedia events. As you may guess, the started event represents when an instance has entered the STARTED state. The endofmedia event is delivered when no more media is left to play (or record/stream). This event is delivered each time an instance that is set to loop reaches the end of the media for each loop.

Of course, many more events than the two (or three if you consider the DefaultColorPhone) are fired by this simple example. Table 4-1 lists all the events defined in the MMAPI specification in the `PlayerListener` interface defined as constants.

Table 4-1. *A Complete List of* `Player` *Events Defined in the* `PlayerListener` *Interface*

Player Event Constant	Constant Value	When Fired
`BUFFERING_STARTED`	`bufferingStarted`	When an instance has started buffering media data for processing or playback.
`BUFFERING_STOPPED`	`bufferingStopped`	When an instance has exited the buffering stage.
`CLOSED`	`closed`	When an instance is closed.
`DEVICE_AVAILABLE`	`deviceAvailable`	When a system resource required by a `Player` instance becomes available for use.
`DEVICE_UNAVAILABLE`	`deviceUnavailable`	When a system resource required by a `Player` instance becomes unavailable. This event must precede the previous event.
`DURATION_UPDATED`	`durationUpdated`	When the duration of previously unknown media data becomes available.
`END_OF_MEDIA`	`endOfMedia`	When an instance has reached the end of the media during the current loop.
`ERROR`	`error`	When an error, which is usually fatal, occurs.
`RECORD_ERROR`	`recordError`	When an error occurs during recording (audio or video).
`RECORD_STARTED`	`recordStarted`	When recording of media data has started.
`RECORD_STOPPED`	`recordStopped`	When recording of media data has stopped.
`SIZE_CHANGED`	`sizeChanged`	When the size of a video display has changed for whatever reason.
`STARTED`	`started`	When the instance has entered the STARTED state.
`STOPPED`	`stopped`	When the instance has paused due to the `stop()` method being called.
`STOPPED_AT_TIME`	`stoppedAtTime`	When the instance has paused due to the `StopTimeControl's setStopTime()` method.
`VOLUME_CHANGED`	`volumeChanged`	When the volume of an audio device is changed.

If you look at the signature of the `playerUpdate()` method, you'll see that it takes three parameters. The first is the `Player` instance that has thrown the event, the second is the actual event, and the third is the `eventData` as an `Object`. The `eventData` is interesting because it contains specific information about each event that can help you do something when the particular event is fired. For example, when the `stopped` event is received by this method, the `eventData` is a Long object identifying the media time when the corresponding Player instance is stopped. Similarly, the started event's eventData contains the media time when the media is started. Almost each event carries some useful information in the corresponding eventData; Table 4-2 shows the complete list.

Table 4-2. *Events and Corresponding Event Data*

Event	Event Data
BUFFERING_STARTED	A Long object designating the time when buffering has started.
BUFFERING_STOPPED	A Long object designating the time when buffering has stopped.
CLOSED	Event data is null when this event is fired.
DEVICE_AVAILABLE	A String object that is the name of the device that is now available.
DEVICE_UNAVAILABLE	A String object that is the name of the device that is not available.
DURATION_UPDATED	A Long object designating the new duration of the media.
END_OF_MEDIA	A Long object that contains the media time when the Player instance reached the end of media and stopped.
ERROR	A String that contains the error message.
RECORD_ERROR	A String that contains the error message.
RECORD_STARTED	A Long object that designates the media time when recording has started.
RECORD_STOPPED	A Long object that designates the media time when recording has stopped.
SIZE_CHANGED	A VideoControl control object that contains information about the new size.
STARTED	A Long object designating the media time when the Player instance is started.
STOPPED	A Long object designating the media time when the Player instance is stopped (paused).
STOPPED_AT_TIME	Similar to STOPPED, the eventData contains the media time when the Player instance is stopped in the form of a Long object.
VOLUME_CHANGED	A VolumeControl control object that contains information about the new volume.

Note that in MMAPI all times are measured in microseconds, not milliseconds.

Understanding the Event Delivery Mechanism

The event delivery mechanism in MMAPI is based on an asynchronous model that allows you to create multimedia applications that do not block the main application thread. This means that events are fired using an event delivery thread separate from the main application thread. This thread may or may not be in existence till an actual event is to be delivered. For example, in the Sun's MMAPI reference implementation, this thread is only created when the first event is fired. Even then, this thread remains active only for another five seconds, after which, if no more events are delivered, the thread exits. A new thread is created the next time an event needs to be delivered. Most actual commercial implementations follow a similar model that only differs in the time that they stay alive for; however, they are guaranteed to all follow this asynchronous nature of event delivery.

The MMAPI also guarantees that events will be delivered to their respective listeners in the order they are generated. This way, events that occur very fast after one another are guaranteed to be received by the registered listeners in order, without getting overwhelmed by newer events. For example, suppose you start playing a media file, which would fire a STARTED event. However, if the media file is short, it will end very quickly and generate an END_OF_MEDIA event almost immediately after it sends the STARTED event. The listener is guaranteed to receive the STARTED event before the END_OF_MEDIA event even if it occurs nearly simultaneously.

Of course, if an error occurs at any stage during a Player instance creation or usage so that the instance cannot continue working, the event delivery mechanism sends an ERROR event. The receipt of this event implies that the instance is unusable and is in a CLOSED state.

Creating an Event Handling Class

In Chapter 3, you created a MIDlet that allowed you to select a media audio file from a list to play and control its volume. In this section, you'll create an event handling class and attach it to the functional Player instances created in that MIDlet. This event handling class is basic, but it gives you an idea of how to listen for events, handle them accordingly, and use the event and eventData parameters. Listing 4-2 shows this event handling class, called EventHandler.

Listing 4-2. EventHandler *Is the Listener for Functional* Player *Instances Created in the Previous Chapter*

```
package com.apress.chapter4;

import javax.microedition.media.*;
import javax.microedition.media.control.*;
import javax.microedition.lcdui.StringItem;

public class EventHandler implements PlayerListener {

  private StringItem item;

  public EventHandler(StringItem item) {
    this.item = item;
  }

  public void playerUpdate(Player player, String event, Object eventData) {

    if(event.equals(PlayerListener.VOLUME_CHANGED)) {

      // a player's volume has been changed
      VolumeControl vc = (VolumeControl)eventData;
      updateDisplay("Volume Changed to: " + vc.getLevel());

      if(vc.getLevel() > 60)  {
        updateDisplay("Volume higher than 60 is too loud");
        vc.setLevel(60);
      }
    } else if(event.equals(PlayerListener.STOPPED)) {
```

```
        // player instance paused
        updateDisplay("Player paused at: " + (Long)eventData);
      } else if(event.equals(PlayerListener.STARTED)) {

        // player instance started (or restarted)
        updateDisplay("Player started at: " + (Long)eventData);
      } else if(event.equals(PlayerListener.END_OF_MEDIA)) {

        // player instace reached end of loop
        updateDisplay("Player reached end of loop.");
      } else if(event.equals(PlayerListener.CLOSED)) {

        // player instance closed
        updateDisplay("Player closed.");
      } else if(event.equals(PlayerListener.ERROR)) {

        // if an error occurs, eventData contains the error message
        updateDisplay("Error Message: " + (String)eventData);
      }
    }

    public void updateDisplay(String text) {

      // update the item on the screen
      item.setText(text);

      // and write to error stream as well
      System.err.println(text);
    }

}
```

The EventHandler constructor accepts a StringItem screen item to which it can write updates as it receives events. The playerUpdate() method is where the updates are written to the screen based on the event that has occurred.

If you change the volume of a Player instance, the associated VolumeControl is retrieved from the eventData after casting it appropriately. You can then query the new volume level from this control.

■ Note You can, of course, retrieve the same VolumeControl by querying the associated Player instance with the getControl(" VolumeControl ") method call that returns a reference to the same instance as referenced by the eventData parameter. The direct referencing eventData omits a method call, whereas getControl() method omits the use of a cast.

Here, the handler informs the user that volume over 60 is too loud and resets the volume back to 60. Note that resetting the volume in turn generates another `VOLUME_CHANGED` event!

The rest of the events are handled accordingly, and you can use the associated event data with appropriate casts. The `updateDisplay()` method updates the screen as well as writes message to the error output stream because some of the messages on the screen will happen too quickly.

The event generating `Player` instances now need to be told to send the instances to this handling class. This is done in the `CachingAudioPlayerCanvas` class where these instances are first created. This class is now modified to add a `StringItem` to display the messages from the event handler, create the `EventHandler` class, and set each `Player` instance up with this class as the listener. These changes are shown in bold in Listing 4-3.

Listing 4-3. *Enabling Event Handling in the* `CachingAudioPlayerCanvas` *Class*

```
package com.apress.chapter4;

import java.util.*;
import javax.microedition.lcdui.*;
import javax.microedition.media.*;
import javax.microedition.media.control.*;

public class CachedAudioPlayerCanvas implements ItemStateListener {

  // the parent MIDlet
  private CachingAudioPlayer parent;

  // form that contains canvas elements
  private Form form;

  // gauge to allow user to manipulate volume
  private Gauge gauge;

  // the volume control
  private VolumeControl volume;

  // the player used to play media
  private Player player;

  // is the player paused?
  private boolean paused = false;

  // to display event info
  private StringItem eventInfo;

  // the event handler
  private EventHandler handler;

  private Hashtable players;
```

```
public CachedAudioPlayerCanvas(CachingAudioPlayer parent) {
  this.parent = parent;

  // create form and add elements and listeners
  form = new Form("");
  gauge = new Gauge("Volume: 50", true, 100, 50);
  eventInfo = new StringItem("", null);
  form.append(gauge);

  // add the event info string item
  form.append(eventInfo);

  // create the EventHandler
  handler = new EventHandler(eventInfo);

  form.addCommand(parent.exitCommand);
  form.addCommand(parent.backCommand);
  form.setCommandListener(parent);

  // a change in volume gauge will be handled by this class
  form.setItemStateListener(this);

  players = new Hashtable();
}

public void playMedia(String locator) {

  try {

    // first look for an existing instance
    player = (Player)players.get(locator);

    if(player == null) {

      // create the player for the specified string locator
      player = Manager.createPlayer(
        getClass().getResourceAsStream(locator), "audio/x-wav");

      // add the EventHandler as a listener
      player.addPlayerListener(handler);

      // fetch it
      player.prefetch();

      // put this instance in the Hashtable
      players.put(locator, player);
```

```
      }

      // get the volume control
      volume = (VolumeControl)player.getControl("VolumeControl");

      // initialize it to 50
      volume.setLevel(50);

      // initialize the gauge
      gauge.setValue(volume.getLevel());
      gauge.setLabel("Volume: " + volume.getLevel());

      // play it twice
      player.setLoopCount(2);

      // start the player
      player.start();

      // set the title of the form
      form.setTitle("Playing " + locator);

    } catch(Exception e) {
      e.printStackTrace();
    }
  }

... rest of the code omitted as it doesn't change from Listing 3-4 ...
```

A single EventHandler instance is used for all three Player instances that are created. Because playerUpdate() receives the instance that generated the event, it's easy to distinguish between these instances, if necessary.

Handling a Custom Event

As you may realize by now, there is no special event class in the MMAPI. That is, events are distinguished as String constants in the PlayerListener interface. To create, rather to handle, a custom event, you do not need to extend any other class.

Custom event creation is primarily designed for MMAPI implementations. This means that the MMAPI specification, having designed its own mandatory events, makes it open for MMAPI implementations to create and broadcast their own events. The description of these events would be made clear in the documentation for each implementation, and the events are likely to be named in the reverse domain name convention. For example, the MMAPI reference implementation from Sun defines a custom event called com.sun.midi.lyrics, which is a Sun-specific event for karaoke lyrics.

Although the PlayerListener interface provides for events that are most common, in some special cases, you may want to define your own. For example, let's say you wanted to do something special that requires an event to be raised whenever an audio file has been played halfway through. None of the predefined events will satisfy this requirement, so you'll need to raise and handle your own custom event. But how do you actually create and raise an event?

The short answer is that you can't. Unless you are ready to implement your own version of a `Player` instance that handles the type of media that you are after. This is not an easy task and requires you to handle all the steps required in realizing, prefetching, and decoding, not to mention interfacing with the controls that it exposes. Further, you have to use your own version over the version supplied with the MMAPI implementation that you are working with. After you have accomplished these difficult tasks, you may be able to plug in and raise your own event.

Handling custom events is, as you may expect, much easier. You only need to know the name of the event and the type of `eventData` that it exposes to be able to use it in the `playerUpdate()` method. Thus, the following code fragment will catch the `com.sun.midi.lyrics` event, and the event data exposed will be a `byte` array:

```
if(event.equals("com.sun.midi.lyrics")) {
  byte[] data = (byte[])eventData;
}
```

Note that the MMAPI specification states that to catch standard events in the `playerUpdate()` method, you should use the reference equality check, and for custom events, you should use the object equality check. Thus, `(event == PlayerListener.CLOSED)` should be preferred over `event.equals(PlayerListener.CLOSED)`, and `event.equals("com.sun.midi.lyrics")` must be used for custom events. Standard events are automatically interned because they are constants; therefore, using the reference check will be faster than the object equality check. However, the same cannot be guaranteed for custom events, so you must always use the object equality test. The `EventHandler` in Listing 4-2 used the object equality test and is now converted to use the reference check in Listing 4-4 to make it more responsive.

Listing 4-4. *Converting* `EventHandler` *to Use Reference Checking Instead of Object Equality*

```
package com.apress.chapter4;

import javax.microedition.media.*;
import javax.microedition.media.control.*;
import javax.microedition.lcdui.StringItem;

public class EventHandler implements PlayerListener {

  private StringItem item;

  public EventHandler(StringItem item) {
    this.item = item;
  }

  public void playerUpdate(Player player, String event, Object eventData) {
```

```
  if(event == (PlayerListener.VOLUME_CHANGED)) {

    // a player's volume has been changed
    VolumeControl vc = (VolumeControl)eventData;
    updateDisplay("Volume Changed to: " + vc.getLevel());

    if(vc.getLevel() > 60)  {
      updateDisplay("Volume higher than 60 is too loud");
      vc.setLevel(60);
    }
  } else if(event == (PlayerListener.STOPPED)) {

    // player instance paused
    updateDisplay("Player paused at: " + (Long)eventData);
  } else if(event == (PlayerListener.STARTED)) {

    // player instance started (or restarted)
    updateDisplay("Player started at: " + (Long)eventData);
  } else if(event == (PlayerListener.END_OF_MEDIA)) {

    // player instance reached end of loop
    updateDisplay("Player reached end of loop.");
  } else if(event == (PlayerListener.CLOSED)) {

    // player instance closed
    updateDisplay("Player closed.");
  } else if(event == (PlayerListener.ERROR)) {

    // if an error occurs, eventData contains the error message
    updateDisplay("Error Message: " + (String)eventData);
  }
}

public void updateDisplay(String text) {

  // update the item on the screen
  item.setText(text);

  // and write to error stream as well
  System.err.println(text);
}
```

```
}
```

Due to device fragmentation, not all MMAPI implementations support reference check for events. Instead, you have to use `equals()` for comparison from Listing 4-2, instead of the improved code from Listing 4-4. The trick is to test your target device(s) for what is supported and optimize accordingly.

Summary

The several different states that a `Player` instance goes through in processing and playing media data allows developers to gain control over these states, provide feedback, and process events at these stages. These states are UNREALIZED, REALIZED, PREFETCHED, STARTED, and CLOSED, and the transitions between them are well defined and accessible.

In this chapter, you learned the background behind these states, the how and why of the transitions that take place between them, and how to respond to the various events generated during these transitions. You learned to create an event handling class and also how to listen to custom events.

The next chapter will introduce you to accessing media data over the network using MMAPI, a task that must be handled efficiently and cleanly for responsive multimedia MIDlets.

CHAPTER 5

Accessing Media Over the Network

The greatest advantage of applications built on mobile devices is that they can be run anywhere any time. These applications are truly mobile lifestyle choices because they allow us to extend our lifestyles by bringing these applications wherever we go, whether for fun or business. Applications that keep all data on mobile phones have the added advantage of being complete without requiring network access to function or update. However, truly mobile applications take advantage of available networks to provide an enhanced user experience.

Take the case of accessing multimedia files over a network. Although games and other fun applications can work with small embedded sound and other audio files, for an even, all-encompassing experience, the user requires network connectivity for his application to stream media over the network. A good reason for streaming over storing media files locally is the size of these files, video especially. Also streaming over stored media is used to provide updated files and to maintain digital rights over the provided content.

Whatever the reasons, accessing multimedia data over a network reliably is an important aspect of learning to use MMAPI. Although the issues involved are not unique to accessing multimedia data per se, they do need to be taken care of.

In this chapter, you'll learn about these common issues and how they affect multimedia data access over the network using MMAPI. You'll learn how to overcome these issues to create MIDlets that can access the network reliably and consistently. Finally, you'll see examples of these issues and the solutions to them.

Understanding Threads in Java ME

The threading environment in Java ME is slightly different from the normal environment in Java SE. The JVM in Java ME does not create a separate application thread for your MIDlet, which is contrary to what happens in an application being run on Java SE, where an application gets its own application thread separate from the system thread. All processing in a MIDlet takes place inside the main system thread. Thus, methods that take a long time to complete hog this single thread and create a bottleneck for a functional MIDlet.

Any threads that you create yourself within your MIDlet are, of course, separate from the system thread and therefore not restrictive. These threads can do their own thing independent of the main system thread. Of course, you have to strike a fine balance between the number of threads required versus the number of threads that the limited resources operating system can handle. Thread creation and management is a processor- and memory-hungry task and should be carefully used, especially in the Java ME environment, which runs on constrained devices.

To understand this better, take a look at Listing 5.1. When started, the MIDlet in this listing displays the name of the current system thread, which is the main MIDlet thread. When the user clicks the command for a new thread, the MIDlet creates a new thread, which displays an alert momentarily with its own name. It then simulates a long activity by sleeping for 4 seconds.

Listing 5-1. *Understanding Threads in MIDlets*

```
package com.apress.chapter5;

import javax.microedition.midlet.*;
import javax.microedition.lcdui.*;

public class ThreadTest extends MIDlet implements CommandListener {

  private Form form;
  private StringItem text;
  private Display display;

  public ThreadTest() {
    form = new Form("Thread Test");

    // displays the name of the current system thread
    text = new StringItem(
      "Current Thread:",
      Thread.currentThread().getName());

    form.append(text);

    // commands to exit and create new threads
    Command exit = new Command("Exit", Command.EXIT, 1);
    Command newThread = new Command("New Thread", Command.SCREEN, 1);

    form.addCommand(exit);
    form.addCommand(newThread);

    form.setCommandListener(this);

    display = Display.getDisplay(this);
  }

  public void startApp() {
    display.setCurrent(form);
  }
```

```
  public void pauseApp() {
  }

  public void destroyApp(boolean unconditional) {
  }

  public void commandAction(Command cmd, Displayable disp) {
    if(cmd.getLabel().equals("Exit")) {
      notifyDestroyed();
    } else {
      System.err.print("Starting new thread ... ");

      // create a new thread
      Thread runner = new Thread(new ThreadRunner(display));

      // and start it
      runner.start();

      System.err.println("Done");
    }
  }
}

class ThreadRunner implements Runnable {

  // the parent MIDlet's display
  Display display;

  ThreadRunner(Display display) {
    this.display = display;
  }

  public void run() {

    System.err.print(
      "New thread ( " + Thread.currentThread().getName() + " ) running .. ");

    display.setCurrent(
      new Alert(Thread.currentThread().getName()));

    try {
      Thread. sleep(3000);
    } catch(Exception e) {}

    System.err.println("Done");
  }
}
```

Caution The getName() used in this listing for the Thread class is a CLDC 1.1 method. This listing will not work in CLDC 1.0 devices.

Figure 5-1 shows the MIDlet running in the Motorola emulator across a few actions, along with the output.

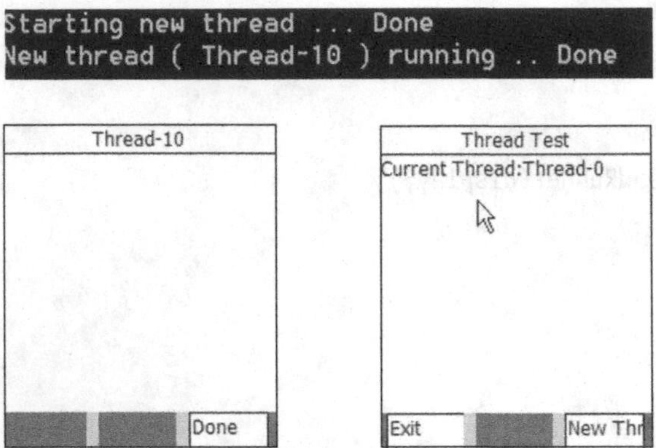

Figure 5-1. *Screen and console output for the* ThreadTest *MIDlet on Motorola emulator*

The MIDlet identifies the way threads work in the Java ME environment. The simulation of a long activity inside a new thread doesn't lock up the main MIDlet thread waiting for this activity to finish. The main MIDlet thread continues its processing after creating and starting the new thread. This concept is further established in Figure 5-2, which shows the main system thread and a new thread's activity and actions.

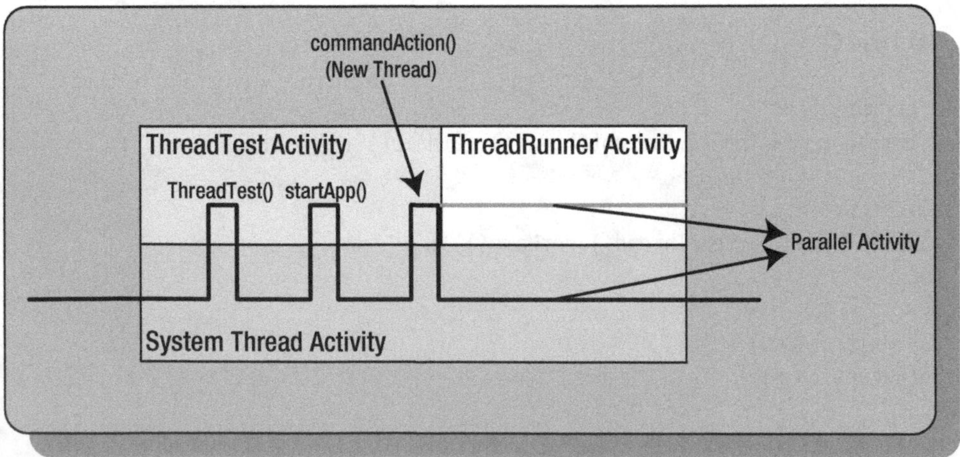

Figure 5-2. *System and new thread activity*

At this stage, you may be wondering if an understanding of thread activity in MIDlets has anything to do with using the MMAPI over a network. It does because network access of multimedia files (and all network activity) should only be done in a separate thread, distinct from the system thread. This is to make sure that network access of these files doesn't leave the main application unresponsive to the user. This is discussed further later in this chapter.

Understanding Permissions for Network Access

Whereas creating responsive MMAPI MIDlets with separate threads is one aspect of accessing network based media, another issue relates to permissions for media access over the network. MIDlets don't automatically have permissions to grab files over the network, so this must be explicitly or implicitly configured.

MIDlets run in a protection domain, which provides access to individual permissions based on whether or not the user grants (or denies) these permissions for the current MIDlet session or for the life of the MIDlet. Individual permissions must be requested explicitly, but not from within the MIDlet code. The permissions that are interesting for MMAPI development are `javax.microedition.io.Connector.http` and `javax.microedition.io.Connector.https`. This section focuses on these permissions, which allow retrieval of media files over the Web.

When any attempt is made to retrieve media files over the network, for example, by specifying an HTTP locator for the `createPlayer()` method, the MIDlet's protection domain kicks in. Because `javax.microedition.io.Connector.http` is a restricted permission, the user of the MIDlet must decide whether to grant access to the network.

As an example, consider the MIDlet in Listing 5-2, which wants to make a connection to a remote server to retrieve and play an audio file.

Listing 5-2. *Playing an Audio File Over the Network*

```
package com.apress.chapter5;

import javax.microedition.midlet.*;
import javax.microedition.lcdui.*;
import javax.microedition.media.*;

public class NetworkTest extends MIDlet implements CommandListener {

  private List list;
  private StringItem text;
  private Display display;

  public NetworkTest() {

    list = new List("Press Play", List.IMPLICIT);
```

```
    // commands to exit and play
    Command exit = new Command("Exit", Command.EXIT, 1);
    Command play = new Command("Play", Command.SCREEN, 1);

    list.addCommand(exit);
    list.addCommand(play);

    list.setCommandListener(this);
    display = Display.getDisplay(this);
  }

  public void startApp() {
    display.setCurrent(list);
  }

  public void pauseApp() {
  }

  public void destroyApp(boolean unconditional) {
  }

  public void commandAction(Command cmd, Displayable disp) {
    if(cmd.getLabel().equals("Exit")) {
      notifyDestroyed();
    } else {
      try {
        Player player =
          Manager.createPlayer(
        "http://www.mmapibook.com/resources/media/audio/chapter5/siren.wav");
        player.start();
      } catch(Exception e) { System.err.println(e); }
    }
  }
}
```

The bold code is where a `Player` instance is created by making a network connection for file retrieval. When you run this listing, the MIDlet needs to be granted permission by the user. Figure 5-3 shows how this permission is granted in the three different environments (Sun Java ME emulator, Motorola C975 emulator, and the Motorola C975 device, respectively).

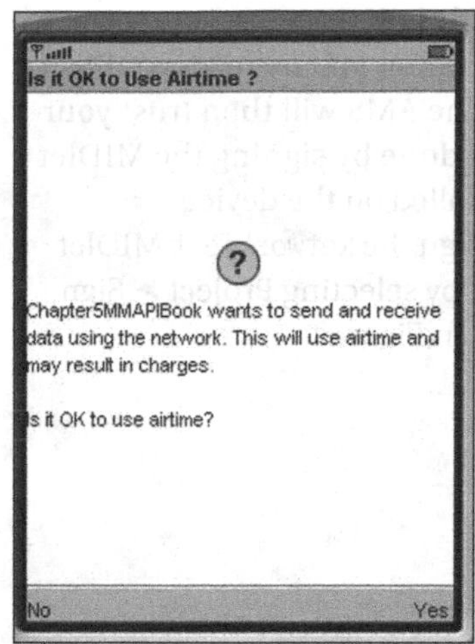

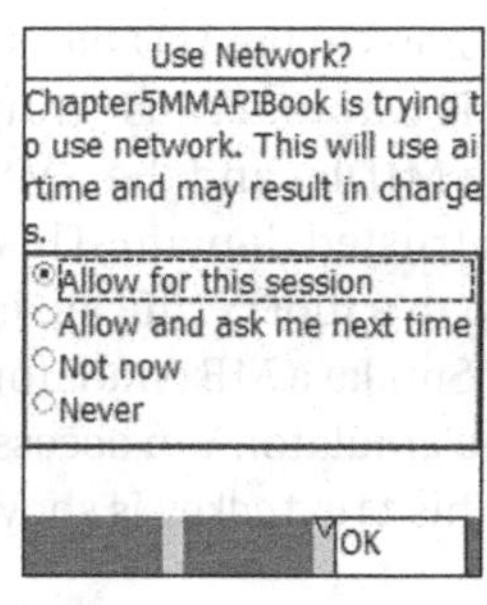

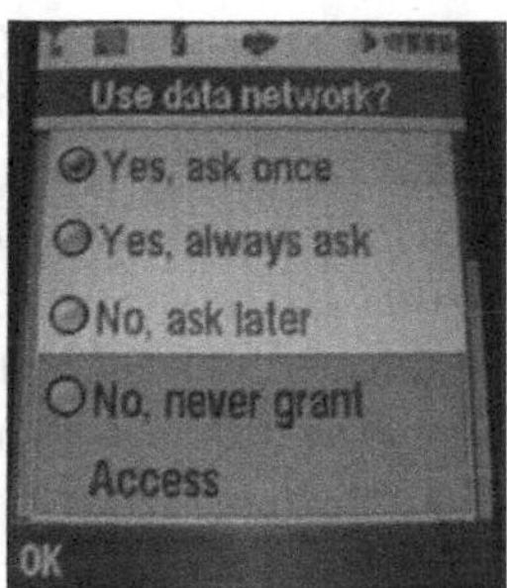

Figure 5-3. *Granting network access permission*

Most users who trust your MIDlet will want to select the Yes, Ask Once choice (or similar), so they won't be bothered the next time they run your MIDlet. By default, all MIDlets are run in an untrusted protection domain, where the user is always consulted for granting network access permission rights. You'll need to establish a level of trust for the device to run your network accessing MIDlet without requiring interaction from the user.

Trust is established by signing your MIDlet and putting it in a trusted domain. The complete details of how you do that is beyond the scope of this book, but this section outlines the steps required to get the `NetworkTest` MIDlet working without needing to request permission to access the network from the user.

To start with, you'll need to modify the JAD manifest file for this MIDlet and add an entry to request permission for HTTP access, as shown here:

```
MIDlet-Permissions: javax.microedition.io.Connector.http
```

If the connection to access the file will be over a secure connection, you need to request HTTPS access. If you're not sure, you can request both permissions.

```
MIDlet-Permissions:
  javax.microedition.io.Connector.http, javax.microedition.io.Connector.https
```

■ **Note** The preceding code lines should not be broken into two lines during coding; they are broken here due to space concerns.

Now when this MIDlet is being installed on a device, the AMS will fail the installation if it's unable to provide these permissions to the MIDlet. This means that if AMS is unable to put this MIDlet in a trusted domain, it halts the installation.

Of course, simply requesting permissions in the JAD file is only half the story. Any rogue MIDlet could request the permission this way and cause trouble. You still need to establish some sort of trust principle between the MIDlet and the AMS; the AMS will then trust your MIDlet enough to let it be installed in a trusted domain. This is done by signing the MIDlet with a certificate that can be validated up to a root certificate installed on the device.

To complete this test, at least on the Sun Java ME emulator, sign the `NetworkTest` MIDlet with the `trustedkey` key installed with the emulator. You access it by selecting Project ➤ Sign in the emulator as shown in Figure 5-4. This `trustedkey` is shown in Figure 5-5.

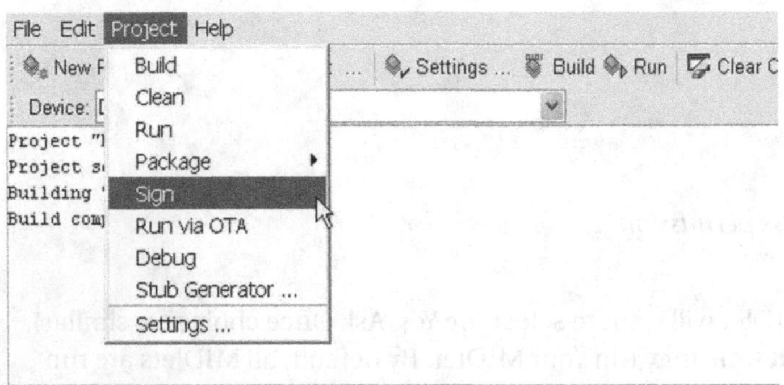

Figure 5-4. *Signing the* `NetworkTest` *MIDlet in the Sun Java ME emulator*

Sign MIDlet Suite

Action

Sign MIDlet Suite... New Key Pair... Generate CSR ... Import Certificate ... Import Key Pair...

Alias List: trustedkey

J2SE Key Details

```
Creation Date: Wed Mar 16 20:43:39 EST 2005
Certificate chain length: 1
Certificate [1]
Subject: CN=cName, OU=orgUnit, O=org, L=city, ST=state
Issuer : CN=cName, OU=orgUnit, O=org, L=city, ST=state
Serial number: 42380ddb
Valid from Wed Mar 16 20:43:39 EST 2005 to Mon Dec 10 20:43:39 EST 2007
Certificate fingerprints:
  MD5: 04:4f:5b:14:ed:81:6b:12:cb:1f:7a:cd:22:a5:b0:37
  SHA: b2:79:46:c6:60:7c:54:ca:b7:ae:be:3a:d5:cb:cd:40:45:5b:ed:a2
```

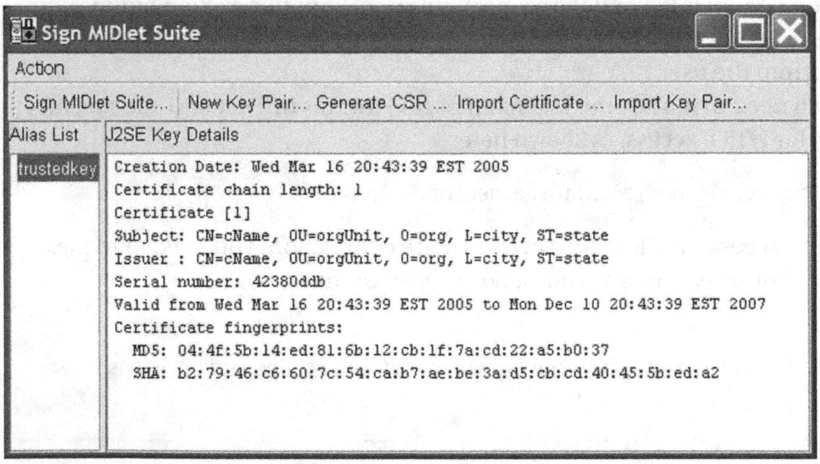

Figure 5-5. *The* `trustedkey` *used to sign the* `NetworkTest` *MIDlet*

After the MIDlet is signed, you can test it by using the Run via OTA menu option shown in Figure 5-6. You don't use the Run menu option like you have been doing so far because when you run the MIDlet locally (by selecting the Run menu option), it does not get installed into a protection domain. Only when installed via the Run via OTA option does your MIDlet gets a chance to be installed into a requested domain, which is the domain that you request by specifying permission for it in the JAD file.

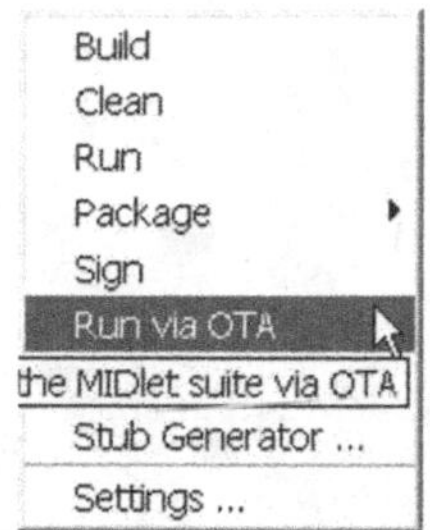

Figure 5-6. *Running* NetworkTest *MIDlet via Over the Air provisioning*

Of course, so far, you've only tested in the Sun Java ME emulator platform. Testing on the Motorola C975 emulator and device is only possible if you have a certificate containing a key-pair that can be trusted to a root certificate installed on the emulator and device, respectively. Even then, the actual device may only keep your MIDlet in a third-party trust domain that will never be fully trusted. To get it to a higher trust level, you need to sign it with a certificate supplied by either a manufacturer (Motorola) or an operator (for example, Vodafone). An alternate mechanism is to use the Java Verified Program, which certifies your application for deployment on devices that support this program. See more details of this program at *http://www.javaverified.com*.

To summarize, using MMAPI across a network requires looking at two issues:

- Network operations can be time consuming and should be done in a separate thread from the main application thread.
- Network access requires permission from the user. To gain this permission and then acquire a level of trust, your MIDlet must request this permission implicitly and be signed with a certificate that can be traced to a root certificate. Alternatively, explicit permission from the user is required when network access is attempted, which the user may not give.

You just learned about the second item in the preceding list; the next section covers the first issue in the list in more detail, expanding on what you've learned so far.

Putting It Together

The MIDlets created in the previous chapters have accessed their media files through the JAR file in which they are bundled. In this section, you'll create a Player instance that will access a media file over the network via HTTP. You'll create a separate thread from the main MIDlet thread to handle the task of creating and realizing the Player instance.

Listing 5-3 shows the code for the ThreadedMIDlet that initiates the playback. When requested by the user, it creates a new thread using the NetworkPlayerManager class, shown in Listing 5-4.

Listing 5-3. ThreadedMIDlet *Creates a New Thread to Play Back a Media File*

```
package com.apress.chapter5;

import javax.microedition.midlet.*;
```

```
import javax.microedition.lcdui.*;
import javax.microedition.media.*;

public class ThreadedMIDlet extends MIDlet implements CommandListener {

  private List list;
  private StringItem text;
  private Display display;

  private NetworkPlayerManager mgr;
  private Command cancel = new Command("Cancel", Command.CANCEL, 1);

  public ThreadedMIDlet() {

    list = new List("Press Play", List.IMPLICIT);

    // commands to exit and play
    Command exit = new Command("Exit", Command.EXIT, 1);
    Command play = new Command("Play", Command.SCREEN, 1);

    list.addCommand(exit);
    list.addCommand(play);

    list.setCommandListener(this);
    display = Display.getDisplay(this);
  }

  public void startApp() {
    display.setCurrent(list);
  }

  public void pauseApp() {
  }

  public void destroyApp(boolean unconditional) {
  }

  public void commandAction(Command cmd, Displayable disp) {
    if(cmd.getLabel().equals("Exit")) {
      notifyDestroyed();
    } else if(cmd.getLabel().equals("Cancel")) {
      mgr.cancel();
      display.setCurrent(list);
    } else {
      try {
        mgr = new NetworkPlayerManager(display, cancel, this);
        Thread runner = new Thread(mgr);
        runner.start();
```

```
      } catch(Exception e) { System.err.println(e); }
    }
  }
}
```

As you can see, Listing 5-3 is built on top of Listing 5-2. The changes are marked in bold. A new command is added to allow users to cancel a request to play the media file, in case it takes too long or the user changes his mind. The code to handle this command is added in the `commandAction()` method. More importantly, the default handling of the play command is now changed. A new class, `NetworkPlayerManager`, is created, and because it implements the `Runnable` interface, it can be started as a thread. Before going forward, let's take a look at this class in Listing 5-4.

Listing 5-4. `NetworkPlayerManager` *Class Implements the* `Runnable` *Interface and Makes Network Connections for Media Playback*

```
package com.apress.chapter5;

import javax.microedition.lcdui.*;
import javax.microedition.media.*;

public class NetworkPlayerManager implements Runnable {

  private Display display;
  private Form form;
  private StringItem msg;

  private boolean cancel = false;

  private Player player = null;

  public NetworkPlayerManager(
    Display display, Command cancelCmd, ThreadedMIDlet parent) {

    this.display = display;

    form = new Form("Network Player Manager");
    msg = new StringItem("Please Wait ... ", null);
    form.append(msg);
    form.addCommand(cancelCmd);

    form.setCommandListener(parent);
  }

  public void run() {

    display.setCurrent(form);
    boolean connected = false;
```

```
    try {
      player =
        Manager.createPlayer(
          "http://www.mmapibook.com/resources/media/audio/chapter5/siren.wav");

      player.realize();

      connected = true;
    } catch (Exception e) {
      msg.setText("Failed: " + e.getMessage());
      System.err.println(e);
      return;
    }

    if(connected && !cancel)
      msg.setText("Connected. Starting playback...");
    else {
      msg.setText("Unable to connect.");
      return;
    }

    try {
      player.start();
    } catch(Exception pe) {
      msg.setText(pe.getMessage());
      System.err.println(pe);
    }
  }

  public void cancel() {
    cancel = true;
    if(player!= null) player.deallocate();
  }
}
```

When a new instance of the `NetworkPlayerManager` class is created, it creates a `Form` instance and appends a `StringItem` for displaying messages. The cancel command is attached to this form, but the command listener for this command is still the calling MIDlet.

When the thread is started, the `run()` method takes over. It makes the `form` instance as the current display and tries to realize the `Player` instance for playback of the media file. If connection can be established, the message on the screen is updated and the playback is initiated. If, for some reason, the connection cannot be established, an error message is displayed and the display returns to the calling MIDlet.

Connection may not be established for a variety of reasons. The device may not allow your MIDlet access to the network if it isn't signed and in a correct domain, as you learned in the previous section. A path to the remote server may not be available.

While the MIDlet is trying to connect to the remote server, the user must be given a chance to cancel the request. The user can do this by issuing the cancel command. When this happens, the `cancel()` method is called, which deallocates the `Player` instance. Recall from Chapter 4 that calling `deallocate()` on an instance that is blocked at the realize call results in the instance being returned to the UNREALIZED state. Thus, if the network is intermittent or taking too long, the user can cancel the request. If the `Player` instance has already reached the REALIZED state, calling cancel will not affect anything.

If you sign this MIDlet and put it in the correct domain, you will not be asked permission to access the network when you run it. Figure 5-7 shows running a MIDlet over the Sun Java ME and the Motorola C975 emulators.

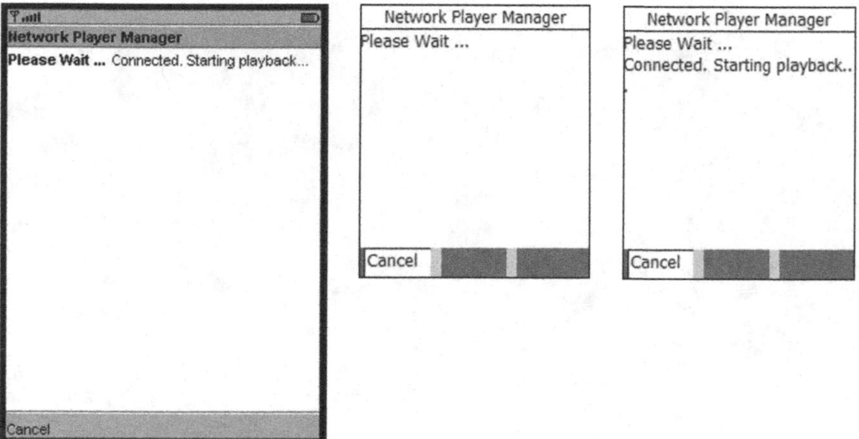

Figure 5-7. *Network access of a media file using a separate thread over Sun's DefaultColorPhone and Motorola C975 emulators*

Summary

Accessing media data over the network requires careful consideration because it involves two issues. First, network access should be done in a separate thread from the main thread, because accessing the network may block the main thread for a long time, leading to an unresponsive MIDlet. Second, network access requires permission from the user of the MIDlet as it may lead to charges from the network operator.

This chapter showed you how to overcome these two issues by explaining threads in Java ME and how they affect network access. The chapter also explained the concept of protection domains and how to overcome them for requesting permissions for network access. The chapter finished with an all-encompassing example that solved those two issues together.

The next chapter covers generating and playing tones using MMAPI with the help of the `ToneControl` control.

CHAPTER 6

Creating and Playing Tones Using ToneControl

The MMAPI is unique in providing a genuine capability to play synthetic tones on mobile devices. We all recognize the sometimes annoying, but practical, ring tones on most mobile phones. With MMAPI, you can program your own tones to build a ring tone that plays when an event occurs, to embed in a game as a musical accompaniment to the main action, or just for plain fun.

In this chapter, you'll learn how to use the built-in tone generator mechanism in MMAPI to generate and distribute synthetic tones. You'll start with the single note generator provided by the `Manager` class. You'll then learn about the `ToneControl` class, which provides mechanisms to generate complex tones based on user-defined sequences. Finally, you'll learn how to distribute these tone sequences using the JTS file structure.

First, however, you need to understand the basics of synthetic tones. Let's start with some background on this topic.

Understanding Synthetic Tones

Synthetic tones, as the name suggests, are tones generated synthetically, or more specifically, by a computer system. A ring tone is a dominant example of synthetic tones, but computer systems have been capable of generating these tones for quite some time. The ring tone industry has popularized the enormous push for this technology to enhance capabilities of mobile phones, resulting in first, monophonic, and now, polyphonic ring tones.

A synthetic tone is a musical note that has a defined duration. Monophonic ring tones only play one note of music at a time. Before the start of the next note, the previous note is cut off. Older synthesizers and almost all mobile phones and devices can play monophonic tones.

Note In music, a *note* is the unit of fixed pitch that has been given a name, or the graphic representation of that pitch in a notation system. In English, notes are given seven names: A, B, C, D, E, F, and G (in order of rising pitch).

Comparatively, polyphonic ring tones can play multiple tones at the same time, thereby providing the effect of multiple instruments playing together. Not only does it resemble a more convincing musical background, but also it's pleasing to the ears. Most modern mobile devices are capable of playing polyphonic tones.

As far as MMAPI is concerned, a single tone is specified using the note, duration, and volume. These three must be specified for the underlying engine to be able to play the tone. MMAPI provides the capability to play either a single tone using the static method `Manager.playTone(int note, int duration, int volume)` or more complex tone sequences (ring tones are nothing but sequences of tones) using the `ToneControl` interface. You'll see examples of both of these shortly.

Understanding Note, Pitch, and Frequency

To better understand how MMAPI plays tones, you must differentiate between different notes of music by understanding how notes relate to pitches and how their representation is used in MMAPI.

As stated earlier, in English seven notes are represented by the symbols A, B, C, D, E, F, and G. Each of these represents an increasing frequency of music. However, frequency is a physical term, as far as human understanding of music is concerned, and therefore, it is replaced with the more generic term of pitch. Thus, musically, pitch is the perception of the frequency of a note, and the symbols A to G represent notes in order of rising pitch. Symbol A represents a lower pitched musical note than symbol B, which is lower than symbol C, and so on.

Mathematically, each symbol is related to a frequency value, because each symbol represents a pitch. Table 6-1 shows the frequency value of each symbol.

Table 6-1. *Frequency Values for the Basic Notes*

Note Symbol	Frequency (in Hertz (Hz))
A	440
B	493.92
C	523.28
D	587.36
E	659.28
F	698.48
G	784

Of course, things are not this simple. There are a large number of variations on the basic symbols, so let's clarify some of the more important ones.

Even though notes are represented using only these seven symbols, the symbols are repetitive for frequencies that are an octave above or below them. This is better explained with an example.

■Note An *octave* is the interval between one musical note and another with half or double the frequency.

Consider the symbol A. Although it represents the frequency 440, it also represents the frequencies 220 (= 440 / 2) and 880 (= 440 * 2). Further, it represents the frequencies 110 (= 220 / 2), 55 (= 110 / 2), and 27.5 (= 55 / 2) as well. All these frequencies are an octave interval apart because they are double or half of the frequency before or after them, respectively. Thus, A is a musical note that represents the frequencies 27.5, 55, 110, 220, 440, and 880. To distinguish between the different octaves, a number is placed after the symbol. A4 represents the fourth octave for the musical note A, which is 440 Hz. Table 6-2 summarizes some of these symbols.

Table 6-2. *The Different Octaves for the Musical Note A*

Symbol	Frequency (Hz)
A0	27.5
A1	55
A2	110
A3	220
A4	440
A5	880

The other seven symbols are similarly modified to arrive at different corresponding octaves. As an example, Table 6-3 shows some of the different octaves for the musical note C.

Table 6-3. *The Different Octaves for the Musical Note C*

Symbol	Frequency (Hz)
C0	16.35
C1	32.70
C2	65.41
C3	130.82
C4	261.64
C5	523.28

When no number is placed after a musical symbol, it usually means the fourth octave. Thus, A implies the frequency at 440 Hz (A4), and C implies the frequency at 261.64 (C4).

Besides octaves, the notes can differ by a semitone. If an octave difference in frequency is double or half of each frequency, a semitone is a musical interval that is one-twelfth of an octave. Alternatively, an octave contains 12 semitones.

Note A *semitone* is one-twelfth of an octave and is also known as half step. It is the smallest musical interval.

Thus, if a musical note differs from another by a semitone, it is modified into either a *sharp* or a *flat*. A sharp raises the pitch of a note by a semitone interval, whereas a flat lowers the pitch by a semitone interval. Using musical notation, a sharp is denoted by # while b is used to denote a flat. Thus, C# (pronounced C-sharp) denotes the musical note that is a semitone above C_4 and equals 277.183 Hz. This symbol may also be written as $C_4^{\#}$, but C# is more common.

The figure of 277.183 for a pitch that is a semitone above C4 (261.64 Hz) comes from the fact that a semitone is one-twelfth of an octave, and an octave above a frequency means doubling over the previous frequency. This implies that a semitone above (or sharp as it is called) a frequency means multiplying it by the twelfth root of 2. The twelfth root of 2 equals 1.059463. Therefore, 261.64 * 1.059463 = 277.183.

Similarly, a flat pitch implies dividing the frequency by the twelfth root of 2. Therefore, C_4^{b} equals 261.64 / 1.059463 = 246.95.

Given any note, you can thus arrive at the note higher or lower than that by multiplying or dividing it by the constant 1.059463.

Using a MMAPI Formula to Calculate Note Values

With this brief interlude into musical mathematics complete, let's return to the tone support in MMAPI. To play a single tone, you can use the `Manager` class static method `playTone(int note, int duration, int volume)`. The second and third parameters are self explanatory, but the first one needs an explanation. With the background in mind from the previous section, the first parameter cannot be the frequency of a note because it is only an `int` value, whereas frequencies can have a decimal part.

The Javadoc for this method defines that the `note` parameter can be a value between `0` and `127`, both inclusive. It also provides a formula to arrive at these values as well, based on the frequency of the desired note to be played as a tone by this method. This method is shown here:

```
note = ln(freq/8.176)*(17.31234049066755)
```

The value `17.31234049066755` is called the `SEMITONE_CONST` and is arrived at with the formula:

```
SEMITONE_CONST = 1/(ln(2^(1/12)))
```

Note that `ln` in both these formulas means log to the base 'e,' also called the natural logarithm of a number (as opposed to the common logarithm, which is log to the base 10).

Using this formula, let's calculate the corresponding `int note` parameter value for the note represented by C#. As you learned in the last section, the frequency of C# is equal to 277.183.

```
note (C#) = ln(277.183/8.176) * (17.31234049066755) = 61 (after rounding)
```

To play C# using MMAPI, you use the value `61`. Listing 6-1 shows a MIDlet that will play this value when run.

Listing 6-1. *Playing C# for 5 Seconds at Max Volume*

```
package com.apress.chapter6;

import javax.microedition.midlet.MIDlet;
import javax.microedition.media.Manager;
import javax.microedition.media.MediaException;

public class CSharpMIDlet extends MIDlet {
  public CSharpMIDlet() {
  }
```

```
  public void startApp() {
    try {
      // plays C# (frequency of 277.183 for 5 seconds at max volume)
      Manager.playTone(61, 5000, 100);
    } catch(MediaException me) { System.err.println(me); }
  }

  public void pauseApp() {
  }

  public void destroyApp(boolean unconditional) {
  }

}
```

The outcome on all three of our test environments will be the same sound being played for a maximum of 5 seconds at the loudest permissible volume. Not terribly exciting, but it demonstrates the basic way of using this method to play tones.

You don't have to manually calculate the integer value of a note given its frequency. Listing 6-2 shows a simple Java class that does this for you using the formula provided earlier. The class also contains a method for doing the reverse; that is, given the integer value of a note, it will tell you the corresponding frequency of the note/tone. Finally, this Java class contains a method that will print all the 128 notes along with their corresponding frequencies.

■ **Caution** Listing 6-2 cannot be run in a Java ME environment because Java ME doesn't contain the methods `ln(double val)` and `exp(double val)` in the `Math` class. Therefore, this method must be run in a Java SE environment.

Listing 6-2. *A Simple Java Class to Calculate Note Frequencies and* `int` *Values*

```
package com.apress.chapter6;

public class NoteCalculator {

  public static final double SEMITONE_CONST = 17.31234049066755;
  public static final double ARBIT_CONST = 8.176;

  public static int getNoteAsInt(double freq) {
    return (int)Math.round((Math.log(freq/ARBIT_CONST) * SEMITONE_CONST));
  }

  public static double getNoteFreq(int note) {
    return (ARBIT_CONST * Math.exp(note/SEMITONE_CONST));
  }
```

```
public static void printAllNoteFreq() {
  for(int i = 0; i < 128; i++) {
    System.err.println(i + " : " + getNoteFreq(i));
  }
}

public static void main(String[] args) {

  try {
    if(args.length == 2) {
      if(args[0].equals("1")) {
        double freq = new Double(args[1]).doubleValue();
        System.err.println(args[1] + " Hz : " + getNoteAsInt(freq));
      } else {
        int note = new Integer(args[1]).intValue();
        System.err.println(args[1] + ": " + getNoteFreq(note));
      }
    } else {
      System.err.println("Usage: NoteCalculator convType convVal \r\n" +
      " where convType: 1 for freq in Hz and 2 for note value in int \r\n" +
      " and convVal is the actual value");
    }
  } catch(Exception e) {
    System.err.println(e);
  }

  // print all notes from 0 to 127
  printAllNoteFreq();
 }
}
```

Using the methods of this class, Table 6-4 lists the integer note values for the basic notes defined in Table 6-1.

Table 6-4. *Integer Note Values for the Basic Notes*

Basic Note	Integer Note Value
A	69
B	71
C	72
D	74
E	76
F	77
G	79

Using the playTone() Method

playTone() is a nonblocking method, which means that after it is called, it returns immediately. Your MIDlet continues to play the tone for the time you specify with the duration parameter. Listing 6-3 shows an example MIDlet that will play all the notes from 0 to 127 sequentially.

Listing 6-3. *Playing All Notes Sequentially*

```
package com.apress.chapter6;

import javax.microedition.midlet.MIDlet;
import javax.microedition.media.*;
import javax.microedition.lcdui.*;

public class AllTonesPlayer extends MIDlet implements CommandListener {

  Form displayForm = new Form("Playing all tones");
  StringItem info = new StringItem("", "");
  Command exit = new Command("Exit", Command.EXIT, 1);
  Thread runner;
  boolean stop = false;

  public void startApp() {

    displayForm.append(info);
    Display.getDisplay(this).setCurrent(displayForm);
    displayForm.addCommand(exit);
    displayForm.setCommandListener(this);

    // create and start a new thread to play all the notes
    runner = new Thread(new TonePlayer(info));
    runner.start();
  }

  public void pauseApp() {
  }

  public void destroyApp(boolean unconditional) {
    if(runner != null) stop = true;

  }
```

```
  public void commandAction(Command cmd, Displayable disp) {
    // only exit command defined in this MIDlet
    destroyApp(true);
    notifyDestroyed();
  }

}

// Plays all notes sequentially
class TonePlayer implements Runnable {

  StringItem info;
  AllTonesPlayer midlet;

  public TonePlayer(StringItem info, AllTonesPlayer midlet) {
    this.info = info;
    this.midlet = midlet;
  }

  public void run() {
    try {
      for(int i = 0; i < 128; i++) {
        // wait a second before playing the next note
        Thread.sleep(1000);
        info.setText("Playing: " + i);
        Manager.playTone(i, 500, 100); // play for 500 milliseconds at max vol
        if(midlet.stop) break;
      }

    } catch(Exception me) { System.err.println(me); }
  }
}
```

The MIDlet starts playing the tones as soon as it's started. The `playTone()` method is called sequentially after every 1 second to play the note for 500 milliseconds. The note generation part is separated from the main MIDlet system thread into its own thread using the `TonePlayer` class to allow easy termination of this thread, and consequently, the tone generation sequence from the main system thread. Figure 6-1 shows the output on the Sun Java ME DefaultColorPhone emulator.

Figure 6-1. *Playing all tones in the Sun Java ME DefaultColorPhone emulator*

The `playTone()` method can throw a `MediaException` if the note can't be played due to a hardware problem with the underlying mobile device. This usually occurs if the device doesn't support the playback of tones or if the device is using the built-in tone generator (by ringing to indicate an incoming call, for example). The method also throws the runtime `IllegalArgumentException` if the `duration` parameter is set to a negative value. Setting the `volume` parameter to a negative value results in the volume being set to 0 and 100 for any value over 100.

Using Tone Sequences with `ToneControl`

Of course, playing single tones isn't very useful in itself, except in games and applications where you may want to emphasize a critical point by playing a note of high pitch to draw the user's attention. Of more interest to most developers is the ability to play tones in a sequence that resembles popular songs so they can integrate them as ring tones on mobile devices or as background tones in games.

In the last section, you saw an example of playing tones in a sequence using the `playTone()` method. The underlying hardware was told to play single tones after a predefined interval, which is hardly suitable for realistic and continuous music.

The MMAPI defines the `ToneControl` interface to play tones in a sequence. You specify the notes that you want played in any sequence that you want, including repetitive blocks, along with tempo, volume, and duration using a `byte` array. A `Player` instance for playing tones can then be used like a normal `Player` instance, including using all control and lifecycle methods that you have learned about so far.

Before you learn how to create a `Player` instance for tone playback, you need to learn how to create tone sequences using the proprietary format defined by MMAPI.

Defining Tone Sequences

Tone sequences are defined using a slightly complicated format. Basically, a tone sequences is a collection of notes and durations values as you have learned in the previous sections. Note values range from 0 to 127 representing the various frequencies, but the value of the duration for each note is defined differently than before.

For tone sequences, the duration of each note is specified using *resolution*, as opposed to measuring it in milliseconds, which you've seen so far. To understand resolution, you need to know about another standard measurement of music using the beats present in musical notes.

Understanding Time Signature

A beat, as you may know, is the pulse of music. A *time signature* is used to define how many beats are in each *bar* (segment of time) of music along with how many note values constitute one beat. Just remember that time signature is a way to quantify musical work using the beats and the notes duration that constitute one beat.

Time signature is written as a fraction. The numerator indicates the number of beats in a bar and the denominator specifies the notes/beat (that is, the fraction of note duration that makes up one beat). The most common time signature is 4/4 (called *common time*), which means that there are 4 beats in a bar and 1/4 of a note makes up a beat.

Caution Make sure it is 1/4 of a note, not 4 notes.

In other words, common time written as 4/4 implies that there will be 4 beats per measure (musical measure or bar), with each beat composed of a quarter note.

Calculating Duration Using Resolution and Tempo

Let's say you want to play a tone for 1 second. To completely specify the duration, you also need to specify the tempo of the tone of the note because tempo, which represents the beats per minute of a note, varies the way the tone is heard. Let's say the tone that you want to play for 1 second should correspond to the common time you read about in the last section. That is, there should be 4 beats (one whole note) in the tone. Then, the resolution (which is a measure of duration) is specified using the following formula:

```
duration (milliseconds) * default resolution * default tempo / 240000 = resolution
```

Now, the default resolution equals 64, and the default tempo is equal to 120 beats per minute (bpm). Thus, playing a note for 1 second using the default resolution of 64 and the default tempo of 120 bpm by using the preceding formula equals the duration of

```
1000 * 64 * 120 / 240000 = 32
```

You are, of course, allowed to change the values of the default resolution and tempo. Thus, let's say the default tempo is changed to a faster beat, with 240 bpm as the value. The same tone will have the duration of

```
1000 * 64 * 240 / 240000 = 64
```

and for a slower beat of say 60 bpm:

```
1000 * 64 * 60 / 240000 = 16
```

Similarly, changing the default resolution to say 32 will result in a duration of

```
1000 * 32 * 120 / 240000 = 16
```

If all this seems too complicated for simple tone generation, then just remember to use the duration of a note in multiples of 8, with 8 being the lowest interval for which you want the tone to play and 120 being the longest. (You can use values that are not multiples of 8 as well, but they don't produce accurate results. No duration value can be greater than 127, as the duration is represented as a byte.)

Creating Sequences

Now that you know how to specify the note and calculate the duration for the note, you can now actually create a tone sequence to play using the ToneControl interface. The simplest tone sequence contains the ToneControl version number, which is always 1, followed by note-duration pairs. Thus, the following is a single note tone sequence:

```
ToneControl.VERSION, 1
69, 32
```

The first two values in the sequence must always be ToneControl.VERSION and 1. This identifies the version of this ToneControl (version of the ToneControl, not the sequence that you are describing), and by default is equal to 1 and unlikely to change. Next, you will have a note followed by its duration as described in the previous sections. Thus, the preceding sequence consists of a single note 69 that must be played for duration of 32 resolution.

There is no specific value to end a sequence. The last note-duration pair ends the sequence. Therefore, the preceding sequence is complete and valid. In code, it looks like the following:

```
byte[] sequence = new byte[] {
  ToneControl.VERSION, 1,
  69, 32,
};
```

VERSION is a constant in the ToneControl interface and is assigned a value of -2.

Let's now add more notes to this sequence. Actually, let's try to create the sequence for a popular tune, "Happy Birthday to You."

The tone sequence for the first stanza for this tune is shown here in note-duration pairs:

```
72, 4, 72, 2, 74, 8, 72, 8, 77, 8, 76, 16
```

In code, it looks like this:

```
byte[] sequence = new byte[] {
  ToneControl.VERSION, 1,
  72, 4, // Hap-
  ToneControl.SILENCE, 2,
  72, 2, // -py
  ToneControl.SILENCE, 2,
  74, 8, // Birth-
```

```
  ToneControl.SILENCE, 2,
  72, 8, // -day
  ToneControl.SILENCE, 2,
  77, 8, // to
ToneControl.SILENCE, 2,
76, 16 // you
};
```

To arrive at the note values and their durations for this sequence the trick is to use tone values that are available freely on the Internet for various other formats. However, these formats are different from the MMAPI format described so far, so you need to be able to convert between these formats and the MMAPI format.

The most popular format is the Ringing Tone Text Transfer Language (RTTTL) format, published by Nokia. Various Web sites on the Internet will provide you with the RTTTL format for a song or tune (just search for the name of the song or tune along with the text "RTTTL"). For example, the RTTTL format for the complete "Happy Birthday to You" tune is

```
Happy Birthday Song:d=4,o=5,b=125:16c, 32p, 32c, 32p, 8d, 32p, 8c, 32p, 8f, 32p, e,
 16p, 16c, 32p, 32c, 32p, 8d, 32p, 8c, 32p, 8g, 32p, f, 8p, 16c, 32p, 32c, 32p,
 8c6, 32p, 8a, 32p, 8f, 32p, 8e, 32p, 8d, 32p, 16a#, 32p, 32a#, 32p, 8a, 32p, 8f,
 32p, 8g, 32p, f
```

After you get the format for your particular song/tune, you need to convert it to the MMAPI format. You could try to understand the RTTTL format before you start to convert it to the MMAPI format, or you could just use the `RingToneConverter` class provided by Sun to do this for you.

Converting RTTTL to MMAPI Format Using `RingToneConverter`

The `RingToneConverter` class is provided with the examples in the Wireless Toolkit. This class is present in the MMADemo application as a standalone Java ME class. It converts the RTTTL format to the MMAPI format and is very handy. Listing 6-4 shows a MIDlet called `ConverterMIDlet` that uses this class to load and parse the RTTTL format of the "Happy Birthday to You" tune from a file. At this stage, it simply prints the equivalent MMAPI format.

Listing 6-4. *Using the* `RingToneConverter` *Class to Parse RTTTL Formats to MMAPI Format*

```
package com.apress.chapter6;

import javax.microedition.midlet.*;

import javax.microedition.media.*;
import javax.microedition.media.control.*;


public class ConverterMIDlet extends MIDlet {
```

```
public void startApp() {
  try {

    // Load the RTTTL format of the file as an InputStream
    RingToneConverter rtc =
      new RingToneConverter(
        getClass().getResourceAsStream(
          "/media/misc/happybday.rtttl"), "Happy Birthday");

    // get the equivalent sequence
    byte[] seq = rtc.getSequence();

    // print it
    printSequence(seq);

  } catch (Exception e) {
    System.err.println(e);
  }
}

private void printSequence(byte[] seq) {

  // print the sequence in a user friendly format
  byte bite = 0;
  for(int i = 0; i < seq.length; i++) {
    // the first control structure or the note value
    bite = seq[i];
    if(i % 2 == 0) {
      if(bite == ToneControl.VERSION)
        System.err.print("ToneControl.VERSION, ");
      else if(bite == ToneControl.TEMPO)
        System.err.print("ToneControl.TEMPO, ");
      else if(bite == ToneControl.SILENCE)
        System.err.print("ToneControl.SILENCE, ");
      else if(bite == ToneControl.RESOLUTION)
        System.err.print("ToneControl.RESOLUTION, ");
      else if(bite == ToneControl.SET_VOLUME)
        System.err.print("ToneControl.SET_VOLUME, ");
      else
        System.err.print(bite + ", ");
    }
    else {
      // the value of a control structure or the note duration
      if(i != (seq.length - 1))
        System.err.println(bite + ", ");
```

```
        else
          System.err.println(bite);
      }
    }

  }

  public void pauseApp() {
  }

  public void destroyApp(boolean unconditional) {
  }
}
```

Several constructors for the `RingToneConverter` class allow you to load the RTTTL format from a variety of sources. In this case, the RTTTL format for the "Happy Birthday to You" tune is stored in a text file called `happybday.rtttl`, and the `RingToneConverter(InputStream is, String tuneName)` constructor is used to load it. You can also use the `RingToneConverter(String url, String name)` constructor to load the file from a URL, or if you have the RTTTL format for a tune in a byte[] array, you can use the `RingToneConverter(byte[] data, String tuneName)` constructor directly. All constructors ultimately use the last constructor to parse the data.

Because the constructor also does the parsing of the RTTTL format, after it returns successfully, the corresponding MMAPI sequence is easily available by calling the `getSequence()` method. This method returns the MMAPI format in a byte array sequence, perfect for use with the `ToneControl`. You can print this sequence out using the `printSequence()` method in a format that makes it easy to copy and paste the resulting MMAPI sequence format in code.

Note the other constants from the `ToneControl` class that we've used besides the `ToneControl.VERSION` constant as listed in Table 6-5.

Table 6-5. `ToneControl` *Constants*

`ToneControl` Constant	`ToneControl` Value	`ToneControl` Description
`ToneControl.VERSION`	-2	The first control in a sequence and denotes the `ToneControl` version. Always equal to 1.
`ToneControl.TEMPO`	-3	The second control in a sequence and used to set the tempo of the following sequence. Default value is 30.
`ToneControl.RESOLUTION`	-4	The third control in a sequence and used to set the resolution of a sequence, as defined earlier. Default equals 64.
`ToneControl.SET_VOLUME`	-8	Can be used at any stage in a sequence to set the volume of the notes following it.
`ToneControl.SILENCE`	-1	Can be used at any stage in a sequence to indicate a silent note value. It must, of course, be followed by a duration value.

Other constants will be discussed in the coming sections.

Creating, Defining, and Playing Blocks of Sequences

Ring tones that have repetitive stanzas don't need to define these stanzas separately each time they are required to be played. The MMAPI format allows you to define a repetitive block once and then refer to it whenever and wherever you want it played.

Sticking with the "Happy Birthday to You" tune, let's say you wanted the first stanza played a couple of times before moving on to the rest of the tune. This first stanza is the "Happy Birthday to You" part and is reproduced here:

```
72, 4, ToneControl.SILENCE, 2, 72, 2, ToneControl.SILENCE, 2, 74, 8,
ToneControl.SILENCE, 2, 72, 8, ToneControl.SILENCE, 2, 77, 8,
ToneControl.SILENCE, 2, 76, 16
```

To mark this as a block, start by putting the `ToneControl` control constant `BLOCK_START` with a number to identify this block and end with `BLOCK_END` using the same number:

```
ToneControl.BLOCK_START, 0,
72, 4, ToneControl.SILENCE, 2, 72, 2,
ToneControl.SILENCE, 2, 74, 8, ToneControl.SILENCE, 2, 72, 8,
ToneControl.SILENCE, 2, 77, 8, ToneControl.SILENCE, 2,  76, 16,
ToneControl.BLOCK_END, 0
```

The sequence has been marked as block `0`. This block can now be played anywhere in the sequence by using the `ToneControl` control constant `PLAY_BLOCK` followed by the number identifying the block. Thus, the following placed anywhere in a sequence after the block definition will play the block just defined:

```
ToneControl.PLAY_BLOCK, 0
```

Of course, you can't play a block that hasn't been defined. Therefore, all block definitions must come before an attempt to play them is made. There is no limit to the number of blocks that you can define.

The following byte array shows the sequence of playing the first two stanzas of "Happy Birthday to You," with the first stanza repeated once.

```
byte[] sequence = new byte[] {
  ToneControl.VERSION, 1,
  ToneControl.BLOCK_START, 0,
  72, 4, ToneControl.SILENCE, 2, 72, 2, ToneControl.SILENCE, 2, 74, 8,
  ToneControl.SILENCE,  2, 72, 8, ToneControl.SILENCE, 2, 77, 8,
  ToneControl.SILENCE, 2, 76, 16,
  ToneControl.BLOCK_END, 0,
  ToneControl.PLAY_BLOCK, 0, // plays block 0
  ToneControl.SILENCE, 4,  72, 4, ToneControl.SILENCE, 2, 72, 2,
  ToneControl.SILENCE, 2, 74, 8, ToneControl.SILENCE, 2, 72, 8,
  ToneControl.SILENCE, 2, 79, 8,
  ToneControl.SILENCE, 2, 77, 16, // plays the second stanza
  ToneControl.PLAY_BLOCK, 0 // plays block 0 again
}
```

`BLOCK_START`, `BLOCK_END`, and `PLAY_BLOCK` constants have a value of `-5`, `-6`, and `-7`, respectively.

Playing Sequences Using ToneControl and Player

Defining sequences is great, but it's of no use if you can't play them using MMAPI. So let's see how you can play the sequences you have learned to create in the previous sections using a combination of the ToneControl and Player interfaces.

Listing 6-4 showed how to parse a tone file in RTTTL format to the MMAPI format. Let's now add a method (see Listing 6-5) to the ConverterMIDlet defined in this listing that will play this converted tone.

Listing 6-5. *Playing Tone Sequences*

```
private void playSequence(byte[] seq) throws Exception {

  // create a Tone Player
  Player player = Manager.createPlayer(Manager.TONE_DEVICE_LOCATOR);

  // must realize it before getting ToneControl
  player.realize();

  // now get the ToneControl
  ToneControl toneControl = (ToneControl)player.getControl("ToneControl");

  // set the sequence
  toneControl.setSequence(seq);

  // and start the player - this will play the sequence
  player.start();
}
```

After creating or generating a sequence, playing it using MMAPI is relatively simple. You need a Player instance that can play tones. The Manager class provides a constant for creating a tone-based Player instance, which is supplied by the mobile device's hardware. This constant is the TONE_DEVICE_LOCATOR, and its value is equal to device://tone. So a tone-based Player instance is created by supplying this constant as the locator to the createPlayer() method.

This tone-based Player instance will now behave like any other instance. You can start it, stop it, realize it, prefetch it, and so on. To play tones, you need to access the ToneControl control provided by this instance. However, recall from Chapter 4 that an unrealized instance cannot provide any controls. Therefore, in Listing 6-5, the Player instance is realized before the ToneControl control is fetched using the getControl() method.

Finally, ToneControl is supplied the tone sequence by using the setSequence() method. This sequence is the final MMAPI formatted sequence, either created manually or by parsing the RTTTL format.

The Player instance is now ready and can be started when required. In Listing 6-5, the instance is started immediately by using the normal start() method. This instance will behave like any other Player instance; for example, you can pause it using the stop() method, make it repeat using the setLoopCount() method, or listen to events by attaching a PlayerListener.

Distributing Tone Sequences

The tone sequences that you create using the special MMAPI tone sequence format can be distributed using the same file format in a binary mode. This means that the sequence of a tone is dumped into a binary file with the extension of `jts` (Java Tone Sequence). This file can then be downloaded or loaded into any MMAPI-compliant device, and the device will be able to play the tone. To help with the recognition of these files by Web servers and Web browsers, the JTS files have the MIME type of audio/x-tone-seq associated with them.

Creating JTS Files

To create these binary files, you'll need to dump your tone sequence into a file. However, you can't do this within the MIDlet environment because there is no provision to write to a file easily.

The `RingToneConverter` comes to the rescue again by providing a method called `dumpSequence()`, which provides the hexadecimal representation of the tone sequence for you to take and create a binary file out of. To get this representation, simply use `rtc.dumpSequence()` to print the sequence on the standard out. The hex dump sequence for the "Happy Birthday to You" tone is shown here:

```
FE 01 FD 1F 48 04 FF 02
48 02 FF 02 4A 08 FF 02
48 08 FF 02 4D 08 FF 02
4C 10 FF 04 48 04 FF 02
48 02 FF 02 4A 08 FF 02
48 08 FF 02 4F 08 FF 02
4D 10 FF 08 48 04 FF 02
48 02 FF 02 54 08 FF 02
51 08 FF 02 4D 08 FF 02
4C 08 FF 02 4A 08 FF 02
52 04 FF 02 52 02 FF 02
51 08 FF 02 4D 08 FF 02
4F 08 FF 02 4D 10
```

Now, to convert this hexadecimal representation into a binary file, you need to create a Java class that will read this representation from a file, convert it back into a byte array, and write the byte array out to a binary file with the extension of `jts`. Listing 6-6 shows such a class called `CreateJTSFileFromHexString`. Store the hexadecimal representation just shown in a file called `happybday_hex.txt` and compile and run `CreateJTSFileFromHexString` with this file as a parameter.

Listing 6-6. *A Class to Create a Binary JTS File from a Hex Representation*

```
package com.apress.chapter6;

import java.io.*;

public class CreateJTSFileFromHexString {

  public static void main(String[] args) {
```

```
    if(args[0] == null) System.err.println("Usage: java <filename>");

    // initialize streams that we will need
    FileReader fr = null;
    BufferedReader br = null;
    ByteArrayOutputStream bos = null;
    FileOutputStream fos = null;

    try {
      // the argument must be the file containing tone format in hex string
      File hexStringFile = new File(args[0]);

      // create text-based readers on it
      fr = new FileReader(hexStringFile);
      br = new BufferedReader(fr);

      String lineRead;
      String hexString = "";

      // read the file, a line at a time into the hexString variable
      while((lineRead = br.readLine()) != null) {
         hexString += lineRead;
      }

      // remove the spaces within this hexString
      StringBuffer buf = new StringBuffer();
      for(int i = 0; i < hexString.length(); i++) {
        if(!Character.isWhitespace(hexString.charAt(i)))
          buf.append(hexString.charAt(i));
      }

      // the final hexString with spaces removed
      hexString = buf.toString();

      // now write the hexString out to a file as a byte array making it a
      // binary file
      byte[] txtInByte = new byte[hexString.length()/2];
      int j = 0;
      for (int i = 0; i < hexString.length(); i += 2)
      {
        txtInByte[j++] =
          (byte)Integer.parseInt(hexString.substring(i, i + 2), 16);
      }

      // the byte array created, write it to a ByteArrayOutputStream
```

```
      bos = new ByteArrayOutputStream();
      bos.write(txtInByte, 0, txtInByte.length);

      // and create a physical file with the extension jts containing this data
      fos = new FileOutputStream(
        new File(args[0].substring(0, args[0].indexOf(".")) + ".jts"));
      bos.writeTo(fos);

    } catch (Exception e) {
      System.err.println(e);
    } finally {
      try {
        if(fos != null) fos.close();
        if(bos != null) bos.close();
        if(br != null) br.close();
        if(fr != null) fr.close();
      } catch(Exception e) {
        System.err.println(e);
      }
    }
  }

}
```

Remember that this is a normal Java file and not a Java ME class. So this will need to be run in its own Java SE environment, as was the case with Listing 6-2, NoteCalculator.

The output will be a file named happybday_hex.jts. This is a binary file that cannot be viewed in a text editor. However, this file contains the tone sequence for "Happy Birthday to You" in the MMAPI format and can now be distributed and played.

Playing Tone Sequences Stored in Files

Because MMAPI recognizes the jts extension files, you can now create Player instances that can load these files using locator strings. So now it's possible to create a Player instance that loads a tone sequence as a jts extension file from a Web site, using the createPlayer(String locator) method. First, let's load a JTS file stored in a JAR file. Listing 6-7 shows the code for the DistributedToneMIDlet that will load and play the happybday_hex.jts file, created in the previous section, from its JAR file.

Listing 6-7. *Loading and Playing JTS File from JAR File*

```
package com.apress.chapter6;

import javax.microedition.midlet.*;
import javax.microedition.lcdui.*;
import javax.microedition.media.*;
import javax.microedition.media.control.*;

public class DistributedToneMIDlet extends MIDlet {
```

```
  private Player tonePlayer;

  public DistributedToneMIDlet() {
    try {
      tonePlayer = Manager.createPlayer(getClass().getResourceAsStream(
          "/media/misc/happybday_hex.jts"), "audio/x-tone-seq");
    } catch(Exception e) {
      System.err.println(e);
    }
  }

  public void startApp() {
    try {
      if(tonePlayer != null)
        tonePlayer.start();
    } catch(Exception e) {
      System.err.println(e);
    }
  }

  public void pauseApp() {
  }

  public void destroyApp(boolean unconditional) {
  }
}
```

As you can see, this code is not very special. In fact, it's almost identical to the code in Listing 3-1 in Chapter 3, where you learned to play a simple wav file, with changes made for the different content types. Notice that you didn't even need to get the ToneControl and set the sequence on it. By creating a tone-playing instance like this, most of the other things that you learned about earlier are abstracted nicely.

To play the same sequence on a Web site, all you need to do is replace it with the corresponding createPlayer(String locator) method that takes the location of the Web site as a parameter. An example is shown here:

```
tonePlayer = Manager.createPlayer(
  "http://www.mmapibook.com/resources/media/tones/chapter6/happybday_hex.jts");
```

The extension of the file will let MMAPI's Manager class know that it needs to create a TonePlayer and set its sequence to the sequence specified in the JTS file. If there are any errors in the JTS file, you will get an error similar to "bad jts file. Error no <no>." Most of these errors occur if the JTS file hasn't been created correctly, so if you've followed the steps so far, these errors will not occur.

Summary

MMAPI identifies the fact that even the simplest of devices offer the developer and the user some capability of tone generation. MMAPI provides the ability to generate simple tones in its most simple form using the `Manager` class. Of course, if the device supports the full set of the MMAPI implementation, it provides an even richer set of tone-generation, modification, and playback capabilities.

This chapter showed you how to take advantage of this capability in MMAPI. You also learned how to play simple, single tones and to create and distribute more complex tones and tone sequences. You also learned a simple lesson in music theory, which was essential to understanding some of the concepts behind tone generation.

The next chapter covers the basics of MIDI and how MMAPI is capable of handling it.

CHAPTER 7

Managing MIDI Using MIDIControl, TempoControl, and PitchControl

Contrary to popular belief, Musical Instrument Digital Interface (MIDI) is not a representation of music. Rather, it's a communication protocol, designed to transmit information about music digitally across disparate musical systems. Instead of describing audio data directly, MIDI represents it by using events that take place when a sound from an electronic synthesizer is made. This event information is what constitutes a MIDI data/file.

In this chapter, you'll learn about the support MMAPI provides for playing and controlling MIDI. You'll also learn about the different MIDI specifications that are supported and how the different aspects of the specification map to the actual implementation. Extensive examples with `MIDIControl` allow you to use `MIDIControl` effectively. You'll also learn how to play and manipulate MIDI files, without using `MIDIControl`, by using just `TempoControl` and `PitchControl`. You'll understand soundbanks, programs, and other MIDI-related terminology and how to use them.

But first, you need to get a working understanding of MIDI.

Understanding MIDI

Even though you may not realize it, these days MIDI is all around you. Seen a movie at a cinema? The orchestra in the movie was most probably synthesized in MIDI using an electronic keyboard. Been to a concert or a nightclub? The themed lights are in all probability controlled using MIDI messages, synchronized with the music. Love a series on TV? The title music is done using a MIDI synthesizer. How about your cell phone? Your polyphonic ring tone is generated using MIDI!

With such widespread use, it's no wonder that there is a strong industry momentum behind this technology. An audio engineer named Dave Smith proposed the original MIDI standard, and the first specification was published in 1982. Although there have been several updates on this original specification, the current specification is still called MIDI 1.0 with a smaller version number of 96.1 Second Edition (released in November 2001).

Polyphonic ring tones that you have on your mobile phone are based on a variation of the original MIDI specification, called Scalable Polyphony MIDI (SP-MIDI). This specification allows a varying number of notes to define the same MIDI data and, therefore, caters to both high-end and low-end phones with varying polyphonic capabilities.

The official and definitive Web site for keeping up to date with the various facets of the MIDI specification is *http://www.midi.org*. Although it doesn't contain a free copy of the MIDI specification, it still contains a wealth of information. The MIDI specification is available for purchase as a book, although it's available on the Internet in snippets. You can also find useful MIDI-related information at *http://en.wikipedia.org/wiki/MIDI*.

Understanding the MIDI Specification

The MIDI specification has two parts. One deals with the physical hardware interface standard for transmitting MIDI; the other is a software protocol dealing with the communication, transmission, and format of MIDI messages. The physical specification is elaborate and specifies the serial transfer rate of messages (31.25 Kbaud), besides defining characteristics of ports and connector cables for MIDI IN, MIDI OUT, and MIDI THRU. The physical side of the MIDI specification doesn't help much with applying it to MMAPI, so it isn't covered further in this book.

The software specification specifies the MIDI message format, which is used for transmission of messages. Considering that the MIDI specification is a communication protocol, it helps to think of a transmitter and a receiver. A transmitter can be any instrument that is capable of producing synthesized music, such as a computer system or an electronic synthesizer. A receiver can also be another computer system and/or an electronic synthesizer, as long as it contains a MIDI IN port. A transmitter, as expected, should contain a MIDI OUT port. This simple configuration is depicted in Figure 7-1.

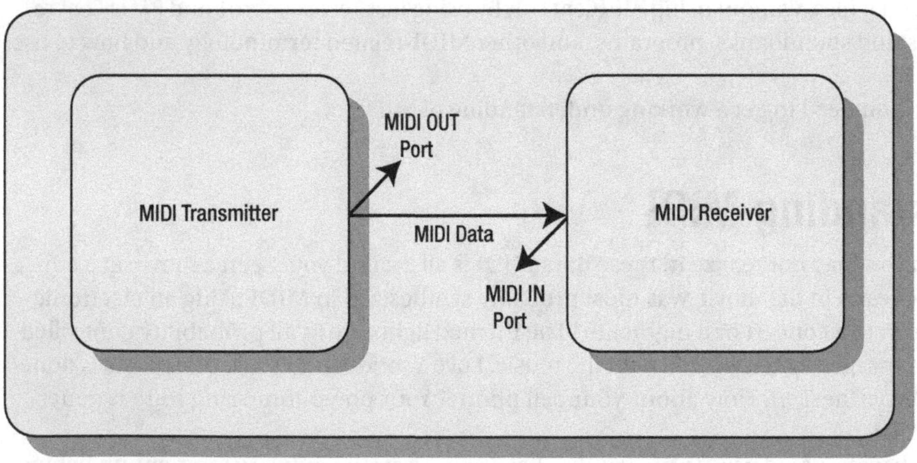

Figure 7-1. *MIDI communication*

As expected, a MIDI transmitter can act as a receiver and vice versa.

The MIDI data in Figure 7-1 is organized into messages. Each message can be thought of as a multi-byte packet that contains information about a particular channel. Think of a channel in MIDI as an exclusive transmission network for the transfer of note information for a particular musical instrument. Transmitters and receivers are primed to send and receive information about 16 possible channels. If any of the channel information is missing, for example, if there is no information about drums being played, then both parties ignore that channel.

The MIDI message format allows the depiction of all notes that can be played by a musical instrument. The MIDI specification assigns notes to particular messages, and any electronic instrument that follows this specification can interpret these messages.

MIDI Message Format

When a musician plays a note on, let's say, a musical keyboard, three events take place:

- Musician presses the key to play the note with a particular volume.
- Musician keeps pressing the key, increasing or decreasing the force with which the note is being played.
- Musician stops playing the note by taking his finger off the particular key.

All three events are transmitted via the MIDI OUT port serially, through a series of three messages, one for each event. Each of these messages is a MIDI message and consists of a multi-byte packet. The first byte in each message is a Status byte, and is followed by 0, 1, or 2 Data bytes. Status bytes have their most significant bit set to 1, and Data bytes have their most significant bit set to 0. This is the standard MIDI message format (see Figure 7-2).

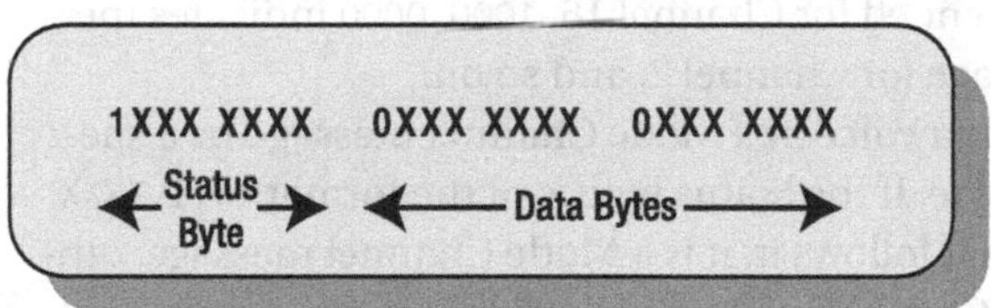

Figure 7-2. *Standard MIDI message format*

These MIDI messages are then divided into two types, depending on whether they are carrying information for a particular channel or whether they are system-wide messages that are intended for all devices that may be interconnected in a MIDI network. These two types of messages are called Channel messages and System messages. These types are further subclassified, with the Channel messages divided into either the Voice or Mode Channel message type, and the System messages divided into Common, Real-Time, or Exclusive System message type. Figure 7-3 shows these classifications.

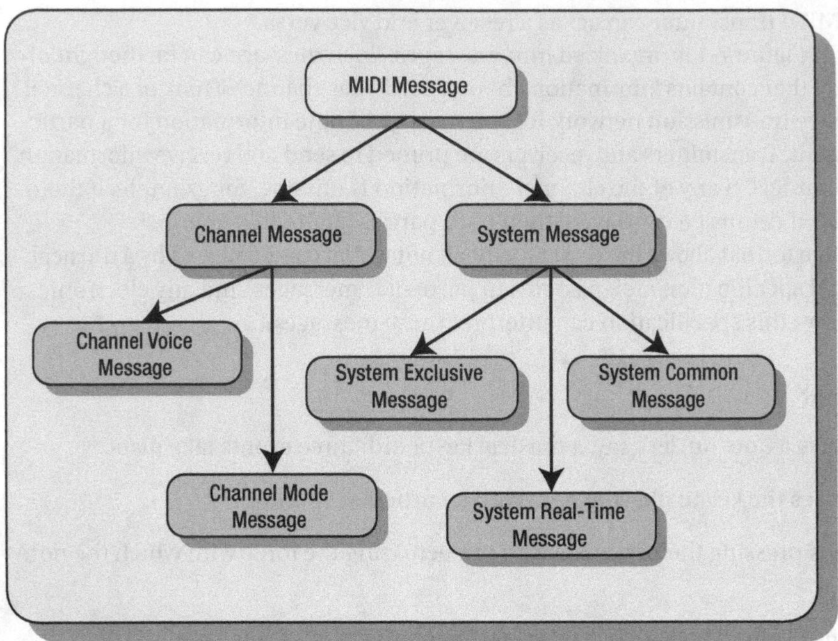

Figure 7-3. *MIDI message classifications*

System messages are differentiated from Channel messages by the presence of 1 in the first 4 bits of the Status byte. That is, if the Status byte is of the format `1111 XXXX`, then the message is a System message; otherwise, it is a Channel message, in which case, the last 4 bits in the Status byte identify one of 16 channels that the message is intended for. For example, `1000 1111` as Status byte in a message indicates that it is intended for Channel 16, `1000 0000` indicates the message is for Channel 1, `1000 0001` is a message for Channel 2, and so on.

Further, a Channel message is classified as a Voice or a Mode Channel message by a specific set of bits in the first 4 bits of the Status byte. If the Status byte is of the format `1011 XXXX` and has a special character in the Data byte that follows it, it is a Mode Channel message; otherwise, it is a Voice Channel message. A Voice Channel message controls a particular channel by starting or stopping the playing of a note, among other things. The Data bytes following this Status byte contain information about the note. The Mode Channel message is a response to the Voice Channel message.

Table 7-1 shows how to spot the different messages discussed so far.

Table 7-1. *Differentiating Between Different MIDI Messages*

First 4 Bits of Status Byte	Last 4 Bits of Status Byte	Message Type	Comment
1111	XXXX	System	
1011	XXXX	Mode Channel message	Only if the Data bytes following this Status byte contain a value between 121 and 127

First 4 Bits of Status Byte	Last 4 Bits of Status Byte	Message Type	Comment
1000			
1001			
1010			
1011			
1100			
1101			
1110	XXXX	Voice Channel message	Only if the Data bytes following this Status byte contain a value between 0 and 120

Continuing on to the three different System message types, their formats are shown in Table 7-2 along with a brief description.

Table 7-2. *The Three Different Types of System Messages in MIDI*

Message Type	Format	Comment
System Real Time	1111 1XXX	XXX is a value between 0 and 7 (000 = 0, 111 = 7). These messages are used to synchronize the whole MIDI system in real time and do not contain any Data bytes.
System Common	1111 0XXX	XXX is a value between 1 and 7. These messages may contain 0 to 2 Data bytes and are intended for an interconnected MIDI network.
System Exclusive	1111 0000	This tracing or debugging message may contain several Data bytes following it with system information.

More About the Voice Channel Messages

The majority of the messages in a MIDI transmission are the Voice Channel messages. These messages contain specific information about notes; how long to play them, what channel to play them on, whether to turn them on or off, how much key pressure is to be applied, and so on. As you have learned so far, these messages consist of a Status byte followed by one or two Data bytes. Let's examine the composition of these Data bytes now.

One of the primary functions of the Voice Channel message is to turn a particular note on or off on a specific channel. This message must also include information about the velocity (roughly equivalent to volume) at which the note was turned on or off. To turn a note on, the message is of the format 1001 XXXX 0YYY YYYY 0ZZZ ZZZZ. As you can see, the first byte is a Status byte followed by two Data bytes, which is indicated by the presence of 0 in the most significant bit. To turn the note off, the format is 1000 XXXX 0YYY YYYY 0ZZZ ZZZZ. The value of the note to turn on or off is indicated by the first Data byte (0YYY YYYY) and can be any value between 0 and 127. The velocity with which to turn the note on or off is indicated by the last Data byte (0ZZZ ZZZZ), and it can be a value between 0 and 127.

■ **Note** See the "Using MMAPI Formula to Calculate Note Values" section in Chapter 6 for an explanation of note values.

As an example, suppose you wanted to compose a MIDI message that would tell a MIDI receiver to turn on the note Middle C (equal to 60) on MIDI Channel 12 at a high velocity (remember velocity roughly means volume) of 100. Start with the Status byte:

```
1001 1011
```

The first 4 bits (from the left) are the Note ON command, and the last four bits represent Channel 12 (Channel 1 is `0000` *not* `0001`). Next, write the first Data byte representing the note Middle C (equal to 60):

```
0011 1100
```

Finally, write the second Data byte, indicating the velocity as equal to 100:

```
0110 0100
```

Putting it all together,

```
1001 1011 0011 1100 0110 0100
```

will start playing the note Middle C at a velocity of 100 on the MIDI Channel indicated by the number 12. This will not stop playing until a corresponding Note OFF message is received:

```
1000 1011 0011 1100 0110 0100
```

Of course, the velocity with which to turn the note off could be made different than the original one in this Note OFF message, but in this example it has been left as is.

Turning notes on and off is not the only Voice Channel message, and Table 7-3 lists all the possibilities along with a brief description.

Table 7-3. *All Possible Voice Channel Messages*

Status Byte	First Data Byte	Second Data Byte	Message	Comment
1000 XXXX	0YYY YYYY	0ZZZ ZZZZ	Note OFF	Turn a note off on a channel with a given velocity.
1001 XXXX	0YYY YYYY	0ZZZ ZZZZ	Note ON	Turn a note on with a given velocity on a particular channel.
1010 XXXX	0YYY YYYY	0AAA AAAA	After-Touch	Key pressure for polyphony; second Data byte indicates the pressure value (0-127).
1011 XXXX	0BBB BBBB	0CCC CCCC	Control Change	First Data byte indicates which control to change (0-121); second Data byte indicates control value (0-127).

Status Byte	First Data Byte	Second Data Byte	Message	Comment
1100 XXXX	0DDD DDDD	No second Data byte	Program Change	Used to change the instrument of a channel to another instrument, so that more than 16 instruments can be used at one time.
1101 XXXX	0EEE EEEE	No second Data byte	Channel Pressure	Changes the pressure of a whole instrument, not just a single note (which is done with After-Touch).
1110 XXXX	0GGG GGGG	0FFF FFFF	Pitch Bend	A shift in a note's pitch in a very small increment or decrement.

The key Voice Channel messages are the first two for turning notes on or off on a channel, and you'll use these more often than the others. The fourth message (Control Change) is also used extensively to effect changes to various controls within the MIDI environment, including main volume (7), modulation wheel (1), and pan controller (10) controls, among others. Finally, you'll use the Program Change message to change instruments before sending the note to be played on a particular channel.

Storing and Distributing MIDI Messages

The format of MIDI messages presented in the previous section is true for live streaming of these messages, which essentially means that messages are played back as they are received in real time. However, MIDI messages can be stored in a file, and distributed for playback later as well. When these messages are stored in a file, they require timing information to be stored with them as well to allow for synchronization of these messages.

The most common format for storing these files is in Standard MIDI file (SMF) format, denoted by the extension `.smf`. These files are created (and read) using sequencer software on computers/electronic instruments and contain a sequence of tracks. Each track contains information about a particular channel and the note sequence to perform, including other meta-level information.

SMF files are generally distributed on the Internet with the extension of `.mid`. Most files with `.mid` (short for MIDI) extensions are compatible with `.smf` files, and you can interchange the use of these files. The distinction lies in the fact that `.mid` extension files correspond to a narrow interpretation of the MIDI file format specification, called the General MIDI specification.

General MIDI Specification

The General MIDI (GM) specification is a tighter, more focused interpretation of the overall MIDI specification that is intended for greater interoperability between MIDI devices. It specifies a general set of features that the GM devices must conform to. The core features of this specification are

- Support for polyphony (GM devices must allow playback of simultaneous, multiple notes on a single channel)
- Definite support for all 16 channels
- Defined and standard program numbers for various instruments

The standard program numbers for various instruments was one of the main driving forces for the adoption of the GM spec. These devices and their corresponding numbers are listed here: *http://en.wikipedia.org/wiki/General_MIDI*.

Note that only 128 instruments can be supported, as per this specification. To support more instruments, the concept of a *bank* was introduced. A soundbank, or bank, is a collection of the 128 instruments that are supported by a particular MIDI device. Soundbanks can be added or removed, and custom soundbanks can be created to support the existing ones in a device.

Using MIDI in MMAPI

Support for MIDI in MMAPI is provided in the form of the `MIDIControl` control and is aided by the use of `PitchControl` and `TempoControl` controls. However, note that `MIDIControl` is an optional control, and MMAPI implementations are not required to support it. Most instances, however, do support this popular control in one form or another. On one hand, at the minimum, if `MIDIControl` is implemented, you are guaranteed support for sending MIDI events to the control, thereby creating your own set of sequences and messages, as you learned in the previous section. If a full `MIDIControl` is implemented, you are allowed to query the installed soundbanks and manipulate them extensively. You'll learn shortly how to find out whether the MMAPI implementation that you are working on supports a minimum or full `MIDIControl` control.

The MMAPI specification states that for basic usage, you don't even need to access the `MIDIControl` control. This is true, as long as you have a basic MIDI file that you want to play as is, without any modifications. Let's try and play such a basic MIDI file.

Playing MIDI Without `MIDIControl`

Even though you may not directly need to access the `MIDIControl` control to play MIDI files, it doesn't mean that `MIDIControl` is not implemented. Behind the scenes, `MIDIControl` is used to access the synthesizer on the device that you are working on, but you won't need to use it directly. Instead, for simple changes, such as pitch and tempo, you can use the `PitchControl` and `TempoControl` controls. For volume changes, simply use the `VolumeControl` control.

Playing a MIDI File

As you may realize by now, playing, controlling, and using MIDI files is similar to playing other file types that you've learned about in previous chapters, thanks to a similar interface. Therefore, playing MIDI files should not require extra effort on your part. Listing 7-1 shows you a simple code listing that plays a local MIDI file.

Listing 7-1. *Playing a Local MIDI File*

```
package com.apress.chapter7;

import javax.microedition.midlet.*;
import javax.microedition.media.*;

public class PlayMIDIMIDlet extends MIDlet {
```

```
  Player midiPlayer = null;

  public PlayMIDIMIDlet() {
    try {
      midiPlayer = Manager.createPlayer(
        getClass().getResourceAsStream(
          "/media/midi/chapter7/cabeza.mid"), "audio/midi");
    } catch(Exception e) {
      System.err.println(e);
    }
  }

  public void startApp() {
    try {
      if(midiPlayer != null) {
        midiPlayer.start();
      }
    } catch(Exception e) {
      System.err.println(e);
    }
  }

  public void pauseApp() {
  }

  public void destroyApp(boolean unconditional) {
  }
}
```

To play the MIDI file, you just need to create a `Player` instance, passing the location of the file to the `Manager` class's `createPlayer()` method, as you learned to do before. The MIME type for the MIDI files is audio/midi or audio/x-midi, as the case may be. For network-based MIDI files, you can simply point to these files by using the `createPlayer(String locator)` method; the MIME type will be specified by the server that is retrieving the file. For example, if the same file was placed at

```
http://www.mmapibook.com/resources/media/midi/chapter7/cabeza.mid
```

you would use the `Manager.createPlayer("http://www.mmapibook.com/resources/media/midi/chapter7/cabeza.mid")` method to retrieve and play this MIDI file, taking care to make sure that the access is done in a separate thread, as you learned in Chapter 5.

■ **Note** The MIDI file (downloaded from the Internet) used here is `cabeza.mid`, which is a MIDI representation of the "Tango Por una cabeza" (the famous Tango, also used in the movie *True Lies*).

Controlling the Pitch, Tempo, and Volume of MIDI Files

Let's now add a few controls to control the pitch, tempo, and volume of a MIDI file. Figure 7-4 shows a MIDlet that allows you to do so (shown in Sun's DefaultColorPhone and Motorola C975 emulators, respectively).

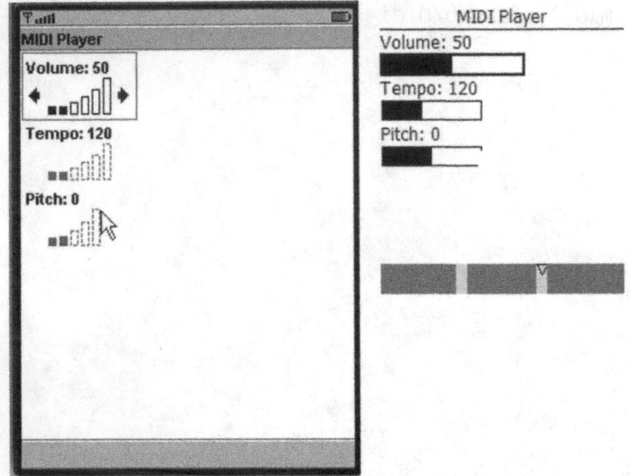

Figure 7-4. *Running* `ControllableMIDIMIDlet` *to control pitch, tempo, and volume in Sun's DefaultColorPhone and Motorola C975 emulators, respectively*

Listing 7-2 shows the code for this MIDlet. An explanation of the code follows this listing.

Listing 7-2. *Controlling MIDI with Pitch, Tempo, and Volume Controls*

```
package com.apress.chapter7;

import javax.microedition.lcdui.*;
import javax.microedition.midlet.*;
import javax.microedition.media.*;
import javax.microedition.media.control.*;

public class ControllableMIDIMIDlet extends MIDlet implements ItemStateListener {

  // the midi player
  Player midiPlayer = null;

  // the controls
  VolumeControl volControl = null;
  PitchControl pitchControl = null;
  TempoControl tempoControl = null;

  // the visual elements
  Form form = null;
```

```
Gauge volGauge = null;
Gauge pitchGauge = null;
Gauge tempoGauge = null;

public ControllableMIDIMIDlet() {
  try {

    // load the midi file
    midiPlayer = Manager.createPlayer(
      getClass().getResourceAsStream(
        "/media/midi/chapter7/cabeza.mid"), "audio/midi");

    // you must prefetch it to get the controls
    midiPlayer.prefetch();

    // extract the controls
    volControl = (VolumeControl) midiPlayer.getControl(
      "javax.microedition.media.control.VolumeControl");
    pitchControl = (PitchControl) midiPlayer.getControl(
      "javax.microedition.media.control.PitchControl");
    tempoControl = (TempoControl) midiPlayer.getControl(
      "javax.microedition.media.control.TempoControl");

    // create the visual elements
    form = new Form("MIDI Player", null);

    // volume is set at a max of 100 with initial value of 50
    volGauge = new Gauge("Volume: 50", true, 100, 50);

    // tempo is set at a max of 30 with 12 (default) as initial value
    tempoGauge = new Gauge("Tempo: 120", true, 30, 12);

    // pitch is set at a max of 5 with initial value of 0, and a min of -5
    // note that because pitch can be negative and positive, the starting value
    // is at 5 (which is pitch 0), with +5 being 10 and -5 being 0.
    pitchGauge = new Gauge("Pitch: 0", true, 10, 5);

    // add the gauges to the form
    form.append(volGauge);
    form.append(tempoGauge);
    form.append(pitchGauge);

    // add the listener to listen to gauge changes
    form.setItemStateListener(this);

    // and set this form as the current display
    Display.getDisplay(this).setCurrent(form);
```

```
    } catch(Exception e) {
      System.err.println(e);
    }
  }

  /**
   * Listens to changes in control gauges and applies them to actual controls
   */
  public void itemStateChanged(Item item) {

    // we are only interested in item state changes of gauges
    if(!(item instanceof Gauge)) return;

    // get the new value of this gauge
    Gauge gauge = (Gauge)item;
    int val = gauge.getValue();

    // and change the control and label accordingly

    // changing volume?
    if(item == volGauge) {
      volControl.setLevel(val);
      volGauge.setLabel("Volume: " + val);
    }

    // changing tempo? make sure that tempoControl is available
    if(item == tempoGauge && tempoControl != null) {
      tempoControl.setTempo((val) * 10 * 1000);
      tempoGauge.setLabel("Tempo: " + (val * 10));
    }

    // changing pitch? make sure that pitchControl is available
    // remember, actual pitch is (val - 5)
    if(item == pitchGauge && pitchControl != null) {
      pitchControl.setPitch((val - 5) * 12 * 1000);
      pitchGauge.setLabel("Pitch: " + (val - 5));
    }
  }

  public void startApp() {
    try {
      // start the MIDI player if it was created
      if(midiPlayer != null) {
        midiPlayer.start();
      }
    } catch(Exception e) {
      System.err.println(e);
    }
  }
```

```
  // standard pause and destroy methods
  public void pauseApp() {
    try {
      if(midiPlayer != null) {
        midiPlayer.stop();
      }
    } catch(Exception e) {
      System.err.println(e);
    }
  }

  public void destroyApp(boolean unconditional) {
    try {
      if(midiPlayer != null) {
        midiPlayer.close();
      }
    } catch(Exception e) {
      System.err.println(e);
    }
  }
}
```

After the Player instance is prefetched, TempoControl, PitchControl, and VolumeControl are extracted using the getControl() method, casting them appropriately. A form is created that contains three gauges, which allow you to control each of the controls individually. The default values of each gauge are set as well. For volume, the default is set at 50 with a maximum value of 100.

For tempo, the default is set at 12, with 30 as the maximum value. These values seem arbitrary, but they are used to show how the TempoControl control works.

How TempoControl Works

TempoControl allows you to vary the tempo of the MIDI file that you are working with. Tempo, which is measured in beats per minute (bpm), is a measure of how fast or slow a piece of music is being played. Using TempoControl, you can vary this speed of playback of a MIDI sequence by using the method setTempo(int milliTempo) and also retrieve the current speed of a sequence by using the getTempo() method. However, setting the tempo doesn't always mean that the desired value will be kept, because a MIDI sequence may contain its own information on the desired tempo. The tempo value in the sequence overrides any value for the tempo that you set using the setTempo() method, if such a value is found in a sequence.

The default tempo of any musical piece (not just MIDI) is usually 120 bpm. With any implementation of TempoControl, you are guaranteed to be able to set the tempo ranging between 10 bpm and 300 bpm. Actual implementations may support more values, specifically over the higher range, but no implementation will support 0 or negative values for the tempo. Instead, most revert to the lowest possible value for the tempo, which in most cases is 10 bpm, but could be as low as 1 bpm.

You can set the tempo using the `setTempo(int milliTempo)` method. Notice that it accepts the value in `milliTempo`. This means, to set the value at 200 bpm, you need to use the method `setTempo(200 * 1000)`. This method returns the actual tempo that was set, expressed as milli-beats per minute.

Returning to Listing 7-2, you can now see that the default value of `12` for the `TempoControl` gauge makes sense. The maximum value is set at `30`. When a change in value of this gauge is detected, the changed value is multiplied by 10 to get the effective value, and then by 1,000 to arrive at the final milli-beats per minute value. This is done in the `itemStateChanged(Item item)` method.

How `PitchControl` Works

As you learned in Chapter 6, pitch is the perception of the frequency of a musical note. The `PitchControl` control allows you to vary the pitch of not only a MIDI sequence, but a normal audio file as well.

Pitch changes are always relative to the original value and can never be set to an absolute value. The changes are specified in semitones; a semitone is one-twelfth of an octave (refer to Chapter 6). Thus, to raise the pitch of a sequence by an octave, you need to raise it by 12 semitones.

The `PitchControl`'s `setPitch(int milliSemitones)` method is used to set the actual value. As you can see, the value is set in milli-semitones. Thus, to raise the pitch by an octave, you need to use the method as `setPitch(12 * 1000)`. To *lower* the pitch by an octave, you use a negative value: `setPitch(-12 * 1000)`.

Of course, you don't have to raise or lower the pitch by an octave. You can change the pitch by any value, down to a single semitone. Just remember that the changes are relative to the original value. To raise by a single semitone, use `setPitch(1000)`; to lower it by a semitone, use `setPitch(-1000)`.

The current *raised* pitch value of a sequence can be queried by using the `getPitch()` method, which returns the value in milli-semitones.

Again, returning to code Listing 7-2, you can see now see why the maximum value of the `PitchControl` gauge is set at `10`, with a default (initial) value of `5`. Due to limitations in the `Gauge` item, negative values can't be set. Thus, the initial, default value of `5` represents `0`, whereas a value of `10` is 5 times the original value, and a value of `0` is –5 times. When you change the value from the default value `5` to, let's say `6`, the code in `itemStateChanged()` method interprets it as raising the pitch by a single octave. The corresponding code is shown here:

```
pitchControl.setPitch((val - 5) * 12 * 1000);
```

Raising the pitch any higher leads to higher octaves, whereas lowering the value below `5` means lowering the pitch by corresponding octaves, so the minimum pitch you can get is five times lower than the original one.

Lowering or raising the pitch up to five octave times the original one is only an arbitrary example that illustrates how to use this control. You can raise or lower the pitch to any values that you desire, which is only limited by the maximum or minimum values that are supported by the particular Player instance. You can get these values by using the methods getMaxPitch() and getMinPitch() methods, respectively.

Differentiating Between TempoControl and RateControl

Figure 7-4 shows how Listing 7-2 plays out in two emulators: Sun's DefaultColorPhone and Motorola C975 emulator. Most MIDlets' working has been shown in a Motorola C975 device as well. However, because the TempoControl control doesn't work on the actual device, it isn't shown here. If you run this listing in an actual C975 device, you won't be able to control the tempo of the MIDI playback.

Tip You would think that the Motorola C975 emulator would exactly mimic the actual device, in terms of functionality and MIDlet support; however, in MIDlet development, what is promised is not always delivered. You should always confirm the working of your MIDlet on the actual device.

In the absence of TempoControl, to control the tempo on the actual device or on devices that don't support TempoControl, you use the superclass of TempoControl, called RateControl.

RateControl is analogous to the PitchControl control in terms of functionality. Like PitchControl, you can use the RateControl as *relative to original* change medium. Thus, RateControl changes the speed of playback relative to the original speed. Rates are specified in milli-percentages and can be negative as well, thereby allowing you to reduce the playback speed, compared to the original playback speed. This is something that you can't do with TempoControl (you can reduce the tempo from the default tempo, however).

It helps to think of TempoControl as a change medium for tempo, where you want an *absolute* value for the speed of playback of your musical piece. Think of RateControl as a *relative* change medium, where you change the speed of playback relative to the original value. Therefore, when using TempoControl, you use the setTempo() method where an absolute value of the desired tempo is required. When using RateControl, you can use the setRate() method where a relative value in percentages is specified.

Using the setTempo() method may not actually result in the desired tempo being set, as the musical sequence may override the tempo value. Using setRate() is guaranteed to succeed as the playback is relative to the original value, which is set against the Player instance's TimeBase and results in media time of the playback passing faster or slower than the original rate.

Besides the setRate() method, the RateControl control provides the getRate() method, which returns the current playback rate of a musical piece. You can also query for the minimum rate by using getMinRate(), and you can query for the maximum rate by using getMaxRate(). All these methods return the actual rate in milli-percentages.

Listing 7-3 (a modified version of Listing 7-2) uses RateControl instead of TempoControl, so that the new listing can be run on the Motorola C975 device, and you can modify the actual speed of playback. A quirk concerning the RateControl implementation in this device is described after the listing.

Listing 7-3. `RateControllableMIDIMIDlet` *Controls Playback Rate*

```
package com.apress.chapter7;

import javax.microedition.lcdui.*;
import javax.microedition.midlet.*;
import javax.microedition.media.*;
import javax.microedition.media.control.*;

public class RateControllableMIDIMIDlet extends MIDlet
  implements ItemStateListener {

  // the midi player
  Player midiPlayer = null;

  // the controls
  VolumeControl volControl = null;
  PitchControl pitchControl = null;
  RateControl rateControl = null;

  // the visual elements
  Form form = null;
  Gauge volGauge = null;
  Gauge pitchGauge = null;
  Gauge rateGauge = null;

  public RateControllableMIDIMIDlet() {
    try {

      // load the midi file
      midiPlayer = Manager.createPlayer(
        getClass().getResourceAsStream(
          "/media/midi/chapter7/cabeza.mid"), "audio/midi");

      // you must prefetch it to get the controls
      midiPlayer.prefetch();

      // extract the controls
      volControl = (VolumeControl) midiPlayer.getControl(
        "javax.microedition.media.control.VolumeControl");
      pitchControl = (PitchControl) midiPlayer.getControl(
        "javax.microedition.media.control.PitchControl");
      rateControl = (RateControl) midiPlayer.getControl(
        "javax.microedition.media.control.RateControl");

      // create the visual elements
      form = new Form("MIDI Player", null);
```

```
    // volume is set at a max of 100 with initial value of 50
    volGauge = new Gauge("Volume: 50", true, 100, 50);

    // rate is set at a max of 10 with 5 (default) as initial value
    rateGauge = new Gauge("Rate: 100%", true, 10, 5);

    // pitch is set at a max of 5 with initial value of 0, and a min of -5
    // note that because pitch can be negative and positive, the starting value
    // is at 5 (which is pitch 0), with +5 being 10 and -5 being 0.
    pitchGauge = new Gauge("Pitch: 0", true, 10, 5);

    // add the gauges to the form
    form.append(volGauge);
    form.append(rateGauge);
    form.append(pitchGauge);

    // add the listener to listen to gauge changes
    form.setItemStateListener(this);

    // and set this form as the current display
    Display.getDisplay(this).setCurrent(form);

  } catch(Exception e) {
    System.err.println(e);
  }
}

/**
 * Listens to changes in control gauges and applies them to actual controls
 */
public void itemStateChanged(Item item) {

  // we are only interested in item state changes of gauges
  if(!(item instanceof Gauge)) return;

  // get the new value of this gauge
  Gauge gauge = (Gauge)item;
  int val = gauge.getValue();

  // and change the control and label accordingly

  // changing volume?
  if(item == volGauge) {
    volControl.setLevel(val);
    volGauge.setLabel("Volume: " + val);
  }
```

```
    // changing rate? Is rateControl available?
    if(item == rateGauge && rateControl != null) {
      val = (val == 5 ? 6 : val);
      rateControl.setRate((val - 5) * 100 * 1000);
      rateGauge.setLabel("Rate: " + ((val - 5) * 100) + "%");
    }

    // changing pitch? make sure that pitchControl is available
    // remember, actual pitch is (val - 5)
    if(item == pitchGauge && pitchControl != null) {
      pitchControl.setPitch((val - 5) * 12 * 1000);
      pitchGauge.setLabel("Pitch: " + (val - 5));
    }
  }

  // the rest of the methods are unchanged from Listing 7-2 and are omitted from
  // the book version for brevity
}
```

The changes from Listing 7-2 are highlighted in bold. For `rateGauge` values 5 and 6, the rate is set at 100%; that is, the rate of playback is not changed. For values higher than that, the rate is increased; for values lower, the playback rate is decreased.

If you run this MIDlet on the actual device, you can increase the rate, but decreasing the rate even by a single value completely stops playing it. This is where the Motorola C975 emulator differs from the actual device. You can confirm this by using the method `getMinRate()`, which returns 100% on the actual device and 500% on the emulator (or negative 500%). A value of 100% on the actual device confirms that the minimum rate will not be lower than the original rate of play.

This quirkiness reemphasizes the need to test your MIDlets on actual devices before distributing them.

Figure 7-5 shows this MIDlet running on the device.

Figure 7-5. `RateControllableMIDIMIDlet` *running on a Motorola C975 device*

Tip `RateControl`, unlike `TempoControl`, can be used to control the rate of all media types, not just MIDI.

Playing MIDI with MIDIControl

MIDIControl allows advanced handling of a MIDI file. In fact, using MIDIControl doesn't even require a MIDI file, although you can use one if required. This control allows you to create your own sequences from scratch. However, doing so requires expert knowledge of the MIDI specification and knowing exactly what commands to call.

Creating a Standalone MIDI Player Instance

Recall from Chapter 6 that to play tones, the Manager class provides a constant that can be used for creating Player instances that fetch a ToneControl, without requiring an actual tone file. Similarly, the Manager class provides a MIDI locator constant that can be used to create a standalone MIDI Player instance, from which you can retrieve a MIDIControl and create your own sequences. This constant is called MIDI_DEVICE_LOCATOR and has a value of device://midi. Using it is pretty straightforward and an example is shown here:

```
Player p = Manager.createPlayer(Manager.MIDI_DEVICE_LOCATOR);
p.prefetch();
MIDIControl mControl =
  (MIDIControl)p.getControl("javax.microedition.media.control.MIDIControl");
```

Of course, because this Player instance doesn't correspond to an actual file, it doesn't have any associated data. If you call the method getDuration() on this instance, it will return a value of 0.

■ **Caution** You can also retrieve the MIDIControl with the getControl("MIDIControl"); method. However, this is not guaranteed to work on all implementations, even though the Javadoc for the getControl(String controlName) method seems to suggest otherwise.

Querying for MIDIControl Capabilities

The "Using MIDI in MMAPI" section earlier in this chapter stated that MMAPI implementations that provide support for MIDIControl may do so in a minimum or full form. At the minimum, if MIDIControl is provided, you are guaranteed support for sending MIDI events to the underlying device. On the other hand, if a full MIDIControl is implemented, you are allowed to query the installed soundbanks and manipulate them as well. Next you'll see how to query the installed MIDIControl for its capabilities.

Listing 7-4 shows a MIDlet that informs whether a full MIDIControl is installed.

Listing 7-4. MIDICapabilitiesMIDlet *Provides Information About* MIDIControl*'s Capability*

```
package com.apress.chapter7;

import javax.microedition.midlet.*;
import javax.microedition.lcdui.*;
import javax.microedition.media.*;
import javax.microedition.media.control.MIDIControl;
```

```
public class MIDICapabilitiesMIDlet extends MIDlet {

  public void startApp() {
    try {

      // create Player using MIDI Device locator
      Player p = Manager.createPlayer(Manager.MIDI_DEVICE_LOCATOR);

      // must prefetch before extracting controls
      p.prefetch();

      // get the MIDIControl
      MIDIControl mControl =
        (MIDIControl)p.getControl(
          "javax.microedition.media.control.MIDIControl");

      // create a message based on whether advanced capabilities are supported
      String msg =
        mControl.isBankQuerySupported() ?
          "MIDIControl is fully supported" : "Minimum MIDIControl is provided";

      // and display message as alert
      Display.getDisplay(this).setCurrent(
        new Alert("Message", msg, null, AlertType.INFO));

    } catch(Exception e) {
      System.err.println(e);
    }
  }

  public void pauseApp() {
  }

  public void destroyApp(boolean unconditional) {
  }
}
```

As you can see, querying for advanced capabilities of a MIDIControl boils down to using the method isBankQuerySupported(), which returns true if these advanced queries are indeed supported and false otherwise. If this method returns true, then you can do the following with your MIDIControl:

- Get a list of all the installed soundbanks on your device. This is done by using the method getBankList(boolean custom), which returns an array of integers, where each int corresponds to an installed soundbank. If the custom parameter is true, only custom soundbanks that you may have installed are returned, otherwise all soundbanks, preinstalled or custom, are returned.

- Get a list of all instruments installed or associated with a given soundbank. Instruments on a soundbank are also called programs. Thus, you can get all the program numbers by using the method `getProgramList(int bank)`, and you can get the name of the instrument/program by using `getProgramName(int bank, int prog)`.
- Get the current instrument/program assigned to a given channel using the method `getProgram(int channel)`. This returns an integer array with two values in it; the first integer represents the soundbank and the second represents the program number on that soundbank.
- Get the name of a key, given the soundbank, program, and key identifications. Thus, using the method `getKeyName(int bank, int program, int key)`, you can get the device-assigned name of this key.

With all the methods, the valid value for the soundbank parameter is `0-16383`, and the value is `0-127` for the program and key parameters.

With the target devices/emulators that you have been using so far, the result of running the MIDlet in Listing 7-4 is shown here:

- *Sun's DefaultColorPhone emulator*: Minimum `MIDIControl` is provided.
- *Motorola C975 emulator*: `MIDIControl` is fully supported.
- *Motorola C975 device*: Minimum `MIDIControl` is provided.

As you can see, the functionality on the emulator differs from the actual device. You'll use the C975 emulator to perform some of the functions provided by a full `MIDIControl`.

All implemented `MIDIControl` controls, minimum or full, can do the functions described in the following sections.

Send a Short MIDI Event to the Device

This means that you can send any MIDI message (refer to Figure 7-3), except System Exclusive to the device, and the device will interpret and react to it accordingly. To send a short MIDI event message, use the method `shortMidiEvent(int type, int data1, int data2)` where the type of the message is specified using the first parameter and the actual data, if any, using the last two parameters.

Refer to Tables 7-1, 7-2, and 7-3 for a list of the possible messages and their formats.

Send a Long MIDI Event to the Device

You can do this to send System Exclusive messages to the device using the `longMidiEvent(byte[] data, int offset, int length)` method.

Change Program and Volume of a Channel

You can set the program/instrument to use on a particular channel and set the volume for the channel as well.

The first is accomplished by the method `setProgram(int channel, int bank, int program)` and the second by `setChannelVolume(int channel, int volume)`. You can do the same using the `shortMidiEvent()` method, as these are really high-level convenience methods that are translated internally to use it. For a minimum `MIDIControl`, the `setProgram()` method uses a value of `-1` for the soundbank, which translates to the default soundbank on the device.

Sending Simple MIDI Messages

By using the `shortMidiEvent()` method, and to a lesser degree, the `longMidiEvent()` method, you can send all types of messages (as described at the beginning of this chapter) to the MIDI player on your device. In effect, you can create sequences of MIDI or create your own user-editable MIDI player.

Single MIDI Message

Let's start with how to send a single MIDI message by expanding on the "More About the Voice Channel Messages" section, where you learned to describe a MIDI message and created the message to turn on the note Middle C on MIDI Channel 12 at the velocity of 100. This complete Note ON command is repeated here:

```
1001 1011 0011 1100 0110 0100
```

The first byte from the left is the Status byte with the first 4 bits representing the Note ON command and the last four bits representing Channel 12 (again, Channel 1 is 0000, *not* 0001). The next Data byte represents Middle C (equal to 60) and the last Data byte is the velocity, equal to 100.

The `shortMidiEvent()` method takes three parameters; first, an integer that is the type of the message, and the next two are any data bytes associated with it. The type of the message is essentially information about the status and the channel that it is intended for, both of which are shown with the first byte. Thus, for the given message, `1001 1011` equals 155, `0011 1100` equals 60, and `0110 0100` equals 100. These are the three parameter values, and `shortMidiEvent(155, 60, 100)` will send the Note ON command for the note Middle C on MIDI Channel 12 at a velocity of 100.

Of course, you don't need to calculate the binary values first to arrive back at the decimal values, but this process illustrates the concept. Also, because it's so frequently used, `MIDIControl` provides a constant for the Note ON command, which you can use to create your Status bytes. For example, if you know your channel, note value, and velocity, you can use the following to send the command:

```
shortMidiEvent(MIDIControl.NOTE_ON | channel, note, velocity);
```

For the current case, this equates to:

```
shortMidiEvent(MIDIControl.NOTE_ON | 11, 60, 100); // 11 means Channel 12 not 11
```

The constant `NOTE_ON` has a value of `144`, as you would expect for the binary upper nibble value of `1001`.

You can send other MIDI messages in a similar way. For example, to send a corresponding Note OFF command, you can either use the actual value of 128 OR'ed with the channel number or send a Note ON command with a velocity of 0. Both examples are shown here:

```
shortMidiEvent(128 | 11, 60, 100);
shortMidiEvent(MidiControl.NOTE_ON | 11, 60, 0);
```

Both examples are equivalent and will achieve the same result.

■ Note Using the `shortMidiEvent()` method means that you don't have to physically start the associated `Player` instance for the event to be played. Sending the event acts on the MIDI device and not on any associated MIDI files.

Control Change Messages

`MIDIControl` provides another constant, `CONTROL_CHANGE`, which can be used to send Control Change messages. From Table 7-3, Control Change messages are used to change a particular control on a particular channel. For example, volume is a control that can be set individually for each channel. The format of Control Change messages is

```
1011 XXXX 0BBB BBBB 0CCC CCCC
```

The Status byte combines a static value with the channel information, while the first Data byte indicates the control that needs to be changed. The last Data byte provides the new value for this control. Thus, to change the volume of Channel 12 to 50, you can use the following command:

```
shortMidiEvent(MIDIControl.CONTROL_CHANGE | 11, 7, 50);
```

The actual value for the control is taken from the table provided by the MIDI organization at *http://www.midi.org/about-midi/table3.shtml.* Table 7-4 shows some of the more useful control numbers taken from this online table. As you can see, the Channel Volume control is given a value of 7.

Table 7-4. *Control Change Messages and Their Values*

Control Function	Control Number
Bank Select	0
Modulation Wheel or Lever	1
Foot Controller	4
Channel Volume	7
Balance	8
Pan	10

Instead of using the `shortMidiEvent()` method to change the volume of a channel, you can use the convenience method `setChannelVolume(int channel, int volume)`, which does the same thing internally.

Program Change Message

If you want to change the current instrument/program that is assigned to a particular channel, you can send one of the Program Change messages. This requires knowledge of the program numbers that can be assigned to each channel, which you can look up at *http://en.wikipedia.org/wiki/General_MIDI.*

The format of the Program Change message as per Table 7-3 is

```
1100 XXXX 0DDD DDDD No second Data byte
```

The new program number is identified by the only Data byte, and the Status byte is a combination of a static upper nibble and the channel number. Thus, as an example, to change the program on Channel 12 to a Xylophone (value 14), you can use:

```
shortMidiEvent(192 | 11, 14, 0);
```

As a convenience, `MIDIControl` provides another method that does the same thing, `setProgram(int channel, int bank, int program)`.

Giving Events Time to Process

One practical issue with using the `shortMidiEvent()` method arises because the method returns almost immediately. Now, this would be okay if the `MIDIControl` implementation was to form a queue of all the event messages arising out of the use of this method. However, there are no guarantees of this occurring. This doesn't mean it won't happen, but you'll rarely find two implementations that work the same way and queue the messages, thus ensuring that a message is received and processed in the order it was sent.

To overcome this issue, you need to give the device's MIDI receiver time to process the event, before sending it another one. Hence, a simple `Thread.sleep(100)` after every event will ensure that the events are received in order and processed in order as well.

Listing 7-5 combines the information from the previous three sections (and this section as well) to create a MIDlet that first sends a Note ON event, followed by a Note OFF event. A Program Change message is then sent to change the program to Xylophone. Finally, a Control Change message to change the volume is followed by a Note ON (and OFF) Message to see the effect of the changes.

Listing 7-5. *The* `shortMidiEvent()` *Method in Action*

```
package com.apress.chapter7;

import javax.microedition.midlet.*;
import javax.microedition.media.*;
import javax.microedition.lcdui.*;
import javax.microedition.media.control.MIDIControl;

public class MIDIEventsMIDlet extends MIDlet {

  Display display = null;
  Alert alert = null;

  public MIDIEventsMIDlet() {
    display = Display.getDisplay(this);
    alert = new Alert("Message");
    alert.setString("Working...");
    alert.setTimeout(Alert.FOREVER);
  }
```

```
public void startApp() {

  // show the alert at startup
  display.setCurrent(alert);

  try {

    // create a MIDI player
    Player p = Manager.createPlayer(Manager.MIDI_DEVICE_LOCATOR);

    // prefetch
    p.prefetch();

    // extract MIDI Control
    MIDIControl mControl =
      (MIDIControl)p.getControl(
        "javax.microedition.media.control.MIDIControl");

    if(mControl == null) throw new Exception("MIDIControl not available");

    // send Note ON for Channel 12 for note MIDDLE C at 100 velocity
    mControl.shortMidiEvent(MIDIControl.NOTE_ON | 11, 60, 100);

    Thread.sleep(100);

    // send Note OFF
    mControl.shortMidiEvent(MIDIControl.NOTE_ON | 11, 60, 0);

    Thread.sleep(100);

    // send program change to Xylophone (14)
    // alternatively, use setProgram(11, -1, 14);
    mControl.shortMidiEvent(192 | 11,14, 0);
    // mControl.setProgram(11, -1, 14);

    Thread.sleep(100);

    // set volume change to 50
    // alternatively, use setChannelVolume(11, 50);
    mControl.shortMidiEvent(MIDIControl.CONTROL_CHANGE | 11, 7, 50);
    Thread.sleep(100);

    // send Note ON for Channel 12 for note MIDDLE C at 100 velocity
    mControl.shortMidiEvent(MIDIControl.NOTE_ON | 11, 60, 100);

    Thread.sleep(100);
```

```
        // send Note OFF
        mControl.shortMidiEvent(MIDIControl.NOTE_ON | 11, 60, 0);

        Thread.sleep(100);

      } catch(Exception e) {
        alert.setString(e.getMessage());
        System.err.println(e);
      }
    }

    public void pauseApp() {
    }

    public void destroyApp(boolean unconditional) {
    }
  }
```

In this code, the main MIDlet thread sleeps for 100 milliseconds each time an event is sent, but you can use a lesser value (and send the events in a separate thread) for better performance and responsiveness. When you run this MIDlet, you will hear a single beep followed by a lesser audible beep made by the Xylophone.

■ **Caution** On the Motorola C975 device, the Program Change message using `shortMidiEvent(192 | 11, 14, 0);` doesn't work, so you'll have to use the alternate method `setProgram(11, -1, 14);`.

Working with Soundbanks

A soundbank, as you learned earlier, is a collection of 128 programs (or instruments) that are supported by a particular MIDI device, to overcome the limitation of only 128 programs. You also learned that not all MIDI devices support the concept of soundbanks, and the subsequent support for soundbank operations is limited, leading to either a full `MIDIControl` or minimum `MIDIControl` implementation.

The method `isBankQuerySupported()` is used to find out whether a full or minimum `MIDIControl` is available. Of the devices/emulators that you have used so far in this book, only the Motorola C975 emulator supports a full `MIDIControl`. Let's exercise this full `MIDIControl` to query the installed soundbank(s).

Figure 7-6 shows a MIDlet running on the C975 emulator, taking advantage of its support for a full `MIDIControl`. The MIDlet first queries the installed soundbanks and then lists the available programs, along with their names. When the user selects a program from the list, a note is played using that particular program.

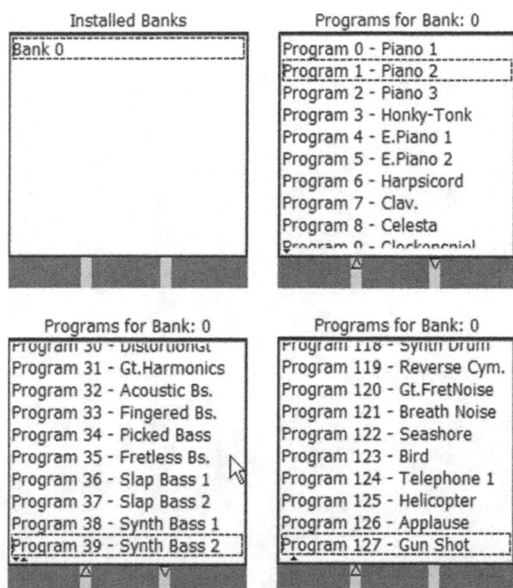

Figure 7-6. *Installed banks and programs on the C975 emulator*

As you can see, only one soundbank is installed, and it has 128 programs installed on it. This list of programs and their names mimics the one mentioned earlier, which is found at *http://en.wikipedia.org/wiki/General_MIDI.*

■ **Note** The fact that you can't query Sun's DefaultColorPhone emulator or the actual Motorola C975 device doesn't mean that no soundbank is installed. There is a default soundbank installed, but querying it is not permitted.

The full code for this MIDlet is shown in Listing 7-6. A brief explanation follows this listing, which should be read along with the comments in the code.

Listing 7-6. `ProgramNamesMIDlet` *Queries Installed Soundbanks/Programs and Plays Notes in Different Programs*

```
package com.apress.chapter7;

import javax.microedition.midlet.*;
import javax.microedition.lcdui.*;
import javax.microedition.media.*;
import javax.microedition.media.control.MIDIControl;

public class ProgramNamesMIDlet extends MIDlet implements CommandListener {
```

```
  // MIDlet's display
  private Display display = null;

  // the bank and program lists
  private List bankList = null;
  private List programList = null;

  // the actual banks and programs (instruments)
  private int[] banks = null;
  private int[] programs = null;

  // the player and MIDIControl
  private Player player = null;
  private MIDIControl mControl = null;

  public ProgramNamesMIDlet() {

    display = Display.getDisplay(this);

    try {
      // create a MIDI player
      player = Manager.createPlayer(Manager.MIDI_DEVICE_LOCATOR);

      // prefetch
      player.prefetch();

      // extract MIDI Control
      mControl = (MIDIControl)player.getControl(
        "javax.microedition.media.control.MIDIControl");

    } catch (Exception e) {
      error(e);
    }
  }

  public void startApp() {

    try {

      // check if we can query the banks
      if(mControl.isBankQuerySupported()) {

        // get the list of banks
        banks = mControl.getBankList(false);

        // create a list to display the banks
        bankList = new List("Installed Banks", Choice.IMPLICIT);
```

```
        // and populate the list
        for(int i = 0; i < banks.length; i++) {
          bankList.append("Bank " + banks[i], null);
        }

        // add this MIDlet as the CommandListener
        bankList.setCommandListener(this);

        // and show the list
        display.setCurrent(bankList);

      } else { // Bank Query not supported
        display.setCurrent(new Alert("Bank Query not supported"));
      }

    } catch(Exception e) {
      error(e);
    }
  }

  public void commandAction(Command cmd, Displayable disp) {

    // only bankList and programList commands are being listened for
    if(disp != bankList && disp != programList) return;

    try {

      // for bankList
      if(disp == bankList) {

        // the selected bank
        int selectedBank = banks[bankList.getSelectedIndex()];

        // get the programs for this selected bank
        programs = mControl.getProgramList(selectedBank);

        // and create a programList
        programList =
          new List("Programs for Bank: " + selectedBank, Choice.IMPLICIT);

        // populate this list
        for(int i = 0; i < programs.length; i++) {
          programList.append("Program " + programs[i] + " - " +
            mControl.getProgramName(selectedBank, programs[i]), null);
        }

        // add this MIDlet as the CommandListener
        programList.setCommandListener(this);
```

```
        // and show this list
        display.setCurrent(programList);

      } else { // can be programList only

        // send command to change program
        mControl.setProgram(
          11, // on channel 11
          banks[bankList.getSelectedIndex()], // the selected bank
          programs[programList.getSelectedIndex()]); // the selected program

        // sleep
        Thread.sleep(100);

        // send a Note ON command
        mControl.shortMidiEvent(MIDIControl.NOTE_ON | 11, 60, 100);

        // sleep
        Thread.sleep(100);

        // send a Note OFF command
        mControl.shortMidiEvent(MIDIControl.NOTE_ON | 11, 60, 0);

        // shorter sleep
        Thread.sleep(20);
      }

    } catch(Exception e) {
      error(e);
    }
  }

  // general purpose error method, displays on screen as well to output
  private void error(Exception e) {
    display.setCurrent(new Alert(e.getMessage()));
    e.printStackTrace();
  }

  public void pauseApp() {
  }

  public void destroyApp(boolean unconditional) {
  }
}
```

The MIDlet starts by finding out whether querying the soundbanks is permitted. If not, a brief message is displayed. Otherwise, the `getBankList(false)` method is used to get a list of all soundbanks. This list is then displayed, and the user can make a soundbank selection (in the case of the C975 emulator, there is only one soundbank). The programs installed on this soundbank are then displayed, along with their names, using the methods `getProgramList (selectedBank)` and `getProgramName(selectedBank, programs[i]), null)`. Finally, when the user selects any program from the list, a Note ON command with Middle C note and velocity 100 is sent after changing the program by using the `setProgram(int channel, int bank, int program)` method.

Mapping key presses on a device to a program in a soundbank should now be fairly easy. This can be used to create a user-controlled MIDI player if you want to do so.

Summary

MIDI is an extensive and diverse communication protocol for transmission of audio messages. It is a widely used protocol for digital music, and MMAPI does well to support MIDI by providing `MIDIControl` as a separate control.

Of course, the exact level of support varies between MMAPI implementations, with the most basic support being the capability to play MIDI files. This chapter introduced you to the concepts of MIDI, including a guide on how MIDI works and an overview of its message structure.

MMAPI allows you to control MIDI files without actually needing to use a `MIDIControl` control, and this chapter showed you how, using `VolumeControl`, `PitchControl`, and `TempoControl` only.

Of course, greater control is provided by using `MIDIControl`, which was shown with the help of various examples, including working with soundbanks, program and control change messages, and the like.

The next chapter will show you how to work with audio and video in MMAPI, one of the most exciting parts of this specification.

CHAPTER 8

Working with Audio and Video

Being able to embed audio and video in your MIDlets provides the biggest advantage that MMAPI brings. The entertainment value provided by multimedia-based options like these is a sure way to get your MIDlets noticed. These MIDlets provide a richer user experience than those without any such visual stimuli.

By being an open-ended API, MMAPI provides a single, simple yet powerful medium to embed audio and video in your MIDlets. Device manufacturers decide which part of the API they want to and can support and consequently provide implementations that take full advantage of the device's features. For example, if the device contains a camera, the MMAPI implementation on it may provide means to capture snapshots or full videos. The point is that the device manufacture is in full control of the capabilities that it wants enabled and can do so with a single API interface.

Whether audio capture or live radio streaming, video capture to video playback, synchronized audio and video, or simple snapshots, MMAPI provides the means using your device. The trick is to find a device that supports all these options so you can create your magical MIDlet. This chapter shows you all the capabilities provided by the MMAPI to support these features.

Querying the Capabilities of Your Device

Before you decide to make an audio/video-enabled MIDlet, you should find out the capabilities of your target device(s). MMAPI provides a simple way of finding out these capabilities, by using the `System.getProperty(String key)` method, which, technically, is a CLDC method.

MMAPI defines several unique properties that you can query for using this method. Table 8-1 gives a list of these properties, along with what they indicate. Almost all these properties relate to the support of audio and video in a particular MMAPI implementation, which is why they are introduced in this later chapter.

Table 8-1. *MMAPI System Properties*

Property Key	Description
`microedition.media.version`	Returns the version of MMAPI that the implementation implements. Currently it returns either 1.1 or 1.0, depending on the implementation that you try it on.
`supports.recording`	Returns true or false, depending on whether either audio and/or video capture is supported by the implementation. Thus, if neither audio nor video can be captured, it returns false; otherwise, true is returned in all other cases.
`streamable.contents`	Returns a list of supported media types, only if the MMAPI implementation supports streaming of media data. In most cases, this returns null, meaning that streaming content is not supported.
`supports.mixing`	Returns true if audio media data can be "mixed" or returns false otherwise. If true, you can have more than one `Player` instance playing audio and/or tones at the same time.
`supports.audio.capture`	Returns true if audio can be captured; returns false otherwise. If true, the following property must not return a null or empty value.
`audio.encodings`	Returns the supported formats for recording audio; returns null if audio capture is not supported.
`supports.video.capture`	Similar to audio, returns true if video capture is supported; returns false otherwise. If true, the following property must not return a null or empty value.
`video.encodings`	Returns the supported formats for recording video content; returns null if video capture is not supported.
`video.snapshot.encodings`	Returns the list of supported formats for taking snapshots with the device camera; returns null if this is not supported.

Listing 8-1 shows a MIDlet that you can use to find out the value of these properties and hence the capabilities of your MMAPI implementation.

Listing 8-1. `CapabilitiesMIDlet` *Lists the Capabilities of a MMAPI Implementation*

```
package com.apress.chapter8;

import javax.microedition.midlet.*;
import javax.microedition.lcdui.*;

public class CapabilitiesMIDlet extends MIDlet {
```

```
// all the possible capabilities
private String[] capabilitiesIdx = {
  "microedition.media.version",
  "supports.mixing",
  "supports.audio.capture",
  "supports.video.capture",
  "supports.recording",
  "audio.encodings",
  "video.encodings",
  "video.snapshot.encodings",
  "streamable.contents"
};

public void startApp() {

  // create a list
  List list = new List("Audio/Video Capabilities", Choice.IMPLICIT);

  // and query the device for each of the properties
  for(int i = 0; i < capabilitiesIdx.length; ++i) {
    list.append(
      System.getProperty(capabilitiesIdx[i]) + " - " +
      capabilitiesIdx[i], null);
  }

  // show this list
  Display.getDisplay(this).setCurrent(list);
}

public void pauseApp() {
}

public void destroyApp(boolean unconditional) {
}
}
```

Finally, Figure 8-1 gives you the result of running this MIDlet in the three development environments used so far in this book: Sun's DefaultColorPhone, Motorola C975 emulator, and Motorola C975 device.

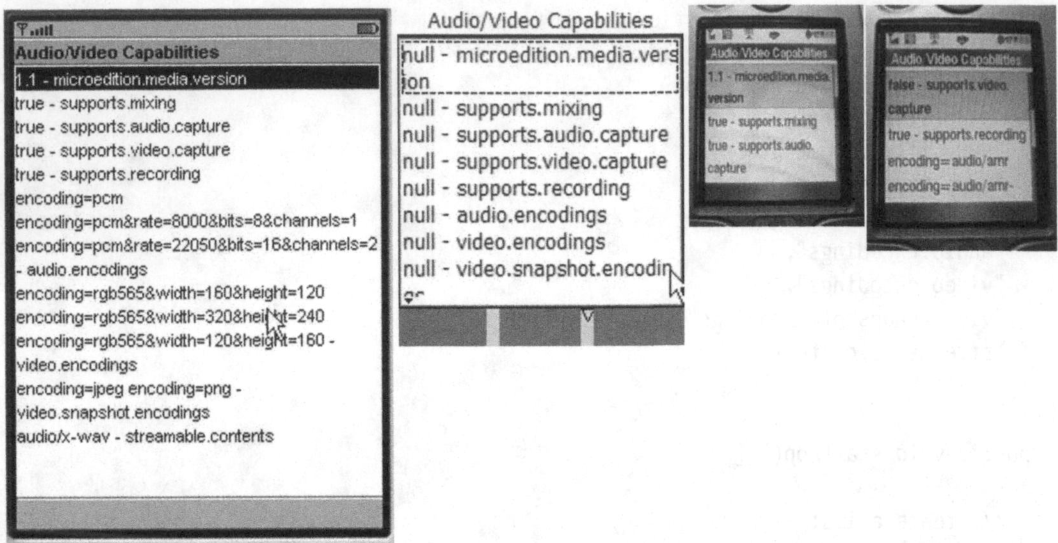

Figure 8-1. *MMAPI capabilities in Sun's DefaultColorPhone emulator, Motorola C975 emulator, and Motorola C975 device (last two figures)*

As you can see, the result of running this MIDlet in various environments is less than encouraging. The Motorola C975 emulator gives a twisted result, returning null for every property, whereas the actual device returns null for `supports.video.capture`, a disappointing result for the continued use of this device for testing in this chapter on audio/video.

■ Note A variance in the output between the Motorola C975 emulator and the actual device must come as no surprise at this stage. Emulator and actual device implementations vary considerably and no MIDlet should be released without testing on target devices.

You may also wonder why the actual device does not support capturing of video, especially if you glance at Table 2-3 from Chapter 2, which shows the result of running `getSupportedContentTypes("capture")`. This table suggests that the Motorola C975 device should support capture of audio, video, and camera (meaning snapshots), yet Figure 8-1 shows that `supports.video.capture` for the actual device is false.

This is the bane of Java ME development. It's one thing to worry about matching the behavior of devices to their emulators, but even devices themselves don't support the MMAPI implementation consistently. Worse, the implementations sometimes give contradictory results, as in this case, which can confuse the developer to no end. All device manufacturers are guilty of this lapse in consistency, lest you believe that it is a Motorola-specific problem.

One reason for this contradiction is that `System.getProperty(String key)` is a CLDC implementation method, whereas `getSupportedContentTypes(String protocol)` is a MMAPI implementation method. Each API may be implemented by different teams, which may result in the said inconsistency. A feeble excuse, but an excuse nonetheless.

Because the Motorola C975 device can't be used to develop video capture MIDlets, the BenQ (formerly Siemens) M75 (*http://www.benqmobile.com/cds/frontdoor/0,2241,hq_en_0_89745_rArNrNrNrN,00.html*) is used in this chapter. The emulator for this device can be downloaded from the BenQ developer site at *http://developer.benqmobile.com/*. This device and the associated emulator are used interchangeably between the Motorola C975 emulator and device for the rest of the MIDlets in this chapter and the next.

Running the MIDlet from Listing 8-1 again in this new emulator and actual device gives the results shown in Figure 8-2.

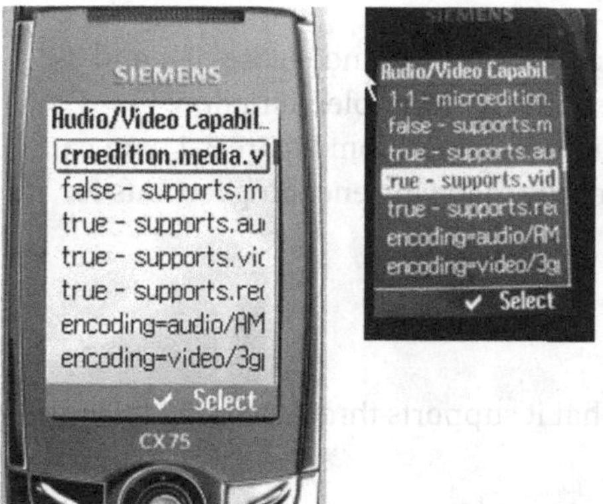

Figure 8-2. *BenQ M75 emulator and device MMAPI capabilities*

Because it may not be very easy to make out the properties completely in Figure 8-2, they are tabulated in Table 8-2. Thankfully, both the emulator and the device support the same set of properties.

Table 8-2. *MMAPI Capabilities on BenQ M75 Emulator and Device*

Property Name	Value
`microedition.media.version`	`1.1`
`supports.mixing`	`false`
`supports.audio.capture`	`true`
`supports.video.capture`	`true`
`supports.recording`	`true`
`audio.encodings`	`encoding=audio/AMR`
`video.encodings`	`encoding=video/3gpp`
`video.snapshot.encodings`	`encoding=jpeg encoding=image/jpeg`
`streamable.contents`	`null`

With the support for audio and video capture, the device/emulator must specify the supported format(s) of the captured media. This is done with the help of `audio.encodings`, `video.encodings`, and `video.snapshot.encodings` properties.

Understanding Media Encodings

Media encoding strings are used for specifying the format of media supported, or desired, for a particular operation. It is explained with the help of a string that has the supported or desired formats separated by a single space. The MMAPI specification states that there are four types of intermixable strings, but in reality, not all are supported, and almost certainly, intermixing of these strings is rare (but possible).

These four types of encoding strings are used to define the format of audio, video, intermixed, and custom media data. The general format for each type is

```
encoding=contentType&encodingParams
```

which resembles the HTTP URL query format. As you saw in Table 8-2 and Figures 8-1 and 8-2, the supported formats vary greatly with the specific device MMAPI implementation.

Audio encodings specify, or request, the correct audio formats. From Figure 8-1, you can see that the Sun's DefaultColorPhone emulator specifies the following encoding formats for the property `audio.encodings`:

```
encoding=pcm encoding=pcm&rate=8000&bits=8&channels=1
encoding=pcm&rate=22050&bits=16&channels=2
```

Using this format, the emulator is informing you that it supports three encoding formats for audio capture:

- PCM (Pulse Code Manipulation), which is a ubiquitous form of storing audio data
- PCM at a frequency rate of 8,000 and 8 bits per sample and a single channel (mono)
- PCM at a frequency rate of 22,050, 16 bits per sample, and dual channels (stereo)

All three formats are separated by a single space, and each starts with the text `encoding=`. This is followed by the content type of the encoding and then the parameters (if any) of the content type that qualifies it. Each parameter and its value are separated by the ampersand sign (&), which also separates the content type from its parameters.

The first encoding is assumed to be the default encoding. That is, as you'll see later, if you don't request a particular encoding, and there are multiple encodings that the device may support for a particular operation, the first returned encoding is the format of the resulting media.

Similarly, the video encodings specify the correct video formats, given by the `video.encodings` property. Again, taking the example from Figure 8-1, Sun's DefaultColorPhone emulator supports the following formats for video capture:

```
encoding=rgb565&width=160&height=120 encoding=rgb565&width=320&height=240
encoding=rgb565&width=120&height=160
```

The content type is the same for all the encodings, and the formats only differ in the size of the capture that is supported. This is only a theoretical possibility with this emulator, as it only simulates video capture and doesn't actually implement it.

Mixed encodings allow you to specify audio and video encodings together in one single string for operations that require specific encodings for mixed formats. Each encoding is separately specified, as if they were being specified for single encodings, and then combined using the ampersand (&) operator. The following is an example of mixed encoding, where the first part is the audio encoding, and the latter (in bold) part is the video encoding:

encoding=pcm&rate=8000&bits=8&channels=1&**encoding=rgb565&width=320&height=240**

Finally, custom encodings allow you to create your own encodings, albeit remaining true to the audio, video, and mixed encodings formats. An example is shown here:

```
encoding=custom&key=value
```

A Brief Overview of Sampled Audio

Digitally recorded audio data is often referred to as sampled audio. This section gives you a brief overview of the concepts behind sampled audio. You can skip this section if you have a fair understanding of this concept.

Sampled audio represents successive *samples* of audio data. Audio data, in physical terms, is represented as a signal (of a sound wave). By taking discrete samples of the amplitude of a sound wave and representing it using bits and bytes, digital audio data is generated. In a sense, sampled audio is only an approximation of the actual sound wave because you are taking samples of the original and not recreating the whole thing.

This implies that the quality of sampled audio depends on how many samples you take per second. This is true; however, the quality of the finished samples also depends on how you represent them digitally. The more bits used to represent each sample, the better it represents the original audio data accurately.

These two measurements are then a representation of sampled audio. The first, which is effectively a measurement of resolution in time, is called the *sampling rate*. The second, which is the resolution in amplitude, is called *quantization* (or just *resolution*). For example, the music on CDs has a sample rate of 44.1 Khz and a quantization of 16 bits per sample. So, sampled audio on a CD has been sampled 44,100 times per second, and each sample is represented using 16 bits. As a comparison, DVD is sampled at 48 Khz to 96 Khz, and professional recording equipment boasts of sample rates of 192 Khz.

This process of producing sampled audio from analog signals is called Pulse Code Manipulation (PCM). The format on its own is not very efficient, because it doesn't deal with redundancy of samples, thereby taking up a lot of space. By using compression algorithms such as MP3, a PCM-encoded sample can be reduced to contain the same amount of data in a smaller sample size. This has led to the tremendous popularity of using MP3, which produces CD-quality (and better) sound in smaller files. In purely technical terms, MP3 is a compression format of the PCM encoded signal and works by discarding samples not considered valuable for hearing.

Storing Sampled Audio

Although sampled audio is mostly encoded using PCM, it can be saved in a variety of formats for transmission, retrieval, and playback. You may be already familiar with the common storage formats, such as WAV, AU, MP3, AIFF, and so on. These file formats contain information about the sampled audio, but may also contain meta information about the file itself, including information about the size, the format, size of frames, and so on. Typically, this information is contained in the file header.

These files are differentiated by the compression offered in the stored data. As stated earlier, MP3 is an example of a compressed file, where the quality of the file is degraded to conserve space by getting rid of some samples. On the other hand, WAV, AIFF, and AU are uncompressed formats and contain the closest representation of the original sampled data; however, the file size is an issue. There are other formats that guarantee not to lose any samples and yet compress the audio data, but these aren't very popular. For one thing, the compression is nowhere near that offered by MP3 compression. An example of such a format is True Audio (TTA).

Another popular format, especially as far as Java ME development is concerned, is the Adaptive Multi-Rate (AMR) format, which is a standard adapted by the 3rd Generation Participation Project (3GPP). This format is like MP3, in that it's a compression algorithm that loses quality of the original samples by dropping samples it considers unnecessary for transmission or playback. It specifies a varying number of bit rates, which is simply the number of bits of the sampled data that it can transmit per second. This format is extended to the AMR–Wide Band (WB), which offers a higher speech quality because of its support for a wider speech bandwidth than the AMR format. For this reason, the original AMR format is also referred to as AMR–Narrow Band (AMR-NB).

One final thing to note here is that the WAV file format cannot be used for streaming audio data, because the format requires the complete file data for calculating header information as opposed to the MP3 or AMR formats, which support streaming seamlessly.

Controlling Sampled Audio

Unlike video, sampled audio doesn't require anything extra, other than what you have already learned, to play it. In fact, the way that MMAPI is designed, tones and MIDI, along with sampled audio, can be played without distinguishing between them. If anything, they differ in the controls that are provided for controlling them. MIDI provides `MIDIControl`, and tones provide `ToneControl`, whereas sampled audio provides a variety of controls, most of which you have already come across in some form or another.

For example, `VolumeControl` was covered in Chapters 4 and 7, and the basics of using it with sampled audio remain the same. The same applies to `RateControl` and `PitchControl`, both of which were covered in Chapter 7. Therefore, this section covers the two controls that haven't been covered yet, `MetaDataControl` and `StopTimeControl`.

■ **Note** `MetaDataControl` and `StopTimeControl` are not exclusively for use with sampled audio, but like `VolumeControl`, their use applies to all media data that supports sampled audio.

Setting Preset Stop Times with `StopTimeControl`

Being able to set a preset stop time for media data may not sound very useful, but it can come in very handy when you want a precise action to happen at a particular instance. This is because when the `Player` instance stops at the preset time, the `STOPPED_AT_TIME` event is fired, which you can capture and act on.

Of course, not all media types, and for that matter, not all implementations, support `StopTimeControl`. This is to say that some MMAPI implementations may support this control, but only for certain media types. It's hard to judge which media types support this control, because unlike the `getSupportedContentTypes(String protocol)` and `getSupportedProtocols(String contentType)` methods, there is no corresponding `getSupportedControls(String contentType)` method. As you know, the `getControls()` and `getControl()` methods only work after a `Player` instance has been prefetched.

Listing 8-2 provides an example of using StopTimeControl. The code creates a Player instance that can be started with or without a StopTimeControl being used to preset a stop time. However, the Player instance remains the same, whether you are using a StopTimeControl or not, and you'll notice varying results due to this. An explanation follows the code listing, and Figure 8-3 shows the MIDlet in use in the Motorola C975 emulator.

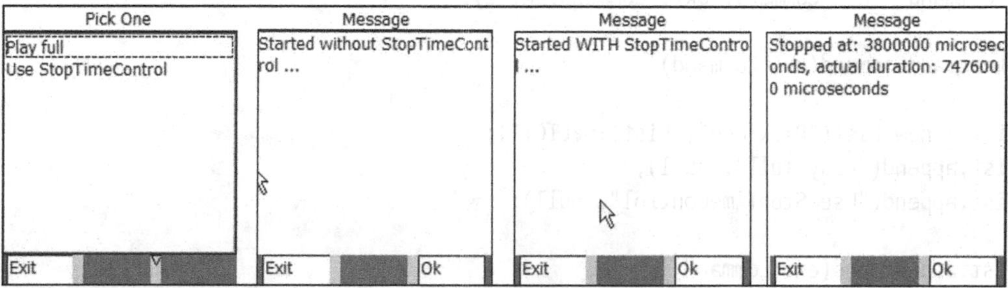

Figure 8-3. *Running* StopTimeControlMIDlet *in Motorola C975*

Figure 8-3 shows the StopTimeControlMIDlet in action, with the two different scenarios played out.

Listing 8-2. StopTimeControlMIDlet *Allows You to Play with the* StopTimeControl

```
package com.apress.chapter8;

import javax.microedition.midlet.*;
import javax.microedition.lcdui.*;
import javax.microedition.media.*;
import javax.microedition.media.control.*;

public class StopTimeControlMIDlet extends MIDlet
  implements CommandListener, PlayerListener {

  // the display items
  private Display display = null;
  private Alert alert = null;
  private List list = null;

  // commands
  private Command exitCommand = null;
  private Command okCommand = null;

  // player and controls
  private Player player = null;
  private StopTimeControl stControl = null;

  public StopTimeControlMIDlet() {
```

```
  // create all the basic stuff
  display = Display.getDisplay(this);

  alert = new Alert("Message");

  exitCommand = new Command("Exit", Command.EXIT, 1);
  okCommand = new Command("Ok", Command.OK, 1);

  alert.addCommand(exitCommand);

  list = new List("Pick One", List.IMPLICIT);
  list.append("Play full", null);
  list.append("Use StopTimeControl", null);

  list.addCommand(exitCommand);
  alert.addCommand(okCommand);

  alert.setCommandListener(this);
  list.setCommandListener(this);

  // create the player and the stoptimecontrol
  try {
    player = Manager.createPlayer(
      getClass().getResourceAsStream(
      "/media/audio/chapter8/printer.wav"), "audio/x-wav");

    player.addPlayerListener(this);

    player.prefetch();

    stControl = (StopTimeControl)player.getControl(
      "javax.microedition.media.control.StopTimeControl");

    // no point continuing if stoptimecontrol is not supported
    if(stControl == null)
      throw new Exception("StopTimeControl is not supported");
  } catch(Exception e) {
    error(e);
  }
}

public void startApp() {
  // show the list of items
  display.setCurrent(list);
}

public void pauseApp() {
}
```

```
public void destroyApp(boolean unconditional) {
}

public void commandAction(Command cmd, Displayable disp) {

  // if exiting
  if(cmd == exitCommand) {
    notifyDestroyed();
    return;
  }

  // if ok command
  if(cmd == okCommand) {
    try {
      // pause the player, so that it can be reused
      player.stop();

      // and redisplay the list
      display.setCurrent(list);
    } catch(Exception e) {
      error(e);
    }
  }

  // implicit list handling
  if(disp == list) {

    // the selected idx
    int selectedIdx = list.getSelectedIndex();

    // show the message
    display.setCurrent(alert);

    try {
      if(selectedIdx == 0) {
        // start player without stoptimecontrol
        if(player != null) player.start();
        alert.setString("Started without StopTimeControl ...");
      } else {

        // start with stoptimecontrol

        // set the stop time as half of the length
        stControl.setStopTime(player.getDuration()/2);

        // start the player
        if(player != null) player.start();
```

```
          alert.setString("Started WITH StopTimeControl ...");
        }
      } catch(Exception e) {
        error(e);
      }
    }
  }

  public void playerUpdate(Player player, String event, Object eventData) {

    // only interested in the STOPPED_AT_TIME event
    if(event == STOPPED_AT_TIME) {
      // give the message
      alert.setString("Stopped at: " + eventData + " microseconds" +
        ", actual duration: " + player.getDuration() + " microseconds");

      // and show the alert
      alert.setTimeout(Alert.FOREVER);
      display.setCurrent(alert);
    }
  }

  // general purpose error method, displays onscreen as well to output
  private void error(Exception e) {
    alert.setString(e.getMessage());
    alert.setTitle("Error");
    alert.setTimeout(Alert.FOREVER);
    display.setCurrent(alert);
    e.printStackTrace();
  }
}
```

If you try this MIDlet in an emulator or a device and test it repeatedly, you'll notice some anomalous results. As per the code, when using the `StopTimeControl`, the `Player` instance is preset to stop playing when exactly half the duration has been reached. Figure 8-4 shows one such anomaly.

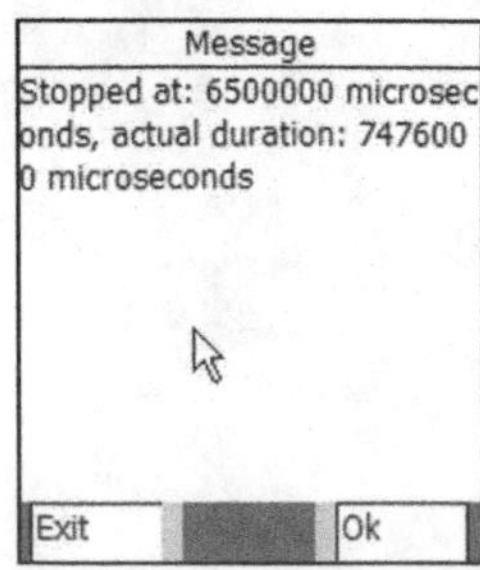

Figure 8-4. `StopTimeControl` *seems to stop after the preset time.*

Figure 8-4 seems to suggest that the Player instance was stopped after the preset time, which being half of the total duration, should be roughly 373,800 microseconds. This happened because in this particular case, the StopTimeControl's setStopTime(long stopTime) method was called *after* the media playback time of the Player instance had passed the preset time. In such cases, that is, when the current media time has already passed the preset time, the Player instance immediately stops at the current media time and generates a STOPPED_AT_TIME event.

You can remove a previously set preset time by using the constant RESET. Thus, setStopTime(StopTimeControl.RESET) will clear any preset times. Calling the getStopTime() method returns the preset time (remember, in microseconds, *not* milliseconds) and RESET if no preset time has been set.

Finally, if you call setStopTime() method on a *started* Player instance, which already has a preset time, an IllegalStateException is thrown. However, you can change the preset time on a stopped Player instance, as is done in Listing 8-2.

Gathering Information Using MetaDataControl

MetaDataControl provides a simple way for Player instances to expose the meta information about media data. This meta information can be exposed with a set of predefined keys, such as Author, Title, Date, and Copyright, or the media may contain its own proprietary keys (with associated values).

As with StopTimeControl, not all media exposes this control. WAV and MP3 in sampled audio and MPEG in video are the most likely candidates that will provide meta information such as this. This doesn't mean that other media doesn't contain this information, just that the MMAPI implementation may not provide the MetaDataControl control for it.

Listing 8-3 shows you an example of using this control, where the information contained in an MP3 is displayed on the screen.

Listing 8-3. *Using* MetaDataControl *to Display Meta Information*

```
package com.apress.chapter8;

import javax.microedition.midlet.*;
import javax.microedition.lcdui.*;

import javax.microedition.media.*;
import javax.microedition.media.control.MetaDataControl;

public class MetaDataControlMIDlet extends MIDlet implements CommandListener {

  // define the display items
  private Display display = null;
  private List list = null;
  private Command exitCommand = null;
  private Alert alert = null;

  // the player instance
  private Player player = null;
```

```
public MetaDataControlMIDlet() {

  // create the display items
  display = Display.getDisplay(this);
  alert = new Alert("Message");
  exitCommand = new Command("Exit", Command.EXIT, 1);
  alert.addCommand(exitCommand);
  alert.setCommandListener(this);

  list = new List("Message", List.IMPLICIT);
  list.addCommand(exitCommand);

  list.setCommandListener(this);

  // create and prefetch the player instance
  try {
    player = Manager.createPlayer(
     getClass().getResourceAsStream(
      "/media/audio/chapter8/frogs.mp3"), "audio/mp3");

    player.prefetch();
  } catch(Exception e) {
    error(e);
  }
}

public void startApp() {

  // if player was created, extract control
  if(player != null) {

    MetaDataControl mControl =
      (MetaDataControl)player.getControl(
        "javax.microedition.media.control.MetaDataControl");

    // if control is provided, show information onscreen
    if(mControl == null) {

      // no info
      alert.setString("No Meta Information");
      display.setCurrent(alert);
    } else {

      // get all the keys of this control
      String[] keys = mControl.getKeys();

      // and append the key and its value to the list
      for(int i = 0; i < keys.length; i++) {
```

```
          list.append(keys[i] + " -- " + mControl.getKeyValue(keys[i]), null);
        }

        // show the list
        display.setCurrent(list);
      }
    }
  }

  public void commandAction(Command cmd, Displayable disp) {
    if(cmd == exitCommand) {
      notifyDestroyed();
    }
  }

  public void pauseApp() {
  }

  public void destroyApp(boolean unconditional) {
  }

  // general purpose error method, displays onscreen as well to output
  private void error(Exception e) {
    alert.setString(e.getMessage());
    alert.setTitle("Error");
    alert.setTimeout(Alert.FOREVER);
    display.setCurrent(alert);
    e.printStackTrace();
  }
}
```

As you can see, to get a list of keys, you use the method `getKeys()`, which returns a `String` array. There are four predefined keys in the `MetaDataControl` class: `AUTHOR_KEY`, `TITLE_KEY`, `COPYRIGHT_KEY`, and `DATE_KEY`. After you have the keys, whether predefined or retrieved using the `getKeys()` method, you can use the `getKeyValue()` method to get the value assigned to each key.

Figure 8-5 shows this MIDlet running in the Motorola C975 device, with only the title key showing a value. The Motorola C975 emulator doesn't support the playback of MP3 audio.

Figure 8-5. *Using* `MetaDataControl` *to display meta information*

Mixing Sampled Audio, MIDI, and Tones

One of the properties listed in Table 8-1, `supports.mixing`, indicates whether a particular MMAPI implementation supports the concept of multiple `Player` instances for sampled audio and tones. If true, it indicates that mixing is supported; in short, you can have multiple `Player` instances for audio, MIDI, and tone playback, playing simultaneously. Multiple `Player` instances mostly equals to a maximum of two or three, although different implementations vary in their support of simultaneous instances. There is no sure way of knowing how many instances you can create for mixing, and the Java ME documentation for your device may give an answer. Of course, you have to be careful creating too many `Player` instances, as this will result in a memory hog, especially prefetched and/or realized instances.

The concept of an implementation supporting mixing is slightly more advanced than just being able to support multiple instances of `Player` objects in memory. When a `Player` instance, created to play back sampled audio, MIDI, or tone, is in the PREFETCHED state, it has acquired the resources required to immediately play back. This means that it has exclusive access to the device's resources, especially the audio output hardware. Thus, the MMAPI implementation that supports mixing must switch intelligently and efficiently between `Player` instances to manage the flow of media data without any errors, using either a software or hardware mixer. This is why most implementations eschew audio mixing, because it becomes too complicated to implement, or provide a simplified version that only caters for specific possibilities.

The Motorola C975 device only implements MIDI mixing (that is, two or more MIDI `Player` instances playing simultaneously) and doesn't support the mixing of either audio or tones, even though it returns a true value for the `supports.mixing` property. However, it does support the mixing of a MIDI file with a WAV file, as long as the MIDI file is started first *and* the WAV file is a PCM encoded, single channel (mono), 8,000 Khz, 8-bit file. Go figure! Siemens M75 doesn't support any mixing and indicates so with a value of false for the property.

■ **Note** This is another case of device manufacturers not sticking with the intent of the MMAPI specification and providing an arbitrary implementation. As per the specification, if `supports.mixing` returns true, the MMAPI implementation must be able to support the playback of two sampled audio `Player` instances simultaneously. For what it's worth, Motorola is not the only device manufacturer guilty of providing an arbitrary implementation.

One of the most common requirements of mixing sampled audio, MIDI, and/or tones is in Java ME games. Most games have a background score playing continuously, while short audio events will accompany some action on the screen. In these cases, you'll have one `Player` instance playing the background score in a loop and other prefetched instances that start playing a short sound such as firing, jumping, opening doors, and so on, depending on the user interaction with the action on the screen.

Listing 8-4 shows an example of mixing a MIDI file with a sampled audio WAV file (as per the Motorola C975 specification!) and another MIDI event. The MIDI event is a fire sound, implemented by issuing the program change (instrument change) of `"Gunshot"` (see Chapter 7, Figure 7-6). The main MIDI sound is a background score that plays continuously, and the audio WAV file is a short sound that mimics a character jumping onscreen. When the user presses the Jump! command, the corresponding `Player` instance is started to play the sound. When the user presses the Fire! command, a `shortMidiEvent()` command is issued. During all this, the background score continues to play.

Listing 8-4. *Mixing MIDI and Sampled Audio*

```
package com.apress.chapter8;

import javax.microedition.midlet.*;
import javax.microedition.lcdui.*;
import javax.microedition.media.*;
import javax.microedition.media.control.MIDIControl;

public class MixingAudioMIDlet extends MIDlet implements CommandListener {

  // define Players and Controls
  private Player backgroundPlayer = null;
  private Player firePlayer = null;
  private Player jumpPlayer = null;
  private MIDIControl mControl = null;

  // define commands and display items
  private Display display = null;
  private Alert alert = null;
  private Command exitCommand = null;
  private Command fireCommand = null;
  private Command jumpCommand = null;

  public MixingAudioMIDlet() {

    // create the display items
    display = Display.getDisplay(this);

    // this is the alert that will be displayed
    alert = new Alert("Message");
    alert.setString("Playing background score. " +
      " Use menu to mix sampled audio and/or other midi");
    alert.setTimeout(Alert.FOREVER);

    // create the commands
    exitCommand = new Command("Exit", Command.EXIT, 1);
    fireCommand = new Command("Fire!", Command.SCREEN, 1);
    jumpCommand = new Command("Jump!", Command.SCREEN, 1);

    // attach the commands to the alerts
    alert.addCommand(exitCommand);
    alert.addCommand(fireCommand);
    alert.addCommand(jumpCommand);

    // and set the command listener
    alert.setCommandListener(this);
```

```
    // finally create the Player instances
    initPlayers();
  }

  private void initPlayers() {

    try {

      // the background player that will play a MIDI file throughout
      backgroundPlayer =
        Manager.createPlayer(getClass().getResourceAsStream(
            "/media/midi/chapter8/cabeza.mid"), "audio/midi");

      // prefetch it and make sure it repeats if it finishes
      backgroundPlayer.prefetch();
      backgroundPlayer.setLoopCount(-1);

      // create another MIDI Player for the firing sound
      firePlayer = Manager.createPlayer(Manager.MIDI_DEVICE_LOCATOR);
      firePlayer.prefetch();

      // extract its MIDIControl
      mControl = (MIDIControl)firePlayer.getControl(
        "javax.microedition.media.control.MIDIControl");

      // set program to the Gunshot sound (See Figure 7-6 in Chapter 7)
      mControl.setProgram(11, -1, 127);

      // create another sampled audio player for jump sound
      jumpPlayer = Manager.createPlayer(getClass().getResourceAsStream(
            "/media/audio/chapter8/jump.wav"), "audio/x-wav");

      // prefetch it as well
      jumpPlayer.prefetch();

    } catch (Exception e) {
      error(e);
    }
  }

  public void startApp() {

    // start background player
    try {
      if(backgroundPlayer != null) {
        backgroundPlayer.start();
      }
```

```
  } catch(Exception e) {
    error(e);
  }

  // and show message
  display.setCurrent(alert);
}

public void commandAction(Command cmd, Displayable disp) {

  // if closing
  if(cmd == exitCommand) {
    destroyApp(true);
    notifyDestroyed();
    return;
  }

  try {

    // if fire command is issued, send the NOTE_ON command
    if(cmd == fireCommand) {
      mControl.shortMidiEvent(MIDIControl.NOTE_ON | 11, 60, 100);
    }

    // if jump command is issued, start the jump player
    if(cmd == jumpCommand) {
      jumpPlayer.start();
    }
  } catch(Exception e) {
    error(e);
  }

}

public void pauseApp() {

  // pause any players if MIDlet is paused
  try {
    if(backgroundPlayer != null) backgroundPlayer.stop();
    if(firePlayer != null) firePlayer.stop();
    if(jumpPlayer != null) jumpPlayer.stop();
  } catch(Exception e) {
    error(e);
  }
}

public void destroyApp(boolean unconditional) {
```

```
      // close players once application is destroyed
      try {
        if(backgroundPlayer != null) {
          backgroundPlayer.close();
          backgroundPlayer = null;
        }
        if(firePlayer != null) { firePlayer.close(); firePlayer = null; }
        if(jumpPlayer != null) { jumpPlayer.close(); jumpPlayer = null; }
      } catch(Exception e) {
        error(e);
      }
    }

    // general purpose error method, displays onscreen as well to output
    private void error(Exception e) {
      alert.setString(e.getMessage());
      alert.setTitle("Error");
      display.setCurrent(alert);
      e.printStackTrace();
    }
  }
```

Figure 8-6 shows this MIDlet playing in the C975 device. The Jump! command is accessed by pressing the Menu button.

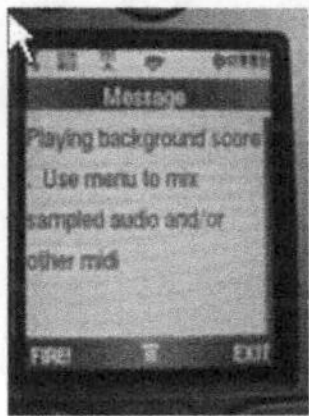

Figure 8-6. *Mixing MIDI and audio in the Motorola C975 device*

Capturing Audio

An implementation supports capture of audio via a MIDlet if it returns true for the `supports.audio.capture` system property. If this property is true, then the `audio.encodings` system property must not return null, but must provide the formats in which audio can be recorded. The Motorola C975 device supports the audio/amr and audio/amr-wb (Wide band) formats.

To capture media, you use the `RecordControl` control, whether for audio or video. This control doesn't distinguish between the media types and is a simple mechanism to start, stop, and control the data recording. It provides several methods to achieve these tasks.

A `Player` instance to capture audio is created by passing the special locator `capture://audio` to the `Manager.createPlayer(String locator)` method, which will then, once realized, give up a RecordControl object for you to use. While creating the locator, you can pass parameters to it, which qualifies the format of the recorded data, as you learned in the "Understanding Media Encodings" section. When no format is specified, the format (content-type) of the recorded data is the default (the first value returned by audio.encodings) format. Thus, for the C975 device, the default recording format for audio is audio/amr.

Of course, recorded data must be either stored somewhere or played back to the user (and then discarded). RecordControl provides two methods for setting the location of recorded data. The setRecordStream(OutputStream stream) directs data to an OutputStream, and setRecordLocation(String locator) directs it to the location in the form of locators used to create Player instances using the Manager.createPlayer(String locator) method. Of course, you should be able to store data at the particular location identified by the locator String.

Tip Recording formats impact the way the MMAPI implementation handles them internally. For formats that can't be streamed, such as WAV for sampled audio and Quicktime for video, the full media data is required before it can be written to any location. This is because some portions in the header of these files require the availability of the full data, and this header will be written to when the complete recorded data is available. When you are recording data like this, the implementation needs to provide an internal buffer that will hold this data till the recording is complete, calculate the missing header information, and then write it to your desired location, either a stream (setRecordStream()) or location (setRecordLocation()). With data that can be streamed, such as MP3 for audio and MPEG for video, this is not a problem, and the data can be written to your desired location at the same time that it's read. This is why you are not likely to find too many devices with MMAPI implementations that support recording in a nonstreamable format.

Recording data itself requires permission from the user. As you saw in Chapter 5, permissions can be requested for in a JAD file (and put in a trusted domain). To record any media (audio or video), the following permission must be available:

```
javax.microedition.media.control.RecordControl
```

Alternatively, the user will be queried to give the permission when the recording commences.

Let's start by creating a MIDlet that will play back whatever you say to it, instead of storing it somewhere.

Timed Capture and Playback

Simple capture and playback of audio can be accomplished easily by using the two streams, ByteArrayOutputStream and ByteArrayInputStream. Because data doesn't need to be stored anywhere, one Player instance can be used to record the raw audio data into the ByteArrayOutputStream's byte array, and another instance created to retrieve data from this buffer using the ByteArrayInputStream. Of course, you can't expect the data to be recorded continuously. For this example, the timed limit is 10 seconds.

Listing 8-5 shows the code for this timed audio capture and playback MIDlet.

Listing 8-5. *Timed Capture and Playback of Audio*

```
package com.apress.chapter8;

import javax.microedition.midlet.*;
import javax.microedition.lcdui.*;
import javax.microedition.media.*;
import java.io.ByteArrayOutputStream;
import java.io.ByteArrayInputStream;
import javax.microedition.media.control.RecordControl;

public class CapturePlaybackAudioMIDlet extends MIDlet
  implements CommandListener {

  // the display items
  private Display display = null;
  private Alert alert = null;
  private Command exitCommand = null;

  // players and controls
  private Player capturePlayer = null;
  private Player playbackPlayer = null;
  private RecordControl recordControl = null;

  // buffers
  private ByteArrayOutputStream bos = new ByteArrayOutputStream();
  private ByteArrayInputStream bis = null;

  public CapturePlaybackAudioMIDlet() {

    // create the display
    display = Display.getDisplay(this);
    alert = new Alert("Message");
    alert.setTimeout(Alert.FOREVER);
    alert.setString("Capturing for 10 seconds. Say something intelligent!");
    exitCommand = new Command("Exit", Command.EXIT, 1);
    alert.addCommand(exitCommand);
    alert.setCommandListener(this);

    try {
      // create the capture player
      capturePlayer = Manager.createPlayer("capture://audio");

      if (capturePlayer != null) {

        // if created, realize it
        capturePlayer.realize();
```

```
        // and grab the RecordControl
        recordControl = (RecordControl)capturePlayer.getControl(
          "javax.microedition.media.control.RecordControl");

        // set the alert as the current item
        display.setCurrent(alert);

        // if it is null throw exception
        if(recordControl == null)
          throw new Exception("No RecordControl available");

        // create the buffer in which recording will be done
        bos = new ByteArrayOutputStream(1024);

        // and set this buffer as the destination for recording
        recordControl.setRecordStream(bos);

      } else {
        throw new Exception("Capture Audio Player is not available");
      }

    } catch(Exception e) {
      error(e);
    }
  }

  public void startApp() {

    try {

      // first start the corresponding player
      capturePlayer.start();

      // and then start the RecordControl
      recordControl.startRecord();

      // now wait 10 seconds
      Thread.sleep(10000);

      // stop recording after time is up
      recordControl.stopRecord();

      // commit the recording
      recordControl.commit();

      // and close the Player instance
      capturePlayer.close();
```

```
      // finished, set the message
      alert.setString("Well done! Now Processing...");

      // flush the buffer
      bos.flush();

      // create an inputstream of this buffer
      bis = new ByteArrayInputStream(bos.toByteArray());

      // create the playback Player instance with this stream,
      // using the specified content type, as given by the RecordControl
      playbackPlayer =
        Manager.createPlayer(bis, recordControl.getContentType());

      // start the playback
      playbackPlayer.start();

      // and set the message
      alert.setString("Playing back ... ");

    } catch(Exception e) {
      error(e);
    } finally {
      try {
        if(bos != null) bos.close();
        if(bis != null) bis.close();
      } catch(Exception ex) {
        error(ex);
      }
    }

  }

  public void pauseApp() {
  }

  public void destroyApp(boolean unconditional) {
  }

  public void commandAction(Command cmd, Displayable disp) {
    if(cmd == exitCommand) {
      notifyDestroyed();
    }
  }

  // general purpose error method, displays onscreen as well to output
  private void error(Exception e) {
    alert.setString(e.getMessage());
```

```
      alert.setTitle("Error");
      display.setCurrent(alert);
      e.printStackTrace();
    }

  }
```

After a `Player` instance is created and realized for capturing audio, the `RecordControl` control is extracted. The `setRecordStream(OutputStream os)` method is used to set a `ByteArrayOutputStream` with an initial buffer size of 1,024 bytes. When the MIDlet is started, recording is started by using the `startRecord()` method of `RecordControl`. You first have to start the underlying `Player` instance by using the `start()` method; otherwise, no recording will actually take place. This is because the `Player` instance is created on the audio microphone on the device, which then releases a `RecordControl` for you to use. If you call `startRecord()` first, then the `RecordControl` will be ready to record, but won't actually record anything till the corresponding `Player` instance is started. Thus, it's best to first start the `Player` instance, and then start the recording by calling the `startRecord()` method.

The recording is done for 10 seconds by making the main application thread sleep. After the 10 seconds are over, the recorded data is put into the `ByteArrayInputStream` after committing the recorded data by calling the `commit()` method and closing the `Player` instance. Note that calling `stopRecord()` is not necessary, as `commit()` calls it internally. When `stopRecord()` is called, the `Player` instance doesn't actually stop, but continues in the STARTED state until it is stopped or closed.

The data is now available in the `ByteArrayInputStream` and a new `Player` instance is created to use this as the `InputStream` for playback. The `getContentType()` method of `RecordControl` is used to specify the content type for this new instance. It's now a simple matter of calling the `start()` method on this instance to play back the captured audio data.

Controlled Capture and Playback

Although timed capture as seen in the previous section shows you the basics of capturing audio, it doesn't show you how to provide controls to better manage the recording time. In this section, you'll add some commands to a modified recording MIDlet created in the previous section, giving you these controls. Listing 8-6 shows the code for this MIDlet, with an explanation following the listing.

Listing 8-6. *Controlling Audio Capture*

```
package com.apress.chapter8;

import javax.microedition.midlet.*;
import javax.microedition.lcdui.*;
import javax.microedition.media.*;
import java.io.ByteArrayOutputStream;
import java.io.ByteArrayInputStream;
import javax.microedition.media.control.RecordControl;

public class ControlledAudioCaptureMIDlet extends MIDlet
  implements CommandListener, PlayerListener {
```

```
// the display items
private Display display = null;
private Alert alert = null;
private Command exitCommand = null;
private Command startCommand = null;
private Command pauseCommand = null;
private Command doneCommand = null;
private Command playbackCommand = null;

// players and controls
private Player capturePlayer = null;
private Player playbackPlayer = null;
private RecordControl recordControl = null;

// buffers
private ByteArrayOutputStream bos = new ByteArrayOutputStream();
private ByteArrayInputStream bis = null;

// Boolean flag to indicate when recording is being done
private boolean recording = false;

public ControlledAudioCaptureMIDlet() {

  // create the display
  display = Display.getDisplay(this);
  alert = new Alert("Message");
  alert.setTimeout(Alert.FOREVER);
  alert.setString("Press Start Recording to capture audio");

  // create the various commands
  exitCommand = new Command("Exit", Command.EXIT, 1);
  startCommand = new Command("Start", Command.SCREEN, 1);
  pauseCommand = new Command("Pause", Command.SCREEN, 1);
  doneCommand = new Command("Done", Command.SCREEN, 1);
  playbackCommand =
    new Command("Playback", Command.SCREEN, 1);

  // and initialize the commands with the alert
  alert.addCommand(exitCommand);
  alert.addCommand(startCommand);

  // set this class as the PlayerListener for command actions
  alert.setCommandListener(this);

  // now set the alert as the current item
  display.setCurrent(alert);
```

```
  try {

    // create the capture player
    capturePlayer = Manager.createPlayer("capture://audio");

    if (capturePlayer != null) {

      // if created, realize it
      capturePlayer.realize();

      // and grab the RecordControl
      recordControl = (RecordControl)capturePlayer.getControl(
        "javax.microedition.media.control.RecordControl");

      // if RecordControl is null throw exception
      if(recordControl == null)
        throw new Exception("No RecordControl available");

      // create the buffer in which recording will be done
      bos = new ByteArrayOutputStream(1024);

    } else {
      throw new Exception("Capture Audio Player is not available");
    }
  } catch(Exception e) {
    error(e);
  }
}

public void startApp() {
  display.setCurrent(alert);
}

public void pauseApp() {
}

public void destroyApp(boolean unconditional) {

  // close any open player instances, underlying controls will be
  // closed by calling the close method
  if(capturePlayer != null)  {
    capturePlayer.close(); // releases the microphone
    capturePlayer = null;
  }
  if(playbackPlayer != null)  {
    playbackPlayer.close();
    playbackPlayer = null;
  }
}
```

```
public void commandAction(Command cmd, Displayable disp) {

  // if exit ..
  if(cmd == exitCommand) {
    destroyApp(true);
    notifyDestroyed();
  }

  // now based on what command is called, take the right action
  try {

    // if starting or restarting recording
    if(cmd == startCommand) {

      // remove other commands
      alert.removeCommand(startCommand);
      alert.removeCommand(playbackCommand);

      // add pause and done commands
      alert.addCommand(pauseCommand);
      alert.addCommand(doneCommand);

      // now, if a playback was being done, close it to preserve
      // system resources
      if(playbackPlayer != null) {
        playbackPlayer.close();
        playbackPlayer = null;
      }

      // are we restarting an existing recording or a new one?
      if(!recording) { // this means a new one

        // set the ByteArrayInputStream to null
        bis = null;

        // initialilze the ByteArrayOutputStream
        bos = new ByteArrayOutputStream(1024);

        // set the output of recording
        recordControl.setRecordStream(bos);

        // and start the underlying player
        capturePlayer.start();
      }

      // now start the recording
      recordControl.startRecord();
```

```
    // set the flag
    recording = true;

    // and show the message
    alert.setString("Recording now. Say something nice" +
      " and then press Pause or Done Recording");

  } else if(cmd == pauseCommand) {

    // pausing an existing recording

    // so remove the pause command and add the start (or restart command)
    alert.removeCommand(pauseCommand);
    alert.addCommand(startCommand);

    // stop the control, this only pauses the recording
    recordControl.stopRecord();

    // and show message
    alert.setString("Recording paused. " +
      " Press Start Recording to restart");

  } else if(cmd == doneCommand) {

    // done recording, so remove commands
    alert.removeCommand(doneCommand);
    alert.removeCommand(pauseCommand);

    // add command to play back or start a new recording
    alert.addCommand(startCommand);
    alert.addCommand(playbackCommand);

    // complete the recording
    completeRecording();

    // show message
    alert.setString("Press Start Recording to capture new audio or " +
      " Playback Recording to playback recorded audio");

  } else if(cmd == playbackCommand) {

    // remove the start recording command
    alert.removeCommand(startCommand);

    // start the playback
    playbackPlayer.start();
```

```
        // and set the message
        alert.setString("Playing back recorded audio");
      }
    } catch(Exception e) {
      error(e);
    }
  }

  private void completeRecording() throws Exception {

    // flush the output buffer
    bos.flush();

    // commit the recording
    recordControl.commit();

    // create the input buffer from the output buffer
    bis = new ByteArrayInputStream(bos.toByteArray());

    // create the playback player
    playbackPlayer =
      Manager.createPlayer(bis, recordControl.getContentType());

    // add a listener on it
    playbackPlayer.addPlayerListener(this);

    // and initialize the recording flag
    recording = false;

  }

  public void playerUpdate(Player player, String event, Object data) {

    // only listening on the playback player
    if(event.equals(PlayerListener.END_OF_MEDIA)) {

      // add the commands back
      alert.addCommand(startCommand);
      alert.addCommand(playbackCommand);
    }
  }

  // general purpose error method, displays onscreen as well to output
  private void error(Exception e) {
    alert.setString(e.getMessage());
    alert.setTitle("Error");
    display.setCurrent(alert);
```

```
        e.printStackTrace();
    }
}
```

Although the listing is long, it shows you how to control the recording using menu commands. Four commands are defined, `startCommand`, `pauseCommand`, `doneCommand`, and `playbackCommand`. The first three control the recording, and the last controls the playback of the recorded data. If you press the `pauseCommand`, it stops the recording for the moment, and when `startCommand` is pressed again, the recording starts from the point that you left off.

The main action takes place in the `commandAction()` method, where the four commands are handled. When the `startCommand` is handled, the recording is checked to see whether it's new or previously paused using the `recording` flag. For new recordings, new buffers are created, the location of the recording data is reinitialized, and the underlying recording `Player` instance is started. For previously paused recordings, all this is ignored, and only `startRecord()` method is called, which takes off from the previously paused recording location.

When the `pauseCommand` is called, the `stopRecord()` method of `RecordControl` is called, which, as you may realize now, only pauses the recording of the media data, while the underlying `Player` instance is still in the STARTED state.

The rest of the commands you should be familiar with, as they mimic the work you did in the previous section. The only other noteworthy code is in the `playerUpdate()` method, where a `Player` instance adds `startCommand` and `playbackCommand` back to the displayed alert, when the `END_OF_MEDIA` event is received.

Figure 8-7 shows the MIDlet in action on the Motorola C975 device.

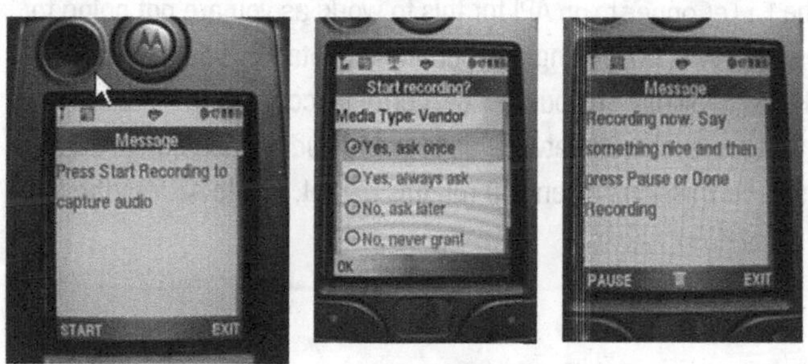

Figure 8-7. *Controlled audio recording MIDlet in action on the Motorola C975*

As you can see, when you press Start, the user must give permission for the recording to be done. Make sure that you select the Yes, ask once option; otherwise, the MIDlet gives an exception if you do multiple recordings (if you select Yes, always ask). The permission is not requested when either the `capturePlayer` or `recordControl` instances are created or initialized, but it is requested when the output stream is set using the `setRecordStream()` method.

Note At this point, the Sun's emulator throws a deadlock issue. Because the `setRecordStream()` method may take a long time to return, it advises you to run this part of the code in a separate thread. This is only an issue on the Sun emulator, however, and most devices don't require separate threads. Creating new threads for simple tasks like this can be counterproductive on small memory footprint devices.

In the next section, you'll learn how to save the recorded data in a particular location, for playback at a later time, and not just in the present MIDlet session.

Saving Captured Audio

Captured audio can be saved to a couple of locations, depending upon the capabilities of your device. The easiest place to save the captured audio is the file system on the device itself, so that you can switch the device (or the MIDlet) off and still come back later and retrieve the recording from this persistent storage.

You can also save the data to another device (most likely a computer) using the serial port. This can be achieved by using the `CommConnection` interface defined in the `javax.microedition.io` package. This interface gives you an `OutputStream` (with the `openOutputStream()` method) to which you can direct the recorded data bytes using the `setRecordStream()` method. Of course, this means that on the other side, the receiving device must have a listener on this serial port that can receive these data bytes and store them for later use. The two devices must also be connected at all times via this port, for data to be stored and later retrieved as well. As you can see, saving this data to another device via the serial port throws several issues and is not the best option.

You can also store the data on the Internet using HTTP. Because the basics remain the same for storing audio, image, or video data, this type of storage is covered in the next chapter. This section shows you how to store the data on the device itself using the `FileConnection` API (JSR-75).

■ **Note** Strictly speaking, you don't need the `FileConnection` API for this to work, as you are not going to use any of the `FileConnection` API classes. However, depending on your implementation, you may or may not need to have this API in your `CLASSPATH` and available on your device. Further, access to the local file system requires permissions from the user that are similar to network access and audio/video/image capture, so you may end up requesting two sets of permissions when you run this MIDlet, one to access the file system, and one to capture audio.

Listing 8-7 shows how to store captured audio on the device's file system and how to retrieve it for playback. Although very similar to Listing 8-5, the difference is in the way the location of the final captured audio is specified.

■ **Tip** Listing 8-7 stores captured audio in the root folder of the device. The root folder can be found by using the `listRoots()` method of the class `FileSystemRegistry` from the `FileConnection` API. As stated before, however, you don't need this API in the `CLASSPATH` to access the file system for Listing 8-7, but you'll need it to find the root folder (unless you can get that information from the documentation for the device).

Listing 8-7. *Storing Captured Audio*

```
package com.apress.chapter8;

import javax.microedition.midlet.*;
import javax.microedition.lcdui.*;
import javax.microedition.media.*;
import javax.microedition.media.control.RecordControl;

public class SaveCapturedAudioMIDlet extends MIDlet
  implements CommandListener {

  // the display items
  private Display display = null;
  private Alert alert = null;
  private Command exitCommand = null;

  // players and controls
  private Player capturePlayer = null;
  private Player playbackPlayer = null;
  private RecordControl rControl = null;

  private boolean error = false;

  public SaveCapturedAudioMIDlet() {

    // create the display
    display = Display.getDisplay(this);
    alert = new Alert("Message");
    alert.setTimeout(Alert.FOREVER);
    alert.setString("Capturing for 10 seconds. Say something intelligent!");
    exitCommand = new Command("Exit", Command.EXIT, 1);
    alert.addCommand(exitCommand);
    alert.setCommandListener(this);

    try {

      // create the capture player
      capturePlayer = Manager.createPlayer("capture://audio");

      if (capturePlayer != null) {

        // if created, realize it
        capturePlayer.realize();

        // and grab the RecordControl
        rControl = (RecordControl)capturePlayer.getControl(
          "javax.microedition.media.control.RecordControl");
```

```
        // set the alert as the current item
        display.setCurrent(alert);

        // if it is null throw exception
        if(rControl == null) throw new Exception("No RecordControl available");

        // and set the destination for this captured data
        // check your device documentation to find out the root.
        // The following will work on devices that have the root
        // specified as shown
        rControl.setRecordLocation("file:///test.wav");

      } else {
        throw new Exception("Capture Audio Player is not available");
      }

    } catch(Exception e) {
      error(e);
    }
  }

  public void startApp() {

    if(error) return;

    try {

      // first start the corresponding recording player
      capturePlayer.start();

      // and then start the RecordControl
      rControl.startRecord();

      // now record for 10 seconds
      Thread.sleep(10000);

      // stop recording after time is up
      rControl.stopRecord();

      // commit the recording
      rControl.commit();

      // stop the Player instance
      capturePlayer.stop();

      // and close it to release the microphone
      capturePlayer.close();
```

```
      // finally, create a Player instance to playback
      playbackPlayer = Manager.createPlayer("file:///test.wav");

      // and start it
      playbackPlayer.start();

    } catch(Exception e) {
      error(e);
    }
  }

  public void pauseApp() {
  }

  public void destroyApp(boolean unconditional) {
    if(capturePlayer != null) capturePlayer.close();
    if(playbackPlayer != null) playbackPlayer.close();
  }

  public void commandAction(Command cmd, Displayable disp) {
    if(cmd == exitCommand) {
      destroyApp(true);
      notifyDestroyed();
    }
  }

  // general purpose error method, displays onscreen as well to output
  private void error(Exception e) {
    alert.setString(e.getMessage());
    alert.setTitle("Error");
    display.setCurrent(alert);
    e.printStackTrace();
    error = true;
  }
}
```

The major changes are highlighted in bold. The code sets the location of the captured audio to a file called `test.wav` on the root folder of the underlying device file system. You'll get an error if this access is not supported. You'll also get an error if the file already exists, as you can see by running the listing twice (without changing the name of the file, see Figure 8-8). The new flag `error` doesn't run the `startApp()` method if there is a problem with either file system access or audio capture.

The location is set using the `setRecordLocation(String locator)` method. This listing runs perfectly on the BenQ M75 but fails on the Motorola C975 because it doesn't support file system access. However, note that the listing saves the file as a WAV file. If you refer to Table 8-2, you'll see that the only supported encoding for audio capture on the BenQ M75 is audio/amr. This seems like an anomaly, but is perfectly acceptable because the MMAPI specification allows implementations to change the format of recorded data. When you set the record location with an extension of WAV, the format conversion is done by the implementation. You can save the data as `test.amr` as well (at least on the M75), without needing to do any format changes.

Figure 8-8 shows this MIDlet running on the M75.

Figure 8-8. *Storing captured audio on BenQ M75*

Capturing Audio from Existing Audio

Until now, you saw how audio is captured using the audio microphone on a device, by creating a `Player` instance using the special locator: `capture://audio`. This is fairly standard practice. The beauty of MMAPI is that you can use any `Player` instance to capture media data from, provided the instance gives you a `RecordControl` instance to work with. This is a great flexibility provided by MMAPI and allows you to, for example, create MIDlets that can read and record data from an existing format and convert to another. Another example may be for a MIDlet to capture media stored on the network and store it locally (with or without the change in formats).

Unfortunately, neither of the two actual devices supports provisioning `RecordControl` for existing audio data, and you'll have to use Sun's DefaultColorPhone emulator to test this in action. This is a simple matter of replacing

```
capturePlayer = Manager.createPlayer("capture://audio");
```

with

```
capturePlayer = Manager.createPlayer("http://www.somesite.com/media/file.amr");
```

or

```
capturePlayer = Manager.createPlayer("file:///root1/file.wav");
```

or

```
capturePlayer =
Manager.createPlayer(getClass().getResourceAsStream("/test.amr"),"audio/amr");
```

or something similar, in any of the listings so far, and you can test the capture of existing media.

Working with Video

A lot of the techniques discussed in the previous sections on audio apply to video as well because of the way the MMAPI is defined. The interfaces remain the same; what you do with the available data based on its type is the only thing that changes. For example, the methods and procedures defined in the previous sections on capturing audio data can be applied to video as well using the same `RecordControl` interface.

The major difference, of course, lies in the display of video. One special control, `VideoControl`, is used for this purpose, and it's augmented by the precise control provided by the `FramePositioningControl` control. `VideoControl` extends `GUIControl`, which is a generic control provided in case MMAPI implementations wanted to provide other methods of controlling and displaying GUI-based media data.

Displaying Video

`VideoControl`, which is the primary control for displaying video, is used to control how the video looks when displayed in a MIDlet, including its positioning and screen focus. As you might expect, the controls for playback, pause, rewind, and forward are provided by the underlying `Player` instance methods, and are therefore, generic.

The video formats you can display depend on your MMAPI implementation. Most implementations support MPEG-4, but an increasing number support 3GPP as well. Some may support proprietary formats. As you know, a full list of supported formats can be queried for by using the `getSupportedContentTypes(null)` method of the `Manager` class, which returns not only the supported formats for video, but the supported formats for all media types. With our target devices, the BenQ M75 supports only the 3GPP and MP4 video formats, whereas the Motorola C975 supports several formats, as you might recall from Chapter 2, Table 2-3, including 3GPP, MP4, and RealVideo.

■ **Note** MPEG-4 and MP4 mean the same thing. Similarly, video/mpeg4 and video/mp4 also define the same content type, however, different implementations may or may not accept one content type over another, so you have to test your videos to make sure the implementation accepts the content type. The same applies to video/3gpp and video/3gp content types.

`VideoControl` provides several methods to control the display of your video. Most of these methods provide control over the positioning of the video, but the main method that initializes the display is the one inherited from `GUIControl`. This method, `initDisplayMode(int mode, Object arg)`, provides the basis on which the video is displayed on the device screen. This method must be called only once for each video display (otherwise an `IllegalStateException` is thrown). Essentially, this method tells the implementation how you plan to display your video: as an embedded item in a `Form` or an independent display in a `Canvas`.

With MIDlet development, this is a powerful choice, and you are given the option to display your video in either a high-level, consistent environment (`Form`), or a low-level, precise display (`Canvas`). When added to a `Form`, the video is just another item in the display, whereas in a `Canvas`, you can work with the video and have more control over its positioning and display, including access to the `Graphics` object.

This choice is expressed using the mode argument. There are two valid constant values defined in the current specification for this argument: USE_GUI_PRIMITIVE and USE_DIRECT_VIDEO. The former is defined in the GUIControl interface, and you use this value when you want to embed your video in a Form. The latter is defined in the VideoControl interface, and you use it when you want to embed video in a Canvas. Because VideoControl extends GUIControl, it also gets to use the USE_GUI_PRIMITIVE mode. By defining USE_GUI_PRIMITIVE in the GUIControl interface, the option is left open for other GUI-based controls to use this mode.

The name USE_GUI_PRIMITIVE suggests that the video must be displayed on a primitive GUI. This is true, and the actual GUI component on which the video will be displayed is returned by the initDisplayMode() method. For Liquid Crystal Display User Interface (LCDUI), it returns an Item object, which can be attached to a Form instance using the append() method. For other environments (for example, CDC, which supports the Abstract Windows Toolkit), it returns a java.awt.Component object. When the mode is USE_DIRECT_VIDEO, the method returns null, because the object on which the video must be displayed is specified by the second parameter to the initDisplayMode() method, and it must be of the Canvas type (or a subclass). For USE_GUI _PRIMITIVE mode, this second parameter can either be null or the fully qualified class name of a GUI primitive (such as java.awt.component if available).

Listing 8-8 creates a MIDlet that allows you to display video on either a Canvas or a Form.

Listing 8-8. *Display Video in a Form or a Canvas*

```
package com.apress.chapter8;

import javax.microedition.midlet.*;
import javax.microedition.lcdui.*;
import javax.microedition.media.*;
import javax.microedition.media.control.*;

public class DisplayVideoMIDlet extends MIDlet implements CommandListener {

  // the list to show the choice - form or canvas
  private List list = null;

  // the canvas to display the video on
  private Canvas canvas = null;

  // the form to add the video to
  private Form form = null;

  // a string item to add to form
  private StringItem descriptionItem = null;

  // the video player
  Player player = null;

  // commands
  private Command backCommand = null;
  private Command exitCommand = null;
```

```
// alert to show messages on
private Alert alert = null;

// and the display
private Display display = null;

// a flag to indicate error
private boolean error = false;

public DisplayVideoMIDlet() {

  // create the visual elements
  display = Display.getDisplay(this);
  exitCommand = new Command("Exit", Command.EXIT, 1);
  backCommand = new Command("Back", Command.ITEM, 1);

  // VideoCanvas is a non public class in this file
  canvas = new VideoCanvas();
  canvas.addCommand(exitCommand);
  canvas.addCommand(backCommand);
  canvas.setCommandListener(this);

  // create the form and add items and commands to it
  form = new Form("Video Form", null);
  descriptionItem = new StringItem("Desc: ", "Sydney Harbour - Bad audio");
  form.append(descriptionItem);
  form.addCommand(exitCommand);
  form.addCommand(backCommand);
  form.setCommandListener(this);

  // create the list
  list = new List("Pick One", List.IMPLICIT);
  list.append("Play Video on Form", null);
  list.append("Play Video on Canvas", null);
  list.addCommand(exitCommand);
  list.setCommandListener(this);

  // and an alert for errors
  alert = new Alert("Error");
}

public void startApp() {
  if(error) return;
  display.setCurrent(list); // show the list if no errors
}

public void pauseApp() {
}
```

```
public void destroyApp(boolean unconditional) {
  // close the player instance
  try {
    if(player != null) player.close();
  } catch(Exception e) {
    error(e);
  }
}

public void commandAction(Command cmd, Displayable disp) {

  // if exit
  if(cmd == exitCommand) {
    destroyApp(true);
    notifyDestroyed();
  } else if(cmd == backCommand) { // if the user clicks back

    // close the player instance
    try {
      if(player != null) player.close();
    } catch(Exception e) {
      error(e);
    }

    // display the list
    display.setCurrent(list);

    // and return
    return;
  }

  // implicit list handling
  try {

    // first load the Player instance
    loadPlayer();

    if(list.getSelectedIndex() == 0) { // form video

      // extract the GUIControl
      GUIControl guiControl = (GUIControl)player.getControl(
        "javax.microedition.media.control.GUIControl");

      // if not found, throw error
      if(guiControl == null) throw new Exception("No GUIControl!!");
```

```
        // add as a video item by initializing it to use GUI Primitive
        Item videoItem =
          (Item)guiControl.initDisplayMode(
            GUIControl.USE_GUI_PRIMITIVE, null);

        // insert at first place
        form.insert(0, videoItem);

        // show the form
        display.setCurrent(form);

        // finally start the player instance
        player.start();
      } else {  // canvas video

        // grab the videocontrol
        VideoControl videoControl = (VideoControl)player.getControl(
          "javax.microedition.media.control.VideoControl");

        // if not found throw error
        if(videoControl == null) throw new Exception("No VideoControl!!");

        // initialize to use direct video and show on canvas
        videoControl.initDisplayMode(VideoControl.USE_DIRECT_VIDEO, canvas);

        // make sure it is displayed full screen
        // not all devices support this, if your device is having trouble
        // showing the video, comment this line
        videoControl.setDisplayFullScreen(true);

        // must make the control visible
        videoControl.setVisible(true);

        // now show the canvas
        display.setCurrent(canvas);

        // and start the player
        player.start();
      }
    } catch(Exception e) {
      error(e);
    }
  }

  private void loadPlayer() throws Exception {
```

```
    // loads the Player on this MP4 file.
    // IMPORTANT: Change content type here for C975 to video/mp4
    // and M75 to video/mpeg4 or use Netbeans device fragmentation
    // feature
    player = Manager.createPlayer(
      getClass().getResourceAsStream(
        "/media/video/chapter8/sydharbour.mp4"), "video/mpeg4");

    player.realize();
  }

  // general purpose error method, displays onscreen as well to output
  private void error(Exception e) {
    alert.setString(e.getMessage());
    alert.setTimeout(Alert.FOREVER);
    display.setCurrent(alert);
    e.printStackTrace();
    error = true;
  }
}

// VideoCanvas that is the container for the video
class VideoCanvas extends Canvas {
  public void paint(Graphics g) {
    // does nothing..
  }
}
```

Tip If you have trouble running this video, comment out the line that sets the video to full screen mode. Many devices don't support full screen mode and throw a `MediaException`.

When the MIDlet is run, it gives you two choices: either run your video in a `Form` or run it in a `Canvas`. The user's choice is handled in the `commandAction()` method, which realizes a `Player` instance with the said video by calling the `loadVideo()` method. This is done each time the choice is made, because once initialized with the display mode, the same `Player` instance can't be reinitialized with the `initDisplayMode()` method. This is also the reason why each `Player` instance is closed when the user presses the Back button.

You'll notice that for the `Form` video, the control extracted from the `Player` instance is of the type `GUIControl`. Although correct, this is not necessary. Instead, you should extract `VideoControl` each time a video `Player` instance is created. Recall that `VideoControl` extends `GUIControl`, so if you wanted to add your video to a `Form` instance, you can still initialize it by using the `initDisplayMode()` method and passing it the inherited constant `USE_GUI_PRIMITIVE`. Further, by using `VideoControl`, you get access to the positioning methods of this control as well (although how useable they may be considering that the video is embedded in a `Form` object is another matter).

Finally, note that when displayed in a Canvas, the setVisible(true) method of the VideoControl must be called for the video to be displayed. By calling the same method with a value of false, you can make the video disappear.

Figure 8-9 shows this MIDlet running in the Motorola C975 device.

Figure 8-9. *Video playback on a canvas on the Motorola C975*

Positioning Video and Controlling Volume

When you're playing back video, you not only get access to the VideoControl, but because there is likely to be an audio component in the video as well, you also get access to all the controls that are accessible to sampled audio media data. Thus, you can easily set the volume or change the pitch of the accompanying audio, provided these controls are exposed.

Changing the volume or the pitch is one thing, and positioning the video is another. To position your video in a Canvas, you need to use the positioning methods provided by VideoControl. These methods, setDisplayLocation(int x, int y), setDisplaySize(int width, int height), and setDisplayFullScreen(boolean fullScreenMode), are only applicable when using direct video on a Canvas (with the USE_DIRECT_VIDEO mode). On a Form, you are restricted by the amount of screen space that the underlying implementation allocates to Form items, and these methods usually return without doing anything.

You can query the size and position of your video by using the size and positioning methods, such as getDisplayHeight(), getDisplayWidth(), getDisplayX(), and getDisplayY(). If you change the position and size of your video to fit in any way on your canvas, you can use the getSourceWidth() and getSourceHeight() methods to find out the actual width and height of your video.

Note that all the size and positioning methods work relative to the component on which the video is displayed, such as a Canvas, and *not* relative to the device screen.

Listing 8-9 shows the code for a MIDlet that allows you to move your video in the vertical space after displaying it in the center of the display screen. It also allows you to mute the volume by using the exposed VolumeControl.

Listing 8-9. *Moving Video in Vertical Space and Muting Volume*

```
package com.apress.chapter8;

import javax.microedition.midlet.*;
import javax.microedition.lcdui.*;
import javax.microedition.media.*;
import javax.microedition.lcdui.game.GameCanvas;
```

```
import javax.microedition.media.control.VideoControl;
import javax.microedition.media.control.VolumeControl;

public class MoveableVideoMIDlet extends MIDlet implements CommandListener {

  // all the controls and containers
  private Player player = null;
  private VideoControl videoControl = null;
  private VolumeControl volControl = null;

  private MovableVideoCanvas canvas = null;
  private Command exitCommand = null;
  private Command stopAudioCommand = null;

  private Display display = null;
  private Alert alert = null;

  private boolean error = false;

  public MoveableVideoMIDlet() {

    // create the alerts, canvas and displays
    display = Display.getDisplay(this);

    alert = new Alert("Error");
    exitCommand = new Command("Exit", Command.EXIT, 1);
    alert.addCommand(exitCommand);
    alert.setCommandListener(this);

    // load the Player and then the Volume and VideoControl
    try {

      // change content type for different devices, mp4 for C975, mpeg4 for M75
      player = Manager.createPlayer(getClass().getResourceAsStream(
        "/media/video/chapter8/sydharbour.mp4"), "video/mp4");
      player.realize();

      // realize the two controls
      videoControl = (VideoControl)player.getControl(
        "javax.microedition.media.control.VideoControl");
      volControl = (VolumeControl)player.getControl(
        "javax.microedition.media.control.VolumeControl");
    } catch (Exception e) {
      error(e);
    }

    if(!error) {
```

```
      // if no error, create the canvas and add commands to it
      canvas = new MovableVideoCanvas();
      canvas.setVideoControl(videoControl);
      stopAudioCommand = new Command("Stop Audio", Command.SCREEN, 1);

      canvas.addCommand(exitCommand);
      canvas.addCommand(stopAudioCommand);
      canvas.setCommandListener(this);

      // initialize the VideoControl display
      videoControl.initDisplayMode(VideoControl.USE_DIRECT_VIDEO, canvas);

      // and position it in the center of the canvas
      int halfCanvasWidth = canvas.getWidth()/2;
      int halfCanvasHeight = canvas.getHeight()/2;

      try {
        videoControl.setDisplayFullScreen(false);
        videoControl.setDisplaySize(halfCanvasWidth, halfCanvasHeight);
        videoControl.setDisplayLocation(halfCanvasWidth/2, halfCanvasHeight/2);
        videoControl.setVisible(true);
      } catch(Exception e) {
        error(e);
      }
    }
  }

  public void startApp() {

    if(error) return;

    try {
      player.start();
    } catch(Exception e) {
      error(e);
    }
    display.setCurrent(canvas);
  }

  public void pauseApp() {
  }

  public void destroyApp(boolean unconditional) {
    try {
      if(player != null) player.close();
    } catch(Exception e) { error(e); }
  }
```

```
  public void commandAction(Command cmd, Displayable disp) {
    if(cmd == exitCommand) {
      destroyApp(true);
      notifyDestroyed();
    } else if(cmd == stopAudioCommand) { // if stop audio, mute VolumeControl
      if(volControl != null) volControl.setMute(true);
    }
  }

  // general purpose error method, displays onscreen as well to output
  private void error(Exception e) {
    alert.setString(e.getMessage());
    alert.setTitle("Error");
    display.setCurrent(alert);
    e.printStackTrace();
    error = true;
  }
}

// MovableVideoCanvas that is the container for the video
class MovableVideoCanvas extends GameCanvas {

  // VideoControl that will be managed
  private VideoControl videoControl = null;

  // distance to move
  private int dx, dy = 2;

  public MovableVideoCanvas() {
    super(false); // do not supress key events
  }

  void setVideoControl(VideoControl videoControl) {
    this.videoControl = videoControl;
  }

  public void paint(Graphics g) {
    // clear the screen first
    g.setColor(0xffffff);
    g.fillRect(0, 0, getWidth(), getHeight());

    // and flush off screen buffer to actual screen
    flushGraphics();
  }

  public void keyPressed(int keyCode) {
```

```
    // handles the user's interaction with the screen by capturing key press
    int gameAction = getGameAction(keyCode);
    int y = videoControl.getDisplayY();

    // only move in vertical direction
    if(gameAction == UP) {
      y -= dy;
    } else if(gameAction == DOWN) {
      y += dy;
    }

    // set the new location of the video
    videoControl.setDisplayLocation(videoControl.getDisplayX(), y);

    // and repaint
    repaint();
  }

}
```

This listing uses a Canvas class that is extended from GameCanvas. This class has an offscreen buffer that may help minimize flicker and is better for displaying video in a Canvas than the generic Canvas class, especially when you are going to move the video around as is the case here. When the user presses the Up or Down keys, the VideoControl is positioned and the screen cleared and repainted to display the video in the new up or down location.

The stopAudioCommand is handled by using the exposed VolumeControl and setting it to mute using the setMute() method of this control.

Figure 8-10 shows the resultant video in the Motorola C975 device.

Figure 8-10. *Moving video around and muting audio*

Capturing Video and Images

Capturing video is not terribly different from capturing audio, as you would expect, because both use the same RecordControl control to achieve the result. However, with video, you can also take a snapshot of a video. This is where capturing video differs from capturing audio: Taking a snapshot doesn't require a RecordControl, but is accomplished using a method in VideoControl.

The getSnapshot() method in VideoControl allows you to take a snapshot of the image that is playing on the device screen. Of course, because the getSnapshot() method is a method of the VideoControl class, you can take an image of any video that is playing on a device screen, not just captured video. The method returns the image data as a byte array, which you can then manipulate in any way you want using the LCDUI Image class.

In this section, you'll apply the methods learned in the previous sections, including capturing media data using RecordControl and displaying video using VideoControl. However, as opposed to capturing audio, capturing and displaying video must be done simultaneously so that the user can see what is actually being recorded.

So, can you just hook into the camera, without actually recording anything, to first show the user the view through the video? Of course!

Looking Through the Viewfinder

As you may expect by now, the locator to hook into a device camera takes the form of capture://video. This gives you a Player instance that returns video in the default format. The Motorola C975 doesn't support video capture, but the default (and the only) format supported by the BenQ M75 device is video/3gpp.

■ **Note** As you'll see shortly, even though the Motorola C975 device doesn't support video capture, it allows you to look through the viewfinder of the onboard camera (possibly because it supports camera snapshots).

After you have a Player instance hooked into a video camera, it's a simple matter of extracting a VideoControl from it to look through its viewfinder and display this video to the user. Note that to look through a viewfinder, you need to use a VideoControl and not a RecordControl, because you are not recording anything (yet).

As before, you can use a Canvas to display the video through the viewfinder to the user. Because you are not going to move the video around, you can either use a GameCanvas or a normal Canvas.

Listing 8-10 shows the code for plugging into the device's viewfinder and displaying it on a canvas. At this point, this is all the MIDlet does, but you'll extend it in the next sections to take a snapshot and capture video.

Listing 8-10. *Looking Through a Camera's Viewfinder and Displaying Onscreen*

```
package com.apress.chapter8;

import javax.microedition.midlet.*;
import javax.microedition.lcdui.*;
import javax.microedition.media.*;
import javax.microedition.media.control.VideoControl;

public class CaptureVideoAndImageMIDlet extends MIDlet
  implements CommandListener {
```

```
// initialize the player and the canvas
private CaptureVideoCanvas canvas = null;
Player capturePlayer = null;

// and the other variables
private Alert alert = null;
private Command exitCommand = null;
Display display = null;
private boolean error = false;

public CaptureVideoAndImageMIDlet() {

  // create the display items
  alert = new Alert("Message");
  display = Display.getDisplay(this);
  exitCommand = new Command("Exit", Command.EXIT, 1);

  // create the video capture player
  try {
    capturePlayer = Manager.createPlayer("capture://video");
    capturePlayer.realize();

    // now create the canvas
    canvas = new CaptureVideoCanvas(this);
    canvas.addCommand(exitCommand);
    canvas.setCommandListener(this);
  } catch(Exception e) {
    error(e);
  }
}

public void startApp() {

  // if error, return
  if(error) return;

  // start the player
  try {
    capturePlayer.start();
  } catch(Exception e) { error(e); }

  // and set the canvas as the current item on display
  display.setCurrent(canvas);
}
```

```
  public void pauseApp() {
    try {
      if(capturePlayer != null) capturePlayer.stop();
    } catch(Exception e) {}
  }

  public void destroyApp(boolean unconditional) {
    if(capturePlayer != null) capturePlayer.close();
  }

  public void commandAction(Command cmd, Displayable disp) {
    if(cmd == exitCommand) {
      destroyApp(true);
      notifyDestroyed();
    }
  }

  // general purpose error method, displays onscreen as well to output
  void error(Exception e) {
    alert.setString(e.getMessage());
    alert.setTitle("Error");
    display.setCurrent(alert);
    e.printStackTrace();
    error = true;
  }
}

// the canvas that holds the video
class CaptureVideoCanvas extends Canvas {

  // the base midlet
  CaptureVideoAndImageMIDlet midlet = null;

  // the video control
  private VideoControl videoControl = null;

  public CaptureVideoCanvas(CaptureVideoAndImageMIDlet midlet)
    throws Exception {

    this.midlet = midlet;

    // initialize the video control
    videoControl =
      (VideoControl)midlet.capturePlayer.getControl(
        "javax.microedition.media.control.VideoControl");
```

```
    // if not present, throw error
    if(videoControl == null)
      throw new Exception("No Video Control for capturing!");

    // init display mode to use direct video and this canvas
    videoControl.initDisplayMode(VideoControl.USE_DIRECT_VIDEO, this);

    try { // try and set to full screen
      videoControl.setDisplayFullScreen(true);
    } catch(MediaException me) {
      // but some devices may not support full screen mode
      videoControl.setDisplayLocation(5, 5);
      try {
        videoControl.setDisplaySize(getWidth() - 10, getHeight() - 10);
      } catch(Exception e) {}
      repaint();
    }

    // and make the video control visible
    videoControl.setVisible(true);
  }

  public void paint(Graphics g) {

    // clear background
    g.setColor(0xffffff);
    g.fillRect(0, 0, getWidth(), getHeight());

    // and draw a rectangle with a different color
    g.setColor(0x44ff66);
    g.drawRect(2, 2,  getWidth() - 4, getHeight() - 4);
  }
}
```

When the CaptureVideoCanvas is created, it uses the MIDlet's capturePlayer to extract the VideoControl. CaptureVideoCanvas then initializes this control and tries to set the control to display full screen. If that fails, a display is created that is bounded by a rectangle through the paint() method. As you can see, the listing doesn't require RecordControl to plug in to the camera's viewfinder and just uses the VideoControl control exposed by the camera Player instance.

If you run this listing in the Sun's DefaultColorPhone emulator, you'll get a simulated video capture as can be seen in Figure 8-11.

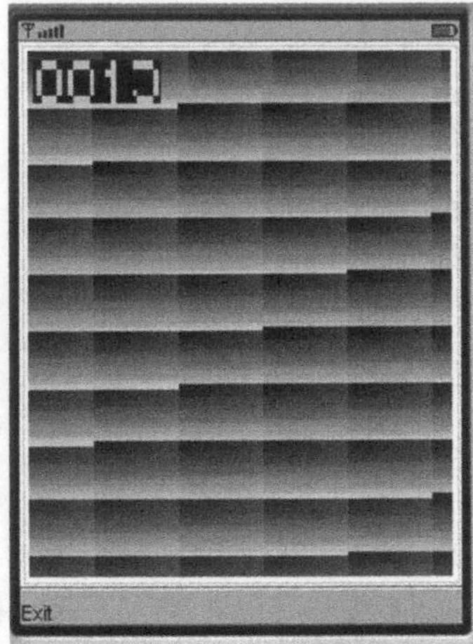

Figure 8-11. *Simulated video capture on Sun's DefaultColorPhone emulator*

Of course, the actual devices don't give simulated but actual views, as can be seen in Figure 8-12. Also note the difference in Figures 8-11 and 8-12 with regard to the screen size. The emulator doesn't support full-screen display (through the `setDisplayFullScreen()` method) whereas the devices do.

Figure 8-12. *Looking through the viewfinder in BenQ M75 and Motorola C975 devices*

Taking Snapshots

Taking a snapshot is now easy, given that you only need to use the `getSnapshot(String imageFormat)` method of the `VideoControl` control. The format of the desired image can be specified using the encoding strings that your device supports, but if you just want the default format, then pass a `null` value. Both the Motorola C975 and BenQ M75 devices support jpeg (or image/jpeg), and this is the only option supplied.

Let's now modify Listing 8-10 and add code that will take a snapshot when the user presses the Action key (also called the Fire key). To accomplish this, the listing needs to add the `keyPressed(int keyCode)` method to the `CaptureVideoCanvas` class. This method is shown here:

```
public void keyPressed(int keyCode) {

  // see what game action key the user has pressed
  int key = getGameAction(keyCode);

  // if fire, take a snapshot
  if(key == FIRE) {
    try {
      // use the control to take the picture, using the default encoding
      byte[] imageArray = vControl.getSnapshot(null);

      // create an image using the LCDUI Image class
      Image image = Image.createImage(imageArray, 0, imageArray.length);

      // make this image a part of an Alert
      Alert imageAlert =
        new Alert("Snapshot", "", image, AlertType.INFO);

      // show this alert for 5 seconds
      imageAlert.setTimeout(5000);

      // and show this alert
      midlet.display.setCurrent(imageAlert);

    } catch(Exception e) {
      midlet.error(e);
    }
  }
}
```

After taking the byte array that the `getSnapshot()` method creates, this method creates an image using the `createImage()` method of the `Image` class (from LCDUI). After this, it really depends on what you want to do with this image. You can save it to a local file system as you saw in the saving audio section, send it to a remote server via HTTP, or as I've done here, simply attach it to an `Alert` object and show the user the captured image for five seconds.

Note that when the device executes the `getSnapshot()` method, it requires permission from the user for taking the image. This permission is `javax.microedition.media.control.VideoControl.getSnapshot` and can be requested in the MIDlet's JAD file, as you saw in Chapter 5.

Capturing Video Clips

Video clips are captured by acquiring a `RecordControl` on the camera `Player` instance, and then following the principles discussed in the "Capturing Audio" section. Of course, after the video is captured, you may need to display it to the user, which requires either a video `Canvas` or a `Form`, the same concepts discussed in displaying video. The following code snippet is added to Listing 8-10 and allows the user to start and stop recording clips by pressing the Up and Down keys on a device. Displaying the clip to the user is left as an exercise for you.

Note The listing adds some new variables that are not in the original listing. The source code contains the full code in the Downloads section of the Apress Web site at *http://www.apress.com*.

```
} else if(key == UP) {

  // start recording
  try {

    // grab a record control
    rControl = (RecordControl)midlet.capturePlayer.getControl(
        "javax.microedition.media.control.RecordControl");

    // if not found, throw exception
    if(rControl == null) throw new Exception("No RecordControl found!");

    // create a ByteArrayOutputStream to store this recorded data in
    bos = new ByteArrayOutputStream();

    // set up the stream
    rControl.setRecordStream(bos);

    // and start recording - no need to start the underlying player
    // as it is already started
    rControl.startRecord();

    // set flag
    recording = true;
  } catch(Exception e) {
    midlet.error(e);
  }
} else if(key == DOWN) {

  try {
    rControl.stopRecord();
    rControl.commit();

    // do what is required with the byte array now, save it, display to user
    // or discard

    // reset the recording flag
    recording = false;
  } catch(Exception e) {
    midlet.error(e);
  }
}
```

This code snippet is added to the keyPressed() method of the CaptureVideoCanvas, along with the FIRE key event discussed in the previous section, to capture snapshots.

Seeking Video Frames with FramePositioningControl

Recall from Chapter 3 that you can fast forward or rewind through a Player instance by using the setMediaTime() method. With video media data, there is another way to go forward or back and that is by using the FramePositioningControl control, which allows you to seek individual frames within this data. Both methods of seeking data inherently do the same thing, that is, move the media time.

The FramePositioningControl control provides a simple way to seek frames by using the method seek(int frameNumber). This method doesn't throw any exceptions, which may be surprising considering that you could pass it any arbitrary value. However, if you pass it a negative value, the video stops at the first frame (the 0th frame); if you give it a value larger than the number of frames in the video, it stops at the last frame. Of course, if the video stops playing because it has reached the last frame, the Player state transitions from STARTED to STOPPED, and the right event is broadcast to registered listeners.

When the frame seek operation is done, you can query the current media time of the video by using the getMediaTime() method of the Player instance, which is updated by the seek() method to reflect time at the new frame. You can skip frames using the skip(int framesToSkip) method, which works similar to the seek() method. The difference is that if skip() is called on a Player instance that is in the STARTED state, then the number of frames that will be skipped cannot be known to an exact degree because a STARTED Player instance is in the process of changing frames when the method is called.

This control also provides methods to convert media time to frame numbers and vice versa. This is useful when you don't actually want to transition to a new frame, but just want to calculate the media time between different frames. You can use the methods mapTimeToFrame (long mediaTime) and mapFrameToTime(int frameNumber) as required. Both these methods will return -1 if mapping is unsuccessful and use microseconds (not milliseconds) as the unit of time measurement.

Streaming Media

Most of you are familiar with streaming media over the Internet. When you play video or audio from a favorite multimedia site, you are streaming media, which in many cases is based on HTTP. Streaming media occurs when the media data isn't downloaded on the host computer, but only sections of it are, leading to on-demand and live broadcast. Streaming media via HTTP is inefficient and doesn't allow seeking operations because it's based on TCP. Most professional streaming media solutions rely on the Real Time Transport Protocol (RTSP), which is User Datagram Protocol (UDP) based. Many MMAPI implementations support RTSP for streaming data, so in this section, you'll learn how to use it.

Note that when you create a Player instance with an HTTP-based locator, depending on the media type, it may resort to streaming as well, instead of downloading the entire contents. HTTP-based streaming doesn't preclude the idea of actually streaming the contents, it's just that it is inefficient.

To plug into streaming data, you need to work with a streaming server. Specialized servers abound, including RealTime Server (*http://www.realnetworks.com*), Apple's Darwin streaming server (*http://developer.apple.com/darwin/projects/streaming/*), and Helix (*http://www.helixcommunity.org*). For the example in this section, the streaming service provided by the BBC's live radio broadcast (*http://www.bbc.co.uk/radio/*) is used.

A streaming media `Player` instance is created by using the special locator string: `rtsp://<path-to-server>/<path-to-file-on-server>`. Thus, RTSP is the protocol, but the rest of the locator string resembles HTTP for accessing files.

Sadly, not many devices support RTSP, including the Motorola C975 (even though it says it does) and BenQ M75. However, you can use Listing 8-11 to run in any device that does support it, and tune into the BBC service.

Listing 8-11. *Streaming Media over the Network*

```
package com.apress.chapter8;

import javax.microedition.midlet.*;
import javax.microedition.lcdui.*;
import javax.microedition.media.*;

public class StreamingMediaMIDlet extends MIDlet {

  private Player player = null;
  private Display display = null;
  private Alert alert = null;

  private boolean error = false;

  public StreamingMediaMIDlet() {

    display = Display.getDisplay(this);
    alert = new Alert("Message");

    // try and create a Player instance for RTSP
    try {

      player = Manager.createPlayer(
        "rtsp://rmv8.bbc.net.uk/radio1/lockup.ra");

      if(player == null)
        throw new Exception("Could not create player for streaming");

      player.realize();

    } catch(Exception e) {
      error(e);
    }
  }
```

```
  public void startApp() {
    if(error) return;

    try {
      player.start();
    } catch(Exception e) {
      error(e);
    }

    alert.setString("Playing streaming radio from BBC");
    display.setCurrent(alert);
  }

  public void pauseApp() {
  }

  public void destroyApp(boolean unconditional) {
    if(player != null) player.close();
  }

  // general purpose error method, displays onscreen as well to output
  private void error(Exception e) {
    alert.setString(e.getMessage());
    alert.setTitle("Error");
    display.setCurrent(alert);
    e.printStackTrace();
    error = true;
  }
}
```

As you can see, there is nothing of note in this code, and you have learned to create `Player` instances like this several times over. This is the beauty of the MMAPI implementation because it permits several protocols and formats to be played using similar coding techniques.

Finally, note that the radio streaming via the BBC service uses the Real Networks real audio file for streaming. This means that the device you run this MIDlet on must not only support RTSP, but be able to recognize and play the real audio content type as well. Of course, this media format doesn't have to be real audio, and can be any other audio or even video format. For video streaming data, you can easily create a `VideoControl` on the data and display it to the user, as you have learned to do in the "Working with Video" section of this chapter. You can even create a `RecordControl` on this data, and record it to the local file system, as discussed in the "Capturing Audio" and "Capturing Video and Images" sections. It just depends on what options are available to your device.

Summary

This chapter should have brought one point to the forefront about MMAPI: It truly is protocol and format agnostic. Different devices support different formats and protocols, but the basics of using these varied formats and protocols remain the same.

This chapter brought to a conclusion the discussion on the various media types that are supported by MMAPI by focusing on the two main types: audio and video. You learned to query, display, control, record, save, and stream these two types using a variety of examples. You also saw the frailty of the MMAPI implementations currently present in the development world. In fact, I had to change devices midstream because one of the chosen devices didn't do what it was supposed to do. This is an important lesson: Test all code in the chosen device!

The next and final chapter will show you a case study that covers some of the concepts discussed so far to create an audio, image, and video blogging MIDlet.

CHAPTER 9

Case Study: Device Blogging

If you haven't been bit by the blogging bug yet, then blogging from your mobile phone is sure to make you give this exciting technology a try. Blogging allows you to post your ideas, experiences, and thoughts in an online journal-like medium, allowing for instantaneous access to the entire world. Couple this with integrated multimedia blogs and, in the case of mobile blogging, anywhere, anytime access, and you provide a richer, more involved user experience.

This chapter is a case study that details how to bring together the knowledge that you have gained in the rest of the book, especially concerned with audio/video/image capture and playback using MMAPI, and put that knowledge to good use by building a mobile blogging MIDlet called Device Blog. Device Blog will allow you to blog text-, audio-, image-, and video-based blog entries directly from your mobile phone or device.

About the Companion Web Site

Creating a mobile blogging application without an actual live Web site against which you can practice is not much fun. The issues that arise in posting blog entries to the server may not impact much on your knowledge of MMAPI, but it's nonetheless instructive to test your ideas in a live environment. Therefore, the companion Device Blog site, which is a very simple blog entries display site, lists the entries posted to it in a sequential order, along with any multimedia components. You can test the Device Blog MIDlet that you will build in this chapter against this site at *http://www.mmapibook.com/deviceblog/index.jsp*.

Besides the index page, the Device Blog site also contains other Java Server Page (JSP) based files, which allow a user to register, log in, and post entries to it. These pages are meant to be accessed from a mobile device, but to keep things simple, no checks are done if requests are made from other direct sources as well.

The Finished MIDlet in Action

Before you learn to build the Device Blog MIDlet, take a look at the final views in some of the devices as shown in the upcoming figures. This storyboard of sorts will also serve as a Use Case for this MIDlet application.

MIDlet Startup

At startup, the MIDlet presents three choices to the user: Login, Register, and Create Blog Entry. This is shown in Figure 9-1 across the Motorola C975 device, the BenQ M75 device, and Sun's DefaultColorPhone emulator.

Figure 9-1. *Starting the Device Blog MIDlet*

Registering with the Device Blog Web Site

The user can choose to register with the Device Blog server by selecting the Register option. The link to register is supplied in the MIDlet's JAD file as a system property: *http://www.mmapibook.com/deviceblog/register.jsp*. When the user selects the Register option, the screen shown in Figure 9-2 appears.

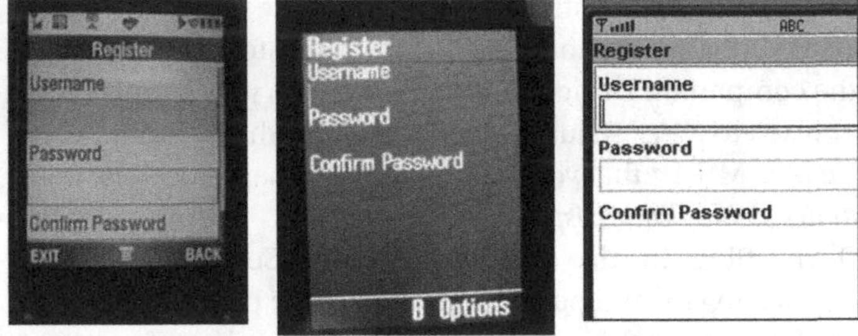

Figure 9-2. *Registering with the Device Blog Web site*

The user enters the desired values, which are just the username and password (with a confirm password field as well), to keep things simple and interaction fast.

Of course, because the mobile device interacts with the server, access over the Internet is required and permission from the user is requested, as shown in Figure 9-3. This applies not just for registration, but for logging in and posting blog entries as well.

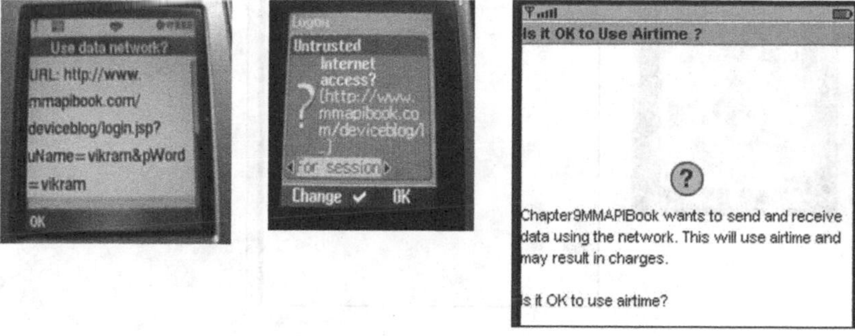

Figure 9-3. *Accessing the Internet requires user permission.*

The server sends back messages such as "Registered" for successful registration, "Username exists" for duplicate usernames, and any other error messages for protocol or network issues. Internet access is not attempted for nonmatching passwords and incomplete fields, which are handled at MIDlet level.

Logging in to Device Blog Web Site

After a successful registration, the user can log in. Note that the user cannot create a blog entry (the third option in Figure 9-1) until the user has registered and/or logged in first. The login screens are shown in Figure 9-4.

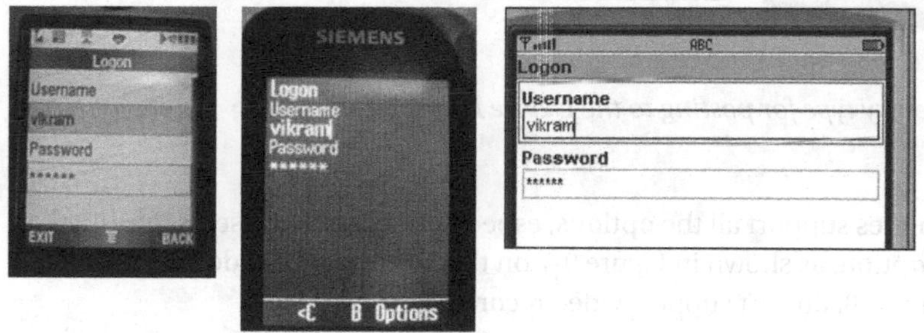

Figure 9-4. *Logging on to the Device Blog Web site*

As you may notice, the login and registration screens look remarkably similar; this common interface keeps things simple.

The login URL is *http://www.mmapibook.com/deviceblog/login.jsp* and is read from the MIDlet's JAD file.

The server's response will be either "Logged In", "Username not found. Please register", or "Invalid Password!", as the case may be. Figure 9-5 shows the screens for a successful login.

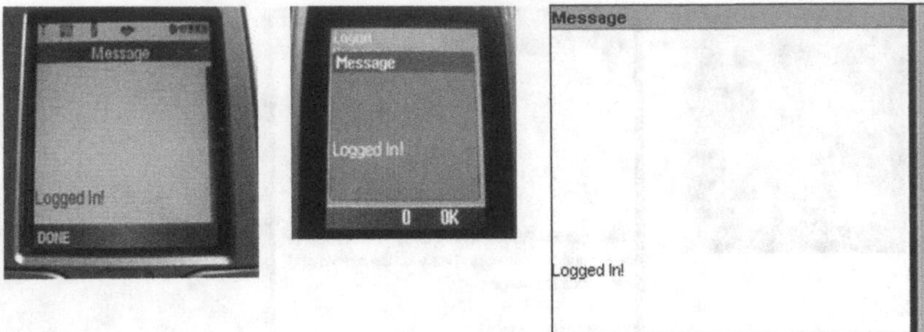

Figure 9-5. *Successful login to the Device Blog Web site*

Creating and Posting Blog Entries

By selecting the Create Blog Entry option, the user is presented with another screen where the choices allow the user to create one of four types of entries: Text Only, Audio, Image, and Video (see Figure 9-6).

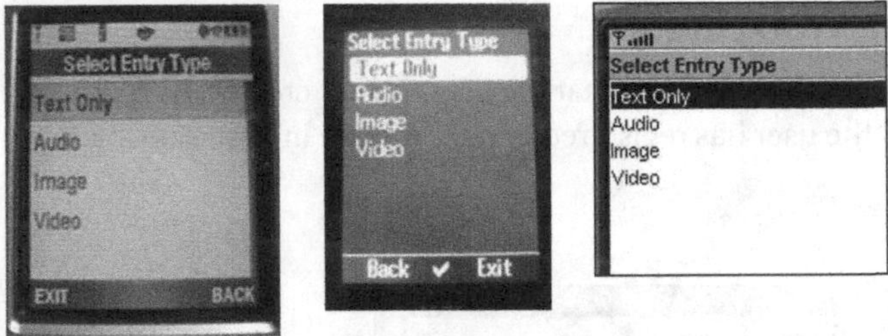

Figure 9-6. *Selecting the entry type for posting to the Device Blog Web site*

Of course, not all phones support all the options, especially, video. The user is informed of this when selecting this option, as shown in Figure 9-7 on the Motorola C975 device, which as you may recall from Chapter 8, doesn't support video recording.

Figure 9-7. *Video recording is not supported on Motorola C975.*

As you may recall, the Sun DefaultColorPhone emulator doesn't support video recording either, and you'll get the same message in that if you select the video option.

Text Only

The text only option is the simplest and allows the user to write a title and an associated message as shown in Figure 9-8.

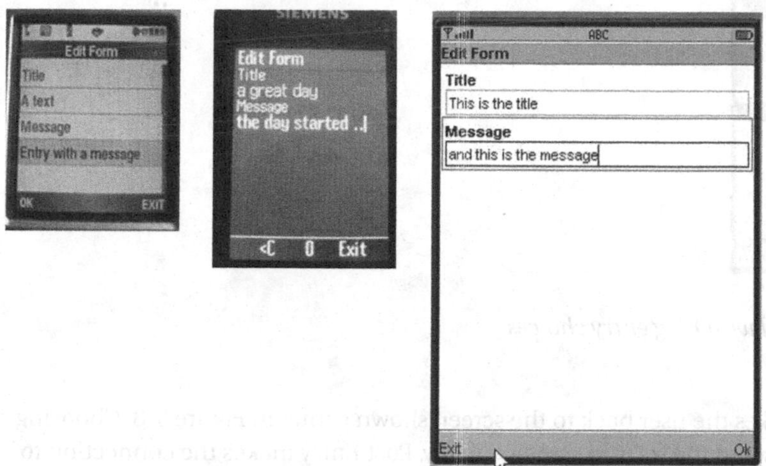

Figure 9-8. *Creating a text-only entry*

After the user selects the OK menu option, a preview of the entry appears as shown in Figure 9-9.

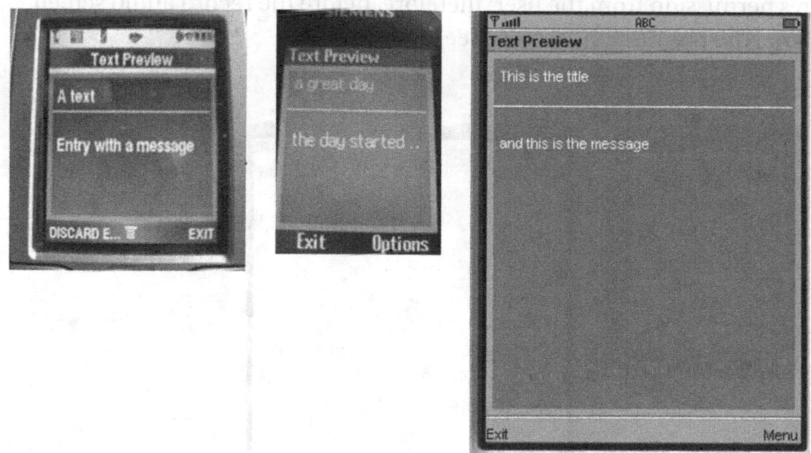

Figure 9-9. *Preview the text-only blog entry.*

At this point, the user can discard this entry, edit the text again, or post the entry to the server. These choices are the same throughout and apply to all types of blog entries. These choices are shown in Figure 9-10 in Sun's DefaultColorPhone emulator.

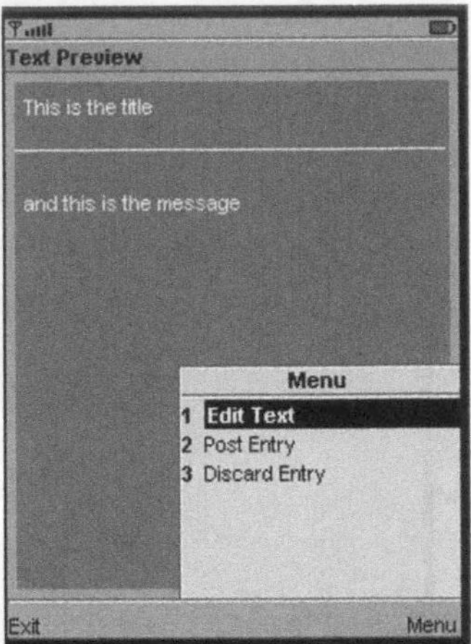

Figure 9-10. *User presented with blog entry choices*

Choosing Edit Text takes the user back to the screen shown earlier in Figure 9-8. Choosing Discard Entry takes the user to the startup screen. Finally, Post Entry makes the connection to the server and posts the entry.

The URL for posting entries is picked up from the JAD file: *http://www.mmapibook.com/deviceblog/postentry.jsp*. The resultant message is shown to the user on the screen; for a successful post, it reads "Posted". At this point, the startup screen is shown to the user.

As expected, these choices and actions remain the same for any type of blog entry.

Audio

Recording audio requires permission from the user; therefore, before the record audio screen is shown, the MIDlet shows the permissions screen (see Figure 9-11).

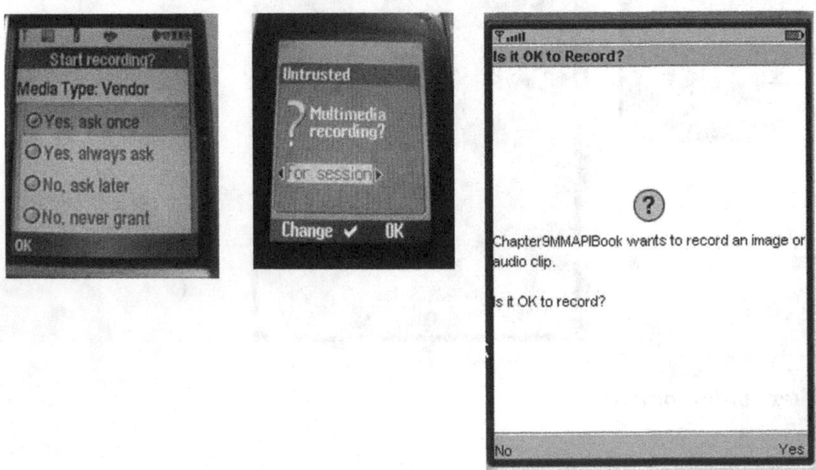

Figure 9-11. *Getting permission from the user for recording audio*

Of course, all three media types require the user to grant these permissions. The user has the choice of granting the permissions only once or for the session, in which case, he won't be prompted for them again.

After the permission is given, the recording canvas is shown, which automatically starts recording audio and doesn't finish until the user selects the Done menu item. These two stages are shown in Figure 9-12 on the Motorola C975 device.

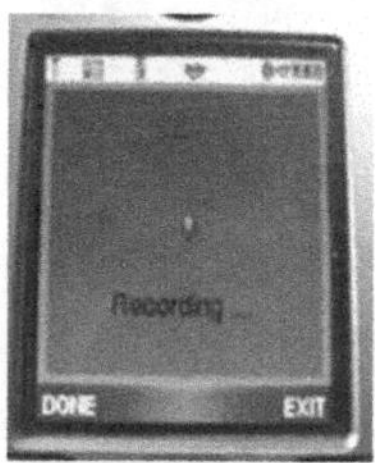

Figure 9-12. *Recording and previewing audio on the Motorola C975 device*

As you can see, when the user presses the Done menu item, the device previews the recorded audio by playing it back. At this point, the user can discard the entry, add text to it by selecting edit text, or post it to the server; the same choices that were discussed in the last section.

Image

For image recording and previewing, first the user is shown the viewfinder of the onboard camera and then shown the associated snapshot that is taken when the user presses the Done menu item. This process is shown in Figure 9-13 on the Motorola C975 device and in Figure 9-14 on the BenQ M75 device.

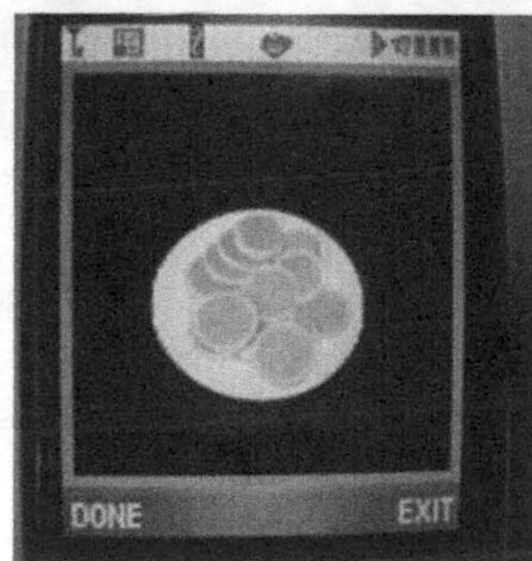

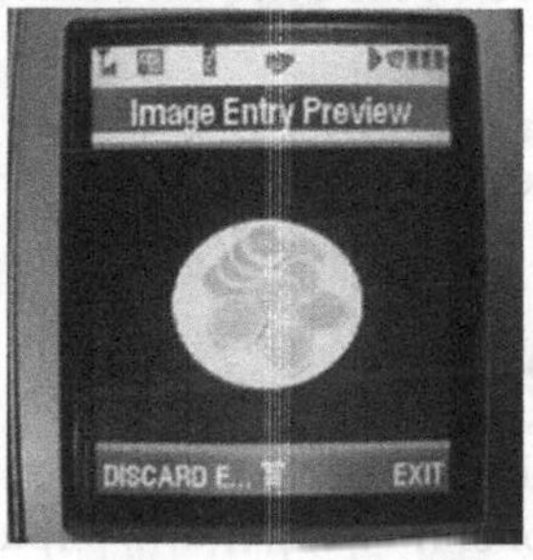

Figure 9-13. *Capturing and previewing images on the Motorola C975 device*

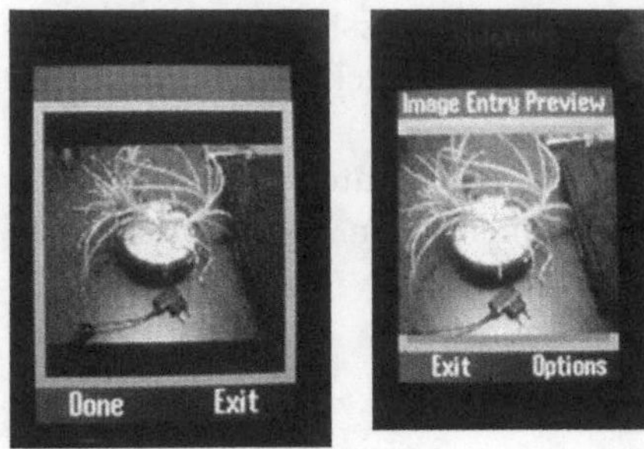

Figure 9-14. *Capturing and previewing images on the BenQ M75 device*

The user choices at this point remain the same as described in the previous sections.

Video

Video capture via MMAPI is not supported on too many devices. Fortunately, the BenQ M75 does support it in a limited way. Figure 9-15 shows the video capture and preview process in this device.

Figure 9-15. *Capturing and previewing video on the BenQ M75 device*

As expected, the options at this point remain the same: Discard Entry, Edit Text, or Post Entry.

Creating the MIDlet Design

To create the finished MIDlet's client application using the storyboard ideas penned in the last section, I'm using the Model-View-Controller (MVC) pattern, popularized by the Struts Web framework. Generalizations and modifications to this pattern need to be made, however, to keep the realities of development on small devices in check.

The Model

Based on what you know so far, a fair crack at building the model for the Device Blog can be attempted. This model is shown in Figure 9-16 using Unified Modeling Language (UML).

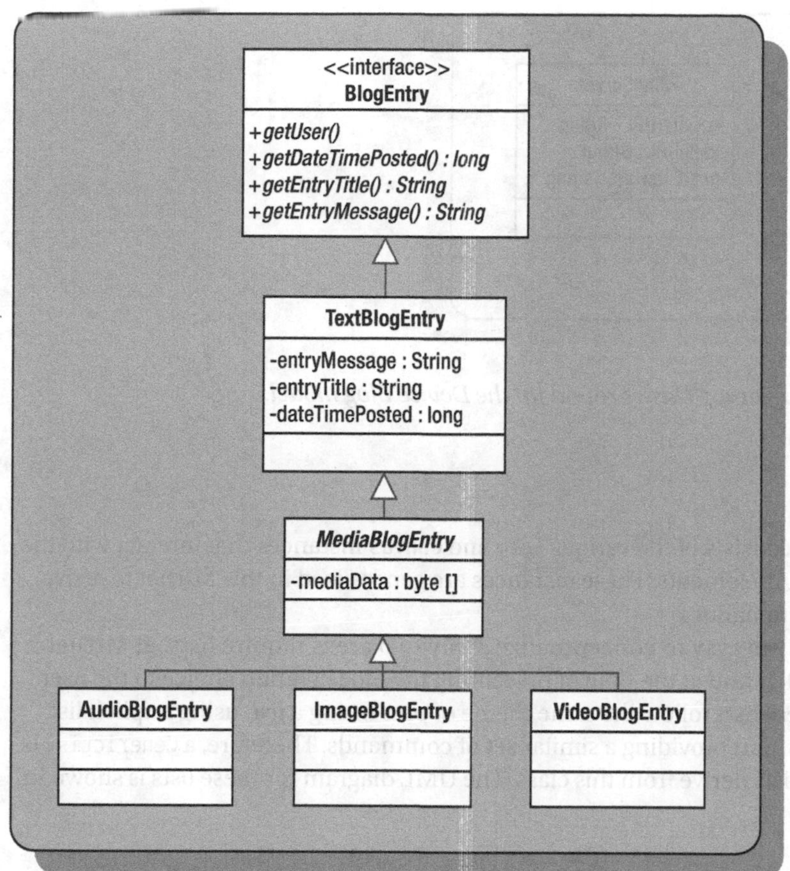

Figure 9-16. *Model for the Device Blog MIDlet application*

A `BlogEntry` interface sits at the top of this model and defines the characteristics of any entry created in this MIDlet. It mandates four self-explanatory methods that must be implemented by its implementations.

The `TextBlogEntry` class is the only implementation for this interface in this model and provides representation for blog entries that are only textual in nature, without any associated media parts. `MediaBlogEntry`, which extends the `TextBlogEntry` class, adds the media part, but is an abstract class. Concrete implementations include representation for each of the three different types of blog entries: `AudioBlogEntry`, `ImageBlogEntry`, and `VideoBlogEntry`. Each of the media blog entries gets a textual part and a media part.

These are not the only classes in the model. You need something to represent the user of the MIDlet and a class to model the server. These two classes are shown in Figure 9-17.

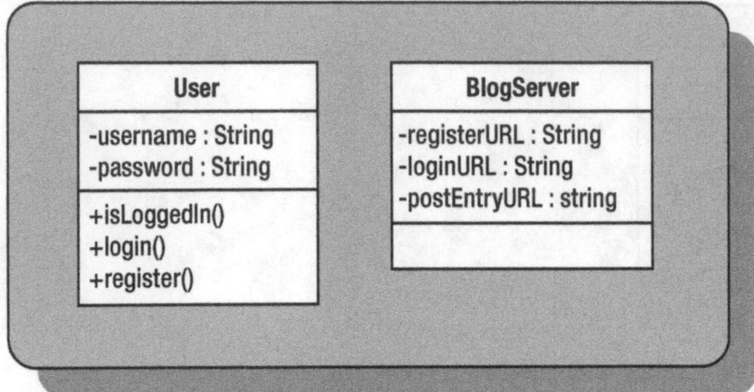

Figure 9-17. `User` *and* `BlogServer` *classes round up the Device Blog model.*

The View

The view of this MIDlet consists of the various `Form` and `Canvas` instances that interact with the user, along with a few `List` elements. These instances are generalized in this MIDlet to arrive at a common set of functionalities.

The `List` instances are easy to conceptualize. Only two areas require lists: at MIDlet startup (refer to Figure 9-1) and at the time of presenting the blog creation choice to the user (refer to Figure 9-6). These lists follow the same theme of presenting a list, using implicit list handling for commands, and providing a similar set of commands. Therefore, a `GenericList` is created, and the actual lists derive from this class. The UML diagram for these lists is shown in Figure 9-18.

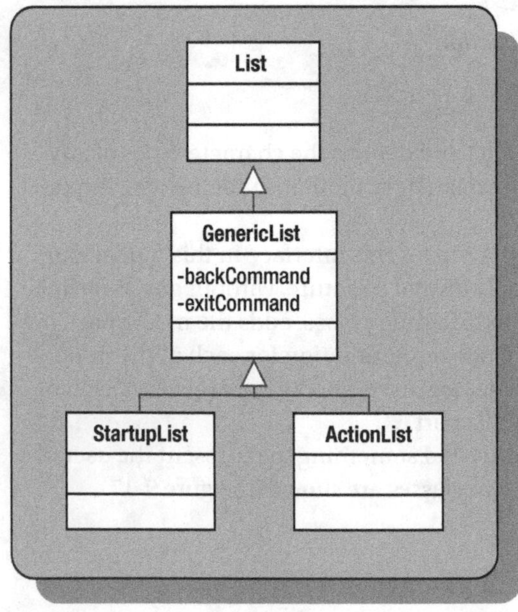

Figure 9-18. *Bundling together common functionalities of a* `List`

The same concept applies to the login and registration `Form` instances, common functionality of which can be put together in a `GenericForm` class. This class adds the commands OK, Exit, and Back, and classes that derive from this class can add their own `Form` items and behaviors. The UML for this structure is shown in Figure 9-19.

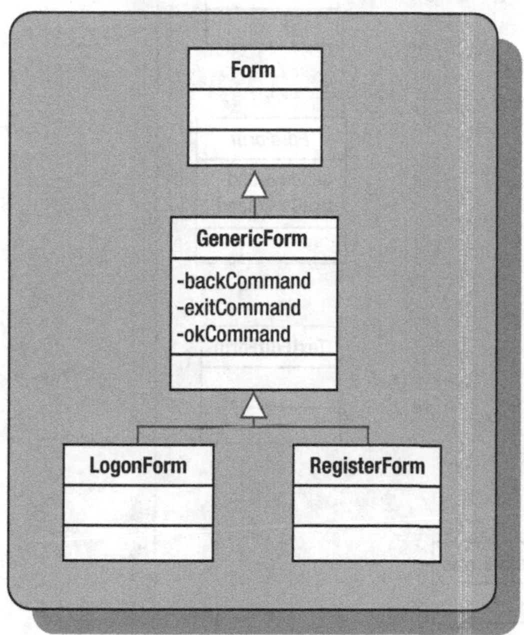

Figure 9-19. *Bundling together common functionalities of a* `Form`

Two sets of views remain to be created: one set for editing blog entries and one for previewing them. For editing (as with preview), it's useful to define a common set of functionalities and behaviors for the view that work similarly across all implementations. With this in mind, `EditableDisplay` is created as an interface that has only one method called `showDisplay()`. All implementations are then free to create their own way of handling the editable parts of the display by providing an implementation for the `showDisplay()` method. For textual entries, it's essential to provide a `Form`-based view, whereas others may provide `Canvas`-based views. The UML for the editing set of classes is shown in Figure 9-20.

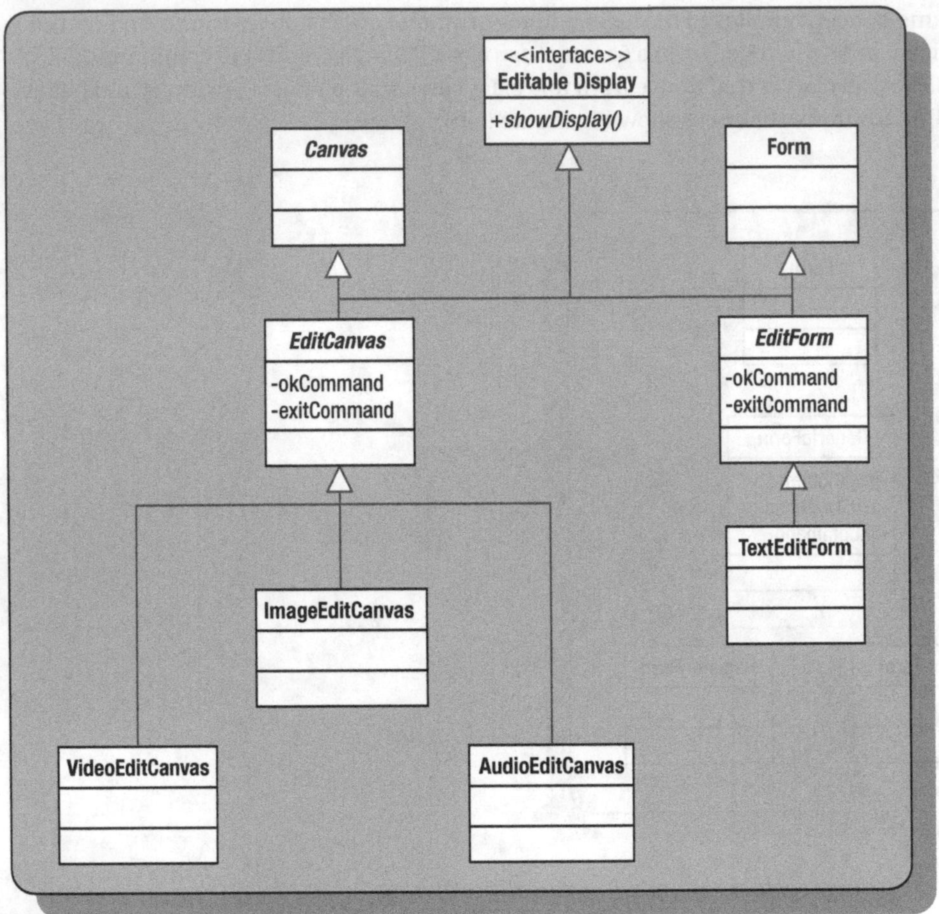

Figure 9-20. *Defining the blog editing set of classes in the Device Blog MIDlet*

As you can see, two abstract classes implement the `EditDisplay` interface. These classes are `EditForm`, which extends the `Form` class and provides the base class for editing textual blog entries, and `EditCanvas`, which extends the `Canvas` class and provides the base class for editing media blog entries.

Similarly, the set of view classes for previewing blog entries can be created. However, no separate distinction needs to be made between text- and media-based entries because everything is to be displayed on a `Canvas`. These set of classes are shown in Figure 9-21.

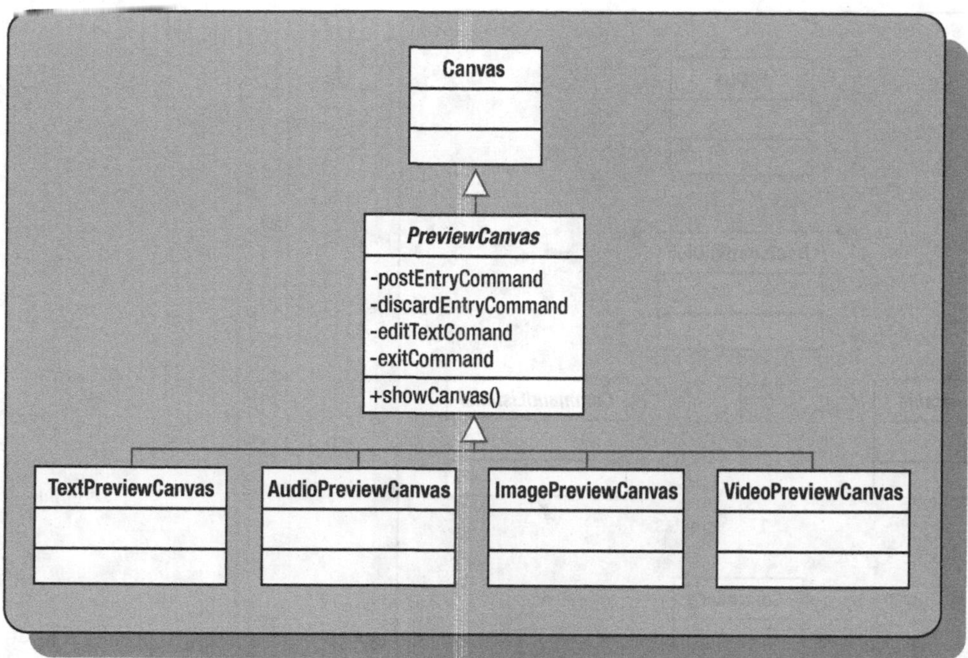

Figure 9-21. *Defining the blog preview set of classes*

As you can see, the `PreviewCanvas` abstract class encapsulates the behavior by providing the commands that are required at this stage of the view in this MIDlet. What remains is for the subclasses to provide an implementation of the `showCanvas()` method to display to the user a preview of the blog entry as the subclasses deem fit.

The Control

The control in this MVC pattern is made up of two classes: the `BootstrapMIDlet` and a specialized class called the `Controller`. The `Controller` class handles the interactions between the view and the model and generally keeps things moving by providing resources, action and error screens, and so on. The `BootstrapMIDlet`, as denoted by the name, is the class that starts this MIDlet application initially. Figure 9-22 shows these two classes.

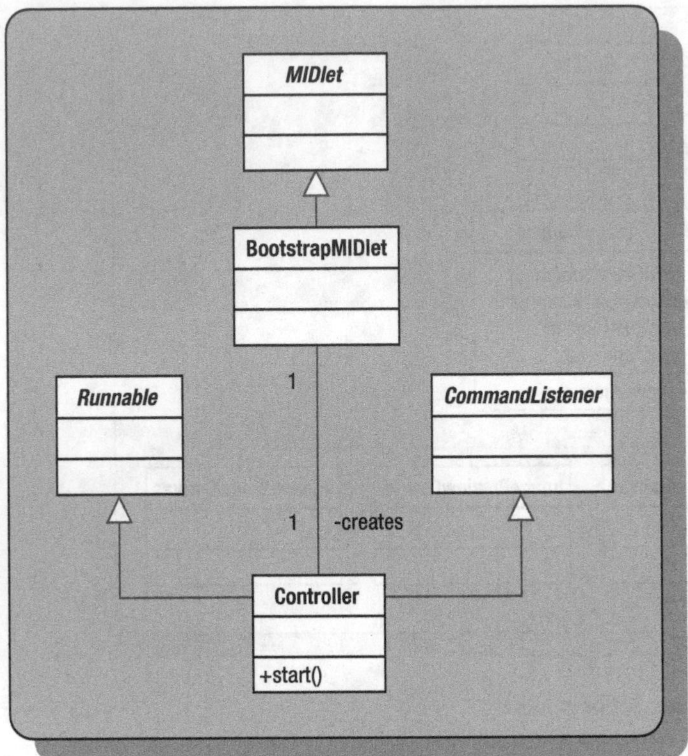

Figure 9-22. *The control classes of the Device Blog MIDlet*

Two other utility classes, `NetworkRunner` and `URLEncoder`, do not fit in any of the classifications so far. `NetworkRunner` provides network connections that are run via a single thread, whereas `URLEncoder` is used to encode the URL query strings.

Creating the MIDlet Code

The previous section provided an idea of what classes are required to create the Device Blog MIDlet application. Let's start by creating the classes of the model, which should be fairly easy because they are essentially Plain Old Java Objects (POJOs).

Creating the Model Classes

The model classes include the `BlogEntry` interface and its sole implementation, `TextBlogEntry`, which is then extended by the abstract class `MediaBlogEntry`. The `AudioBlogEntry`, `ImageBlogEntry`, and `VideoBlogEntry` then provide implementations for this class to represent audio, image, and video blog entries, respectively.

Listing 9-1 shows the code for the `BlogEntry` interface.

Listing 9-1. `BlogEntry` *Interface for All Types of Blog Entries*

```
package com.apress.chapter9.model;



/**
 * BlogEntry is the interface that represents the blog entries as a model
 */
public interface BlogEntry {

  /**
   * The user who is posting this entry
   */
  public User getUser();

  /**
   * The DateTime when the entry was posted
   */
  public long getDateTimePosted();

  /**
   * The title of this entry, if any
   */
  public String getEntryTitle();

  /**
   * The message of this entry, if any
   */
  public String getEntryMessage();

}
```

Listing 9-2 shows the code for `TextBlogEntry`.

Listing 9-2. `TextBlogEntry` *Represents All Entries That Have a Textual Component*

```
package com.apress.chapter9.model;

/**
 * TextBlogEntry implements BlogEntry and represents a TextEntry for the Blog.
 * It also acts as a base class for other media type entries.
 */
public class TextBlogEntry implements BlogEntry {

  // the title of this entry, if any
  private String entryTitle = null;
```

```
  // the message of this entry, if any
  private String entryMessage = null;

  // the time this entry was posted
  private long dateTimePosted = 0;

  // the user who is making this entry
  private User user = null;

  public TextBlogEntry(User user) {
    this.user = user;
  }

  // getter and setters for entry title and message
  public String getEntryTitle() { return this.entryTitle; }
  public void setEntryTitle(String entryTitle) {
    this.entryTitle = entryTitle;
  }

  public String getEntryMessage() { return this.entryMessage; }
  public void setEntryMessage(String entryMessage) {
    this.entryMessage = entryMessage;
  }

  // time posted is immutable
  public long getDateTimePosted() {
    return this.dateTimePosted;
  }

  // the user who is posting this entry
  public User getUser() {
    return this.user;
  }
}
```

Notice that the `getDateTimePosted()` method has only a getter method and is therefore immutable. This makes sense, because once posted, you wouldn't want to change this value. Also note that this value is stored as a `long` type.

Listing 9-3 shows the code for the `MediaBlogEntry` abstract class.

Listing 9-3. `MediaBlogEntry` *Represents Blog Entries That Have a Media Component*

```
package com.apress.chapter9.model;

/**
 * This abstract class encapsulates all the blog entries that have a media
 * component along with any text component. This is why it extends the
 * TextBlogEntry class
 */
public abstract class MediaBlogEntry extends TextBlogEntry {
```

```
  // the mediaData
  protected byte[] mediaData = null;

  // the contentType of the media
  protected String contentType = null;

  protected MediaBlogEntry(User user) {
    super(user);
  }

  public byte[] getMediaData() { return this.mediaData; }
  public void setMediaData(byte[] mediaData) { this.mediaData = mediaData; }

  public String getContentType() { return this.contentType; }
  public void setContentType(String contentType) {
    this.contentType = contentType;
  }

  /**
   * This method tries to guess the extension of the likely media data
   * file that will be gauged from the content type of this data
   */
  public String guessFileExtension() {

    if(contentType == null || contentType.length() == 0) return "";

    contentType = contentType.toLowerCase();

    if(contentType.equals("audio/x-wav")) return "wav";
    if(contentType.equals("audio/amr") ||
       contentType.equals("audio/amr-nb") ||
       contentType.equals("audio/amr-wb")) return "amr";

    if(contentType.equals("jpeg") ||
       contentType.equals("jpg") ||
       contentType.equals("image/jpeg") ||
       contentType.equals("image/jpg")) return "jpg";
    if(contentType.equals("gif") ||
       contentType.equals("image/gif")) return "gif";

    if(contentType.equals("video/mpeg")) return "mpg";
    if(contentType.equals("video/3gpp") ||
       contentType.equals("video/3gp")) return "3gp";

    return "unknown";
  }
}
```

This class contains an interesting method, `guessFileExtension()`. This method analyzes the content type of the media data and returns an appropriate file extension, which is useful when this data is being posted to the server to help the server make an educated guess about the media type. Of course, this extension is guessed based on the content type of the media, which has its own getter and setter methods. The `guessFileExtension()` method may need to be changed to cater for different media types that may be available on your mobile device.

The class also contains getter and setter methods for the media data, which is stored in this class in a `byte` array.

The concrete implementations of `MediaBlogEntry`, `VideoBlogEntry`, `AudioBlogEntry`, and `ImageBlogEntry` are now easy to write and only contain a single constructor. Listing 9-4 shows the code for the `VideoBlogEntry` class. The other implementations are similar and are provided in the source code in the Downloads section of the Apress Web site at *http://www.apress.com* (as is the rest of the code).

Listing 9-4. `VideoBlogEntry` *Extends* `MediaBlogEntry` *and Represents Video Blog Entries*

```
package com.apress.chapter9.model;

/**
 * The VideoBlogEntry extends MediaBlogEntry and represents an entry that
 * has a video component in addition to a text component
 */
public class VideoBlogEntry extends MediaBlogEntry {

  public VideoBlogEntry(User user) {
    super(user);
  }
}
```

The only thing of note here is that while creating an entry, the user who is creating the entry must be provided. A user for this system is created using the `User` class shown in Listing 9-5 and forms part of the model.

Listing 9-5. *User Class Represents the User of the Device Blog MIDlet*

```
package com.apress.chapter9.model;

import com.apress.chapter9.control.Controller;

/**
 * A simple user class to represent a user of this MIDlet. Contains only
 * userName and password. Once created, these values cannot be
 * changed
 **/
public class User {

  // parameters that define this user
  private String userName = null;
  private String password = null;
```

```
// flag to indicate if the user has been successfully logged in
private boolean loggedIn = false;

// the controller
private Controller controller = null;

public User(String userName, String password, Controller controller) {

  // check for invalid values
  if(userName == null || userName.length() == 0 ||
    password == null || password.length() == 0)
    throw new IllegalArgumentException("One of the arguments is invalid");

  this.userName = userName;
  this.password = password;

  this.controller = controller;
}

// getters for the parameters
public String getUserName() { return this.userName; }
public String getPassword() { return this.password; }

/**
 * Tries to log the user into the blog server.
 */
public void login(String loginURL) {

  // use the Network Runner to make the connection
  controller.getNetworkRunner().makeConnection(
    loginURL + "?uName=" + getUserName() + "&pWord=" + getPassword());
}

/**
 * @return true if the user is logged in, false otherwise
 */
public boolean isLoggedIn() {

  if(controller.getNetworkRunner().isLoggedIn()) {
    this.loggedIn = true;
  }

  return this.loggedIn;
}

/**
 * Registers this user with the blog server.
 * Successful registration doesn't log the user in, and login must be
```

```
     * done separately.
     */
    public void register(String registerURL) {

      // use the Network runner to make the connection
      controller.getNetworkRunner().makeConnection(
        registerURL + "?uName=" + getUserName() + "&pWord=" + getPassword());
    }
}
```

The class provides getter and setter methods for the username and password properties and also methods that log on and register the user. The class uses the NetworkRunner class to make the connections; this class will be introduced in the next section.

Finally, the model also contains the BlogServer class, which acts as a container for the server on which blogging will be done. This class is shown in Listing 9-6.

Listing 9-6. BlogServer *Class Acts As a Container for the Blog Server*

```
package com.apress.chapter9.model;

/**
 * BlogServer represents the server on which the blog is hosted, and includes
 * URLs for various actions, such as registration, logging in, and posting entries
 */
public class BlogServer {

  // the URL for registration
  private String registerURL = null;

  // the URL for logging in
  private String loginURL = null;

  // the URL for posting a blog entry
  private String postEntryURL = null;

  public BlogServer(String registerURL, String loginURL, String postEntryURL) {
    this.registerURL = registerURL;
    this.loginURL = loginURL;
    this.postEntryURL = postEntryURL;
  }

  public String getRegisterURL() { return this.registerURL; }
  public String getLoginURL() { return this.loginURL; }
  public String getPostEntryURL() { return this.postEntryURL; }

}
```

The BootstrapMIDlet or the Controller class are responsible for creating the BlogServer class and provide values for the actual URLs. These are listed in the JAD file so that any change in their value doesn't require the MIDlet application to be recompiled.

Creating the Utility Classes

Before moving on to either the view or the control, let's create the utility classes because they are important for testing the MIDlet. Two utility classes are required: NetworkRunner and URLEncoder.

NetworkRunner is required because it acts as a central class for making all connections to the blog server. However, instead of creating a separate thread each time a network connection is required; this class keeps a single thread running. Creating multiple threads is an issue on mobile devices because of small memory footprints, especially in a situation where several connections may be required. Listing 9-7 shows this class.

Listing 9-7. NetworkRunner *Is a Single-Threaded* HTTPConnection *Class*

```
package com.apress.chapter9.utils;

import java.io.IOException;
import java.io.InputStream;
import java.io.OutputStream;
import javax.microedition.io.Connector;
import javax.microedition.io.HttpConnection;

import com.apress.chapter9.model.BlogEntry;
import com.apress.chapter9.control.Controller;
import com.apress.chapter9.model.MediaBlogEntry;
import com.apress.chapter9.control.BootstrapMIDlet;

public class NetworkRunner extends Thread {

  // the calling MIDlet
  private BootstrapMIDlet midlet = null;

  // the controller
  private Controller controller = null;

  // the reusable connection
  private HttpConnection connection = null;

  // flags
  private boolean cancel = false;
  private boolean running = false;

  // the URL to connect to, this will change
  private String url = null;
```

```
// the BlogEntry that may be sent
private BlogEntry entry = null;

// flags that indicate the success or failure of logging in,
// registration and posting
private boolean logInSuccess = false;
private boolean registerSuccess = false;
private boolean postSuccess = false;

public NetworkRunner(BootstrapMIDlet midlet, Controller controller) {
  this.midlet = midlet;
  this.controller = controller;
  running = true;
}

/**
 * Waits till a request is made for making a connection
 */
public synchronized void run() {
  while(running) {
    try {
      wait();
    } catch(InterruptedException ie) {}

    if(running) connect();
  }
}

/**
 * Calling threads must use this method to make a connection
 * providing the URL to connect to
 */
public synchronized void makeConnection(String url) {
  makeConnection(url, null);
}

public synchronized void makeConnection(String url, BlogEntry entry) {
  this.url = url;
  this.entry = entry;
  notify();
}

/**
 * Tries to make a connection with the network server, using the
 * URL that is provided to the makeConnection method
 */
private void connect() {
```

```
InputStream in = null;
OutputStream out = null;

 try {

   // first encode the URL String
   controller.activityMessage("Encoding URL ...");
   String encodedURL = URLEncoder.encodeURL(this.url);

   // next get an HttpConnection on this URL
   controller.activityMessage("Opening connection ...");
   connection =
     (HttpConnection)Connector.open(encodedURL);

   // now check if this connection contains a media object by way
   // of an Entry object
   // if yes, then make this connection via HTTP POST
   if(this.entry != null) {

     // get the media data from this entry
     byte[] mediaData = ((MediaBlogEntry)entry).getMediaData();

     // set connection type and content length
     connection.setRequestMethod(HttpConnection.POST);
     connection.setRequestProperty(
       "Content-Length", (mediaData.length) + "");

     // open the OutputStream over which the media data will be sent
     out = connection.openOutputStream();

     // write the media data over this stream
     controller.activityMessage("Sending media data ...");
     out.write(mediaData);

     // to actually flush the stream check the response code
     int responseCode = connection.getResponseCode();

     if(responseCode != HttpConnection.HTTP_OK)
       throw new IOException("Transmission failed as server " +
         "responded with response code: " + responseCode);
   }

   // now irrespective of whether it was a POST or GET,
   // simply display to the user the response from the server

   // grab the input stream
   controller.activityMessage("Reading response ...");
   in = connection.openInputStream();
```

```
      // this can take a long time.. so check if the user has cancelled
      // before this
      if(cancel) return;

      // see the response and make sure it is not more than
      // 255 characters long
      int contentLength = (int)connection.getLength();
      if (contentLength == -1) contentLength = 255;
      byte[] data = new byte[contentLength];
      int length = in.read(data);

      // create a response message
      String message = new String(data, 0, length);
      midlet.message(message, 3000);

      // and process the type of the message
      processMessage(message);
    }
    catch (IOException ioe) {
      midlet.error(ioe); // show error
    } finally {

      // close connections
      if (!cancel) {
        try {
          if (in != null) in.close();
          if (out != null) out.close();
          if (connection != null) connection.close();
        }
        catch (IOException ie) {}
      }

      this.cancel = false;

    }
  }

  /**
   * This method is a way for the NetworkRunner to inform the rest of the
   * classes about the state of logging, registering and posting
   */
  private void processMessage(String message) {
    if(message == null) return;

    message = message.trim();

    if(message.equals("Logged In!")) { logInSuccess = true; }
    else if(message.equals("Registered")) registerSuccess = true;
```

```
    else if(message.equals("Posted")) postSuccess = true;
  }

  public boolean isLoggedIn() { return this.logInSuccess; }
  public boolean isRegistered() { return this.registerSuccess; }
  public boolean isPosted() { return this.postSuccess; }

  /**
   * Cancel the network attempt
   */
  public void cancel() {
    try {
      cancel = true;
      if (connection != null) connection.close();
    } catch (IOException io) {} // ignore
  }

}
```

This listing is complete code and makes use of the `Controller`, `BootstrapMIDlet`, and the `URLEncoder` classes, which you'll encounter soon.

When this class is created in a thread and started, the `run()` method kicks into an infinite loop. However, this method lies in wait until `notify()` is called from the `makeConnection()` method. Classes that need to make a connection call this method, providing the URL to connect to. In case the connection needs to be done to post a `BlogEntry` to the server, an instance of that object is provided as well.

The `connect()` method makes the actual connection. All URLs are invoked using the HTTP `GET` method, except when an entry is being posted, in which case, the `POST` method is used. Actual media data is posted by opening an `OutputStream` and sending data across to it (the corresponding server process must accept the opening of such a connection).

The server sends simple strings back, which, in case of successful completion, will be one of three values: "Logged In!", "Registered", or "Posted". In this sense, this class is tied in with the Device Blog MIDlet application. You can remove these values and simply return the message returned by the server to make this class generic and useful in other applications.

In case of error, the `BootstrapMIDlet` is used to convey an error message, whereas the `Controller` class is used to display messages representing system activity that may take a while and that the user could possibly cancel. You'll see these methods shortly.

Before making a connection, the `connect()` method encodes the URL using the `URLEncoder` class. This is important to do because the user may type messages that contain characters that are invalid for use over HTTP. Listing 9-8 shows this class, which contains a single method `encodeURL()`.

Listing 9-8. `URLEncoder` *Class Contains a Single Method to Encode URLs*

```
package com.apress.chapter9.utils;

public class URLEncoder {
```

```
  private static char getHex(int val) {
    if (val < 10) return (char)('0' + val);
    else return (char)('A' + (val - 10));
}

  public static String encodeURL(String url) {

    // the return encoded URL
    StringBuffer returnURL = new StringBuffer();

    // the length
    int size = url.length();

    for(int i = 0; i < size; i++) {

      // iterate over each character
      char ch = url.charAt(i);

      // if alphnumeric, it remains as such
      if ((ch >= '0' && ch <= '9') ||
         (ch >= 'a' && ch <= 'z') ||
         (ch >= 'A' && ch <= 'Z'))
           returnURL.append(ch);
      else {

        // non alphanumeric

        // see first if this is one of the special characters.
        int spec = special.indexOf(ch);

        if (spec >= 0) {

          // this character is not in the special chars
          // String defined later
          returnURL.append(ch);

        } else {

          // use the hex converter for the rest of the characters

          // first add the % character
          returnURL.append('%');

          // next convert the high bits
          returnURL.append(getHex((ch & 0xF0) >> 4));

          // and finally the low bits
          returnURL.append(getHex(ch & 0x0F));
```

```
            }
          }
        }

        // the final encoded url
        return returnURL.toString();
      }

      private static String special = "=&:/?\".-!~*_'()";
    }
```

Creating the View

The view contains several classes, some of which are mundane, such as `GenericList` and `GenericForm`, which serve no purpose by being listed here. (You can see these classes in the Downloads section on the Apress Web site.) Instead, Listing 9-9 shows the code for the `EditableDisplay` interface, which acts as the base from which all editable screens will be created.

Listing 9-9. `EditableDisplay` *Is the Base Interface for All Editable Objects*

```
package com.apress.chapter9.view;

/**
 * An EditableDisplay interface specifies custom objects that can be shown on
 * a screen
 */
public interface EditableDisplay {

  /**
   * The method that all these objects must implement
   */
  public void showDisplay();

}
```

The first class created from this interface is the `EditForm` abstract class. This class is shown in Listing 9-10.

Listing 9-10. `EditForm` *Class Implements* `EditableDisplay`

```
package com.apress.chapter9.view;

import javax.microedition.lcdui.Form;
import javax.microedition.lcdui.Command;
import javax.microedition.lcdui.CommandListener;
```

```
import com.apress.chapter9.model.BlogEntry;
import com.apress.chapter9.control.Controller;

/**
 * The EditForm is the super class for editing form based blog entries.
 * Subclasses have the task of displaying the contents to the user
 */
public abstract class EditForm extends Form
  implements EditableDisplay, CommandListener {

  // the controller object
  protected Controller controller = null;

  // the commands
  protected Command okCommand = null;
  protected Command exitCommand = null;

  // and the blog entry object
  protected BlogEntry entry = null;

  protected EditForm(Controller controller, BlogEntry entry) {
    super("Edit Form");

    // controller and entry are essential, and must not be null
    if(controller == null || entry == null)
      throw new IllegalArgumentException("Controller or entry cannot be null");

    this.controller = controller;
    this.entry = entry;

    // create commands
    okCommand = new Command("Ok", Command.OK, 1);
    exitCommand = new Command("Exit", Command.EXIT, 1);

    // add them to the Form
    addCommand(okCommand);
    addCommand(exitCommand);

    // and set the controller as the listener for commamnds
    setCommandListener(this);
  }

  /**
   * Returns the associated blog entry
   */
```

```
  public BlogEntry getBlogEntry() {
    return this.entry;
  }


}
```

The EditForm class is abstract but provides a concrete protected constructor, which creates items common to all subclasses. This class can now be used as a template for creating editable forms that will have an OK and an EXIT command attached to them. Note that each form will have a corresponding BlogEntry object attached with it, because a form must contain an entry that is being edited. Each form will also have a corresponding handle to the controller object. Listing 9-11 shows the code for the TextEditForm class that extends the EditForm class and will be used to create the screen shown in Figure 9-8.

Listing 9-11. TextEditForm *Used to Create Editable Form Screens for Text Blog Entries*

```
package com.apress.chapter9.view.impl;

import javax.microedition.lcdui.Command;
import javax.microedition.lcdui.TextField;
import javax.microedition.lcdui.Displayable;

import com.apress.chapter9.view.EditForm;
import com.apress.chapter9.model.BlogEntry;
import com.apress.chapter9.control.Controller;
import com.apress.chapter9.view.PreviewCanvas;
import com.apress.chapter9.model.TextBlogEntry;

/**
 * TextEditForm extends EditForm and is used for standalone text entries and
 * for editing text of media-based entries
 */
public class TextEditForm extends EditForm {

  // the title of this blog entry
  private TextField title = null;

  // the message of this blog entry
  private TextField message = null;

  public TextEditForm(Controller controller, BlogEntry entry) {

    super(controller, entry);

    // cast the entry to the right type
    TextBlogEntry textEntry = (TextBlogEntry)entry;
```

```
    // create the TextFields
    title =
      new TextField("Title", textEntry.getEntryTitle(), 255, TextField.ANY);
    message = new TextField(
      "Message", textEntry.getEntryMessage(), 255, TextField.ANY);

    // and append them to this Form
    append(title);
    append(message);
  }

  /**
   * The showDisplay() method displays the text entry fields to the user
   */
  public void showDisplay() {
    controller.getDisplay().setCurrent(this);
  }

  public void commandAction(Command cmd, Displayable disp) {

    int commandType = cmd.getCommandType();

    if(commandType == Command.EXIT) {
      controller.processExit();
      return;
    } else if(commandType == Command.OK) {
      // to be added
    }
  }
}
```

The subclasses of the `EditForm` class are responsible for handling the commands, OK and EXIT. In Listing 9-11, the EXIT command is handled by invoking a method in the controller object. You'll add code for the OK command later.

The constructor for `TextEditForm` creates two text fields and attaches them to the `Form` using the `append()` method. The `showDisplay()` method, inherited from `EditableDisplay`, then simply shows this form on the screen. As expected, the constructor also receives a `BlogEntry` object, which can be cast to an appropriate `TextBlogEntry`. Notice that this class is in the `com.apress.chapter9.view.impl` package, instead of the `com.apress.chapter9.view` package.

It shouldn't be hard to see how to create the `EditCanvas` class, which will be used to create editable canvas subclasses for image, audio, and video as shown earlier in Figure 9-20. Listing 9-12 shows the code for the `EditCanvas` class, which also implements the `EditableDisplay` interface from Listing 9-9.

Listing 9-12. EditCanvas *Class Used As the Base Class to Create Editable Canvases*

```
package com.apress.chapter9.view;

import javax.microedition.lcdui.Canvas;
import javax.microedition.lcdui.Command;
import javax.microedition.lcdui.Graphics;
import javax.microedition.lcdui.CommandListener;

import com.apress.chapter9.model.BlogEntry;
import com.apress.chapter9.control.Controller;

/**
 * The EditCanvas is the super class for editing blog entries. Subclasses
 * have the task of displaying the contents to the user
 */
public abstract class EditCanvas extends Canvas
  implements EditableDisplay, CommandListener {

  // the controller object
  protected Controller controller = null;

  // the commands
  protected Command doneCommand = null;
  protected Command exitCommand = null;

  // the blog entry
  protected BlogEntry entry = null;

  protected EditCanvas(Controller controller, BlogEntry entry) {

    super();

    // controller and entry are essential, and must not be null
    if(controller == null || entry == null)
      throw new IllegalArgumentException("Controller or entry cannot be null");

    this.controller = controller;
    this.entry = entry;

    // create commands
    doneCommand = new Command("Done", Command.OK, 1);
    exitCommand = new Command("Exit", Command.EXIT, 1);
```

```
    // add them to the Canvas
    addCommand(doneCommand);
    addCommand(exitCommand);

    // and set the controller as the listener for commands
    setCommandListener(this);
  }

  public void paint(Graphics g) {

    // first clear the screen
    g.setColor(0xFF8040);
    g.fillRect(0, 0, getWidth(), getHeight());

    // and then make a canvas with a border
    g.setColor(0x808040);
    g.fillRect(5, 5, getWidth() - 10, getHeight() - 10);

    // the rest of the work is left to subclasses

  }

}
```

Of course, `EditCanvas` must override the `paint()` method inherited from the `Canvas` class. However, it only clears the background, and subclasses are left to do the rest of the work. The protected constructor does tasks similar to the `EditForm` class and provides the basic infrastructure for subclasses, which must also provide implementation for the `showDisplay()` method. Listing 9-13 shows the code for the `AudioEditCanvas`, and the rest of the implementations are in code in the Downloads sections of the Apress Web site.

Listing 9-13. `AudioEditCanvas` *Used As the Editable Canvas for Audio Recordings*

```
package com.apress.chapter9.view.impl;

import java.io.IOException;
import java.io.ByteArrayInputStream;
import java.io.ByteArrayOutputStream;

import javax.microedition.lcdui.Image;
import javax.microedition.lcdui.Command;
import javax.microedition.lcdui.Graphics;
import javax.microedition.lcdui.Displayable;

import javax.microedition.media.Player;
import javax.microedition.media.Manager;
import javax.microedition.media.control.RecordControl;
```

```
import com.apress.chapter9.BlogException;

import com.apress.chapter9.model.BlogEntry;
import com.apress.chapter9.model.AudioBlogEntry;

import com.apress.chapter9.view.EditCanvas;
import com.apress.chapter9.view.PreviewCanvas;

import com.apress.chapter9.control.Controller;

/**
 * AudioEditCanvas is used to edit/record audio blog entry
 */
public class AudioEditCanvas extends EditCanvas implements Runnable {

  private Player capturePlayer = null;
  private RecordControl recordControl = null;
  private ByteArrayOutputStream bos = null;

  public AudioEditCanvas(Controller controller, BlogEntry entry) {
    super(controller, entry);
  }

  public void showDisplay() {

    // make this canvas the current display item
    controller.getDisplay().setCurrent(this);

    // repaint
    repaint();

    // and start the audio recording process
    new Thread(this).start();
  }

  public void run() {
    startAudioRecording();
  }

  public void paint(Graphics g) {

    // first call the superclass method
    super.paint(g);

    // now draw the mic image in the foreground
    try {
      g.drawImage(Image.createImage(
        getClass().getResourceAsStream("/media/images/chapter9/mic.gif")),
```

```
        getWidth()/2, getHeight()/2, Graphics.VCENTER | Graphics.HCENTER);
    } catch(IOException ioex) {} // ignore exception

    // also draw a message in white
    g.setColor(0x000000);

    g.drawString("Recording .... ",
      (getWidth()/2), (getHeight()/2) + 30, Graphics.TOP | Graphics.HCENTER);

  }

  private void startAudioRecording() {

    try {

      // create the capture player
      capturePlayer = Manager.createPlayer("capture://audio");

      if (capturePlayer != null) {

        // if created, realize it
        capturePlayer.realize();

        // and grab the RecordControl
        recordControl = (RecordControl)capturePlayer.getControl(
          "javax.microedition.media.control.RecordControl");

        // if RecordControl is null throw exception
        if(recordControl == null)
          throw new BlogException("RecordControl not available for audio");

        // create the buffer in which recording will be done
        bos = new ByteArrayOutputStream();

        // set the output of recording
        recordControl.setRecordStream(bos);

        // start the underlying player
        capturePlayer.start();

        // and the actual recorder
        recordControl.startRecord();

      } else {
        throw new Exception("Capture Audio Player is not available");
      }
```

```
    } catch(Exception e) {
      cleanUp(e);
    }

  }

  public void commandAction(Command cmd, Displayable disp) {

    int commandType = cmd.getCommandType();

    if(commandType == Command.EXIT) {
      controller.processExit();
      return;
    } else if(commandType == Command.OK) {

      // complete the recording

      try {
        // flush the output buffer
        bos.flush();

        // commit the recording
        recordControl.commit();

        // close the player
        capturePlayer.close();

        capturePlayer = null;

      } catch(Exception ex) {
        cleanUp(ex);
        return;
      }

      // set the media data on this entry
      ((AudioBlogEntry)entry).setMediaData(bos.toByteArray());

      // set the media content type
      ((AudioBlogEntry)entry).setContentType(recordControl.getContentType());

      // release the resources
      bos = null;
      recordControl = null;

      // create a preview canvas and set this entry for it
      AudioPreviewCanvas pCanvas = new AudioPreviewCanvas(controller, entry);
```

```
      // and show it
      pCanvas.showCanvas();
    }
  }

  /**
   * This method is used to clean up and release resources on error
   */
  private void cleanUp(Exception e) {

    // release resources on error
    if(recordControl != null) { recordControl = null; }
    if(capturePlayer != null) {
      capturePlayer.close();
      capturePlayer = null;
    }

    // and show the user the message
    controller.message(e.getMessage());
  }
}
```

AudioEditCanvas does a lot of work because it handles the recording of audio as a blog entry. When its showDisplay() method is called, it repaints the screen with a simple image and a message and then starts a thread that actually tries to capture audio via the startRecording() method. When the user is done recording, the OK command handler wraps up the data in the associated AudioBlogEntry using the setMediaData(byte[] data) method. After this is done, it tries to clean up resources such as the RecordControl and the associated Player instances by closing them and then setting them to null, so that the Garbage Collector can reclaim them and free up resources.

After the recording is created successfully, the user should be able to hear it and preview it by creating the AudioPreviewCanvas with the controller and the AudioBlogEntry.

Listing 9-9 didn't have any code for the OK command handler, so Listing 9-13 needs to set the title and message on the associated TextBlogEntry and display the TextPreviewCanvas. This is similar to what you've done with the OK command handler for the AudioEditCanvas. This is shown here:

```
// get the values from the form, and set them in the entry
((TextBlogEntry)entry).setEntryTitle(title.getString());
((TextBlogEntry)entry).setEntryMessage(message.getString());

// create a preview canvas and set the entry for it
TextPreviewCanvas pCanvas = new TextPreviewCanvas(controller, entry);

// and show it
pCanvas.showCanvas();
```

Of course, you haven't created any preview canvases yet. Let's take a look at Listing 9-14, which shows the abstract class, PreviewCanvas.

Listing 9-14. `PreviewCanvas` *Is the Base Abstract Class for All Preview Canvases*

```
package com.apress.chapter9.view;

import javax.microedition.lcdui.Canvas;
import javax.microedition.lcdui.Command;
import javax.microedition.lcdui.Graphics;
import javax.microedition.lcdui.Displayable;
import javax.microedition.lcdui.CommandListener;

import com.apress.chapter9.model.BlogEntry;
import com.apress.chapter9.control.Controller;
import com.apress.chapter9.view.impl.TextEditForm;

/**
 * The PreviewCanvas is the superclass for previewing blog entries to the
 * user. Subclasses have the task of displaying the contents to the user
 */
public abstract class PreviewCanvas extends Canvas
  implements CommandListener {

  // the controller object
  protected Controller controller = null;

  // the BlogEntry
  protected BlogEntry entry = null;

  // the commands
  protected Command postEntryCommand = null;
  protected Command discardEntryCommand = null;
  protected Command editTextCommand = null;
  protected Command exitCommand = null;

  protected PreviewCanvas(Controller controller, BlogEntry entry) {
    super();

    // controller and entry are essential and must not be null
    if(controller == null || entry == null)
      throw new IllegalArgumentException("Controller or entry cannot be null");

    this.controller = controller;
    this.entry = entry;

    // create commands
    postEntryCommand = new Command("Post Entry", Command.OK, 2);
    discardEntryCommand = new Command("Discard Entry", Command.CANCEL, 2);
    editTextCommand = new Command("Edit Text", Command.SCREEN, 2);
    exitCommand = new Command("Exit", Command.EXIT, 1);
```

```
    // add them to the Canvas
    addCommand(postEntryCommand);
    addCommand(discardEntryCommand);
    addCommand(editTextCommand);
    addCommand(exitCommand);

    // and set the controller as the listener for commamnds
    setCommandListener(this);
  }

  /**
   * Partially done paint method, which only paints the background
   */
  public void paint(Graphics g) {

    // first clear the screen
    g.setColor(0xFF8040);
    g.fillRect(0, 0, getWidth(), getHeight());

    // and then make a canvas with a border
    g.setColor(0x808040);
    g.fillRect(5, 5, getWidth() - 10, getHeight() - 10);

    // the rest of the work is left to subclasses

  }

  public void commandAction(Command cmd, Displayable disp) {

    // first grab the type of the command
    int commandType = cmd.getCommandType();

    if(commandType == Command.EXIT) {

      // let the controller process the exit
      controller.processExit();

    } else if(commandType == Command.SCREEN) { // means editing text

      // create a new text edit form with the BlogEntry
      TextEditForm form = new TextEditForm(controller, entry);

      // and show it
      form.showDisplay();

    } else if(commandType == Command.CANCEL) { // means discard entry
```

```
      // simply show the startup list
      controller.getDisplay().setCurrent(controller.getStartUpList());

    } else if(commandType == Command.OK) { // means post entry to server

      controller.postEntry(entry);
    }
  }

  /**
   * Subclasses must implement this method as they see fit to show the contents
   * of this canvas
   */
  public abstract void showCanvas();
}
```

This class is very similar to the EditCanvas, in that it creates a background but leaves the full painting to subclasses. However, this class does offer implementations for handling the various commands that are associated with it. These commands are Exit, Edit Text, Discard Entry, and Post Entry commands, as shown earlier in Figure 9-10. Thus, subclasses only need to worry about painting the partially done canvas as they see fit, leaving command handling to this class.

Listing 9-15 shows the code for the ImagePreviewCanvas. With most of the work handled by the superclass, this class only needs to work on its paint() method to display the image in the associated ImageBlogEntry object.

Listing 9-15. ImagePreviewCanvas *Shows the Associated Image to the User As a Preview*

```
package com.apress.chapter9.view.impl;

import java.io.IOException;
import java.io.ByteArrayInputStream;
import javax.microedition.lcdui.Image;
import javax.microedition.lcdui.Graphics;

import javax.microedition.media.Player;
import javax.microedition.media.Manager;

import com.apress.chapter9.control.Controller;

import com.apress.chapter9.view.PreviewCanvas;

import com.apress.chapter9.model.BlogEntry;
import com.apress.chapter9.model.ImageBlogEntry;

public class ImagePreviewCanvas extends PreviewCanvas {
```

```
  public ImagePreviewCanvas(Controller controller, BlogEntry entry) {
    super(controller, entry);
    setTitle("Image Entry Preview");
  }

  public void showCanvas() {

    // make this canvas as the current display item
    controller.getDisplay().setCurrent(this);

    // and then repaint it
    repaint();
  }

  public void paint(Graphics g) {

    // get the superclass to clear background and repaint it first
    super.paint(g);

    // now simply create an Image from the byte array, and show it on
    // the canvas
    Image snapshot = null;

    try {

      ImageBlogEntry imgEntry = ((ImageBlogEntry)entry);
      byte[] imgData = imgEntry.getMediaData();
      snapshot = Image.createImage(imgData, 0, imgData.length);

    } catch(Exception e) {

      // show the error message to the user
      controller.message(e.getMessage());

      // and return
      return;
    }

    // now draw the image on this canvas
    g.drawImage(snapshot, getWidth()/2, getHeight()/2,
      Graphics.HCENTER | Graphics.VCENTER);
  }

}
```

The showDisplay() method makes this canvas as the current display object and then calls repaint(), where the image data contained in the associated ImageBlogEntry is displayed on the screen using the Graphics object. Similarly, Listing 9-16 contains the code for the

VideoPreviewCanvas, which uses a video Player instance to preview the video to the user by using roughly the same principles.

Listing 9-16. VideoPreviewCanvas *Previews the Video to the User*

```
package com.apress.chapter9.view.impl;

import java.io.IOException;
import java.io.ByteArrayInputStream;
import javax.microedition.lcdui.Image;
import javax.microedition.lcdui.Graphics;

import javax.microedition.media.Player;
import javax.microedition.media.Manager;
import javax.microedition.media.MediaException;
import javax.microedition.media.control.VideoControl;

import com.apress.chapter9.control.Controller;

import com.apress.chapter9.view.PreviewCanvas;

import com.apress.chapter9.model.BlogEntry;
import com.apress.chapter9.model.VideoBlogEntry;

public class VideoPreviewCanvas extends PreviewCanvas {

  public VideoPreviewCanvas(Controller controller, BlogEntry entry) {
    super(controller, entry);
    setTitle("Video Entry Preview");
  }

  public void showCanvas() {

    // make this canvas as the current display item
    controller.getDisplay().setCurrent(this);

    // and then repaint it
    repaint();

    // finally play back the recording
    playbackVideoRecording();

  }

  public void paint(Graphics g) {
```

```
    // get the superclass to clear the background and repaint it first
    super.paint(g);
  }

  private void playbackVideoRecording() {

    VideoBlogEntry vEntry = (VideoBlogEntry)entry;

    ByteArrayInputStream bis =
      new ByteArrayInputStream(vEntry.getMediaData());

    Player player = null;
    VideoControl vControl = null;

    try {

      // create the Playback player
      player = Manager.createPlayer(bis, vEntry.getContentType());

      // realize it
      player.realize();

      // create the playback video control
      vControl = (VideoControl)player.getControl(
        "javax.microedition.media.control.VideoControl");

      // initialize it
      vControl.initDisplayMode(VideoControl.USE_DIRECT_VIDEO, this);

      vControl.setDisplayLocation(5, 5);

      try {
        vControl.setDisplaySize(getWidth() - 10, getHeight() - 10);
      } catch (MediaException me) {} // ignore

      vControl.setVisible(true);

      // start it
      player.start();

     } catch(Exception e) {

      // release this player instance
      if(player != null) { player.close(); player = null; }

      // show the error message to the user
      controller.message(e.getMessage());
```

```
      // and return
      return;
    }
  }
}
```

The AudioPreviewCanvas is similar and is provided in the Downloads section of the Apress Web site.

This finishes the code listings for the view part. The only classes left are those of the control part, which hold the model and the view together.

Creating the Control Classes

As you may recall, the control classes are the BootstrapMIDlet class, which starts the Device Blog MIDlet, and the Controller class, which is the glue that holds this MIDlet together. The BootstrapMIDlet is shown in Listing 9-17.

Listing 9-17. BootstrapMIDlet *Is the Entry Point for the Device Blog MIDlet Application*

```
package com.apress.chapter9.control;

import javax.microedition.lcdui.Alert;
import javax.microedition.lcdui.Display;
import javax.microedition.lcdui.Command;
import javax.microedition.midlet.MIDlet;

import com.apress.chapter9.BlogException;
import com.apress.chapter9.model.BlogServer;
import com.apress.chapter9.utils.NetworkRunner;

/**
 * BootstrapMIDlet is the startup MIDlet that loads the initial data and
 * starts the service. If any initial parameters are missing, it will abort.
 * It requires the URLs for posting, logging, and registering defined in the
 * MIDlet JAD and manifest file.
 */
public class BootstrapMIDlet extends MIDlet {

  // the display
  private Display display = null;

  // the controller that will drive this MIDlet
  private Controller controller = null;

  // the thread in which this MIDlet will be run
  private Thread runner = null;

  // the thread used for creating network connections
  private NetworkRunner networkThread = null;
```

```
// the BlogServer contains the URL information
private BlogServer blogServer = null;

// flag to indicate if any error occurs
private boolean error = false;

public void startApp() {

  if(display == null) {
    // get the display
    display = Display.getDisplay(this);

    // load the initial URL parameters
    try {
      loadParameters();
    } catch(BlogException be) {
      error(be);
    }

    // create the new Controller passing this MIDlet as the reference
    controller = new Controller(this);

    // create the runner thread
    runner = new Thread(controller);

    // create the Network Runner thread
    networkThread = new NetworkRunner(this, controller);

    runner.start();
    networkThread.start();
  }
}

/**
 * loads the URL parameters from the Manifest
 */
private void loadParameters() throws BlogException {

  // the registration URL
  String registerURL = getAppProperty("Blog-registerURL");

  // the login URL
  String loginURL = getAppProperty("Blog-loginURL");

  // the URL for posting entries
  String postEntryURL = getAppProperty("Blog-postURL");
```

```
    // if any of them is null or not defined, throw Exception
    if(registerURL == null || registerURL.length() == 0 ||
       loginURL == null || loginURL.length() == 0 ||
       postEntryURL == null || postEntryURL.length() == 0)
      throw new BlogException("One of the Blog server URL's is not defined.");

    // otherwise create the BlogServer information object
    blogServer = new BlogServer(registerURL, loginURL, postEntryURL);
  }

  // getter for BlogServer
  public BlogServer getBlogServer() { return this.blogServer; }

  // getter for Display
  public Display getDisplay() { return this.display; }

  // getter for NetworkThread
  public NetworkRunner getNetworkRunner() { return this.networkThread; }

  public void pauseApp() {
  }

  public void destroyApp(boolean unconditional) {
  }

  /**
   * General purpose nonerror message display method
   */
  public void message(String msg, int time) {
    Alert alert = new Alert("Message");
    alert.setString(msg);
    alert.setTimeout(time);

    display.setCurrent(alert, controller.getStartUpList());
  }

  /**
   * General purpose error message display method
   */
  public void error(Exception e) {
    Alert alert = new Alert("Error");
    alert.setString(e.getMessage());
    alert.setTimeout(Alert.FOREVER);

    display.setCurrent(alert, controller.getStartUpList());
```

```
      error = true;
    }
  }
```

The BootstrapMIDlet class loads the parameters for the blog server from the JAD file, initializes the Controller class and the NetworkRunner class, starts these threads (all in the startApp() method), and provides utility methods for showing error and normal message to the user.

The Controller actively controls the flow of the MIDlet application. It creates the GenericForm and GenericList classes and handles the commands associated with them. It leaves most of the command handling of the Preview and Edit canvases to these canvases themselves, but it keeps the task of posting entries to the server to itself. In the interest of conserving space, the complete code for this class is not listed here, but only a few code snippets. First, Listing 9-18 shows the code for the postEntry(BlogEntry entry) method.

Listing 9-18. postEntry(BlogEntry entry) *Method of the* Controller *Class*

```
/**
 * Has the responsibility of posting an entry to the server
 */
public void postEntry(BlogEntry entry) {

  // first show the message to the user
  activityMessage("Connecting to server ... ");

  // now get the post entry url
  String postURL = midlet.getBlogServer().getPostEntryURL();

  // construct the parameters in the URL
  postURL += "?title=" + entry.getEntryTitle() +
             "&message=" + entry.getEntryMessage() +
             "&dateposted=" + System.currentTimeMillis() +
             "&uName=" + entry.getUser().getUserName();

  // and use the network runner to post the URL based on the
  // type of the entry
  if(entry instanceof MediaBlogEntry) {

    MediaBlogEntry mediaEntry = ((MediaBlogEntry)entry);

    String type =
      ((mediaEntry instanceof AudioBlogEntry) ? "audio" :
      ((mediaEntry instanceof ImageBlogEntry) ? "image" : "video"));

    getNetworkRunner().makeConnection(
      postURL +
      "&media=" + mediaEntry.guessFileExtension() +
      "&type=" + type +
      "&mediasize=" + mediaEntry.getMediaData().length, entry);
```

```
  } else {
    getNetworkRunner().makeConnection(postURL);
  }
}
```

This method makes a distinction between posting text entries and media entries. If a media entry is being posted, it puts extra information about the entry, including the type of media, the size of the media, and expected file extension in the URL, as a query string. If a text-based entry is being sent, only the normal parameters, such as title, message, date posted, and username, are provided.

Listing 9-19 provides the code snippet of the `Controller` class handling the user selection for the type of blog entry to create, as shown earlier in Figure 9-6.

Listing 9-19. *Handling User Selection of Type of* `BlogEntry`

```
// if the user wants to create an entry
int selectedIdx = actionList.getSelectedIndex();

// initialize the display
EditableDisplay editDisplay = null;

// and the associated entry
BlogEntry blogEntry = null;

// now based on what type of entry it is, create the right
// editable display and entry
switch(selectedIdx) {
  case 0: // text only
  {
    blogEntry = new TextBlogEntry(user);
    editDisplay = new TextEditForm(this, blogEntry);
    break;
  }
  case 1: // audio
  {
    blogEntry = new AudioBlogEntry(user);
    editDisplay = new AudioEditCanvas(this, blogEntry);
    break;
  }
  case 2: // image
  {
    blogEntry = new ImageBlogEntry(user);
    editDisplay = new ImageEditCanvas(this, blogEntry);
    break;
  }
  case 3: // only case left, video
  {
    blogEntry = new VideoBlogEntry(user);
    editDisplay = new VideoEditCanvas(this, blogEntry);
```

```
        break;
    }
}

editDisplay.showDisplay();
```

Based on the user selection, the code creates the appropriate type of BlogEntry and editing form. In the end, the code invokes the showDisplay() method of EditableDisplay interface to display the right editing canvas/form created with the right BlogEntry type.

On the Server Side

The code for the server side contains four very simple JSP-based pages. To keep things simple, this example is using a file-based blogging system instead of blogging entries to a database. The postentry.jsp file receives the entries from the user and files them into user-based directories. This file is shown in Listing 9-20.

Listing 9-20. postentry.jsp *Accepts Blog Entries from the Device Blog and Files Them in the File System*

```
<%@ page contentType="text/plain;charset=UTF-8" language="java"
  import="java.io.File, java.io.*" %>

<%--
  Simple postentry.jsp tries to post an entry to the server
--%>

<%

  String title = (String)request.getParameter("title");
  String message = (String)request.getParameter("message");
  String datePosted = (String)request.getParameter("dateposted");
  String username = (String)request.getParameter("uName");
  String media = (String)request.getParameter("media");
  String type = (String)request.getParameter("type");
  String mediaSize = (String)request.getParameter("mediasize");

  // only username is a required value
  if(username == null || username.length() == 0) {

    out.println("Required parameter username is missing");
    return;
  }

  // now find out the working dir
  String workingDir = System.getProperty("user.dir");
```

```
// try to get to the user directory with the given username
// this assumes a specific working directory, change if you put files in
// different places
File userDir = new File(
  workingDir + "/webapps/MMAPI/deviceblog/users/" + username);

if(!userDir.exists()) {

  out.println("Internal error: no user directory");
  return;

}

// set the title if it is missing
if(title == null || title.equals("null") || title.length() == 0) {
  title = "Untitled " + (type == null ? "Text" : type) + " entry";
}

// try and figure out the date posted value
long datePostedLong = 0L;

if(datePosted == null) datePostedLong = System.currentTimeMillis();
else {
  try {
    datePostedLong = Long.parseLong(datePosted, 10);
  } catch (Exception e) {
    datePostedLong = System.currentTimeMillis();
  }
}

// now the file name for this entry will be based on the datePosted value
// but first create, if it doesn't exist, the entries directory for this user
// and also the media directories

File entriesDir = new File(userDir, "entries");

if(!entriesDir.exists()) {
  if(!entriesDir.mkdir()) {

    out.println("Internal error: could not create entries directory");
    return;

  } else {

    // entries directory created, now create the individual media directories
```

```
      new File(entriesDir, "audio").mkdir();
      new File(entriesDir, "video").mkdir();
      new File(entriesDir, "image").mkdir();

    }
  }

  // now see if this is a media entry, before saving the actual text entry
  if(media != null) {

    // this is a media entry

    InputStream in = null;
    FileOutputStream fos = null;

    try {

      // open up an input stream for media data
      in = request.getInputStream();

      // create a byte array to receive this data in
      byte[] rcdData = new byte[new Integer(mediaSize).intValue()];

      // read from the input stream in this byte array
      in.read(rcdData);

      fos = new FileOutputStream(
        new File(entriesDir, type + "/" + datePostedLong + "." + media));

      fos.write(rcdData, 0, rcdData.length);
      fos.flush();

    } catch(IOException ioex) {

      out.println("Internal error: " + ioex.getMessage());
      return;
    } finally {

      try {
        if(fos != null) fos.close();
        if(in != null)  in.close();
      } catch(IOException ix) { return; }

    }

  }
```

```
    // now save this entry
    File entryFile = new File(entriesDir, datePostedLong + ".txt");

    if(!entryFile.createNewFile()) {

      out.println("Internal error: could not create the entry file");
    }

    // now open this file, and write the title and message to it
    FileWriter fw = null;
    try {
      fw = new FileWriter(entryFile);

      // first the title
      fw.write(title, 0, title.length());
      fw.write("\r\n");

      // now the media file location, if any, if there is no media file,
      // still write an empty line
      if(media == null) fw.write("\r\n");
      else {
        fw.write(type + "/" + datePostedLong + "." + media);
        fw.write("\r\n");
      }

      // see if there is a message, if yes, write it
      if(message != null && !message.equals("null"))
        fw.write(message, 0, message.length());

      // flush the buffer
      fw.flush();

    } catch(IOException ioex) {

      out.println("Internal error: " + ioex.getMessage());
      return;

    } finally {

      if(fw != null) {
        try {
          fw.close();
        } catch(IOException io) { return; }
      }

    }

   out.println("Posted");
%>
```

The listing starts with identifying all the parameters in the request and throwing an error that says the required username is not found. It then proceeds to identify the users directory and create any missing ones. Finally, it checks to determine whether the request contains any media data and, if so, saves this in a specific media folder. The actual entry is saved in a date posted file that is also the name for the media file, if any.

The Web site for the blog lists the entries in the order that they are received, and this is done in the `index.jsp` file. This file, along with the `login.jsp` and `register.jsp` files, is in the source code available in the Downloads section of the Apress Web site.

Figure 9-23 shows the Device Blog server (*http://www.mmapibook.com/deviceblog/index.jsp*) as it looks at the moment!

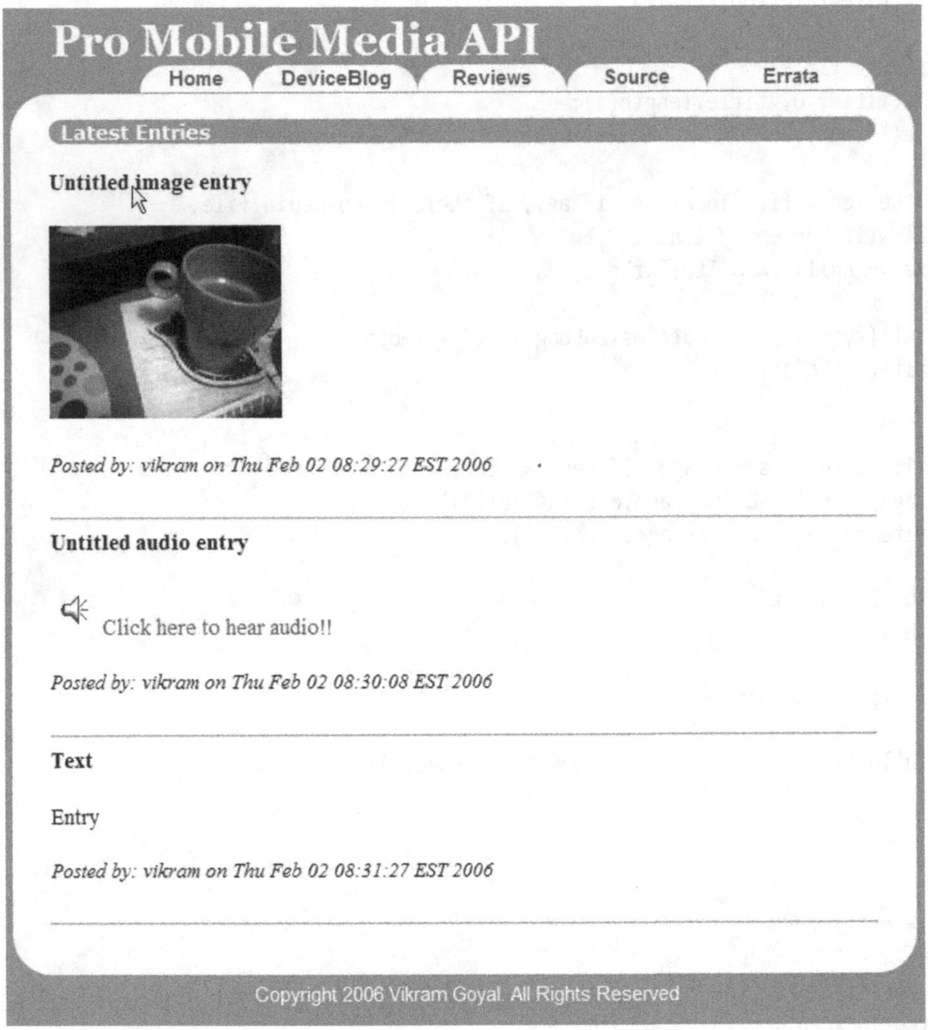

Figure 9-23. *The Device Blog in action!*

Summary

MMAPI is a terrific tool for building purposeful and multimedia-enabled rich applications. However, to make full use of MMAPI, you must know how it works and how it relates to the rest of the APIs in the MIDlet world.

This chapter has culminated the knowledge path that you started in Chapter 1. The Device Blog MIDlet application is a useable and functional application that showcases a thorough use of MMAPI. Device Blog shows that you can successfully integrate MMAPI with the rest of the Java ME API and build business and entertainment applications.

The Device Blog MIDlet application is not complete, however. It can be extended to include MIDI and Tone Blog entries, and the server side can be made more robust and scalable. However, that was not the aim of this case study. It has shown you the way, and you are invited to experiment with it. I look forward to your entries on the Device Blog server!

APPENDIX A

Mobile Media API (MMAPI) Reference

This appendix is a reference to the MMAPI. All classes, interfaces, and exceptions are listed here so that you can find them in one easy-to-use place. The Javadocs, however, remain the best place for getting detailed explanation about each method and class and is used in this appendix to take the one-line explanation of each class, interface, and exception.

This API is listed alphabetically, grouped by package.

Package javax.microedition.media

Interface Control

A Control object is used to control some media processing functions.

```
public interface Control {
  // no methods
}
```

Interface Controllable

Controllable provides an interface for obtaining the controls from an object such as a Player.

```
public interface Controllable {
  // methods
  public Control getControl(java.lang.String controlType);
  public Control[] getControls();
}
```

Class Manager

Manager is the access point for obtaining system-dependent resources such as Player instances for multimedia processing.

```
public final class Manager {
  // Constructors
  public static final java.lang.String MIDI_DEVICE_LOCATOR;
  public static final java.lang.String TONE_DEVICE_LOCATOR;

  // Methods
  public static Player createPlayer(java.lang.String locator)
    throws java.io.IOException, MediaException;
  public static Player createPlayer(
      java.io.InputStream stream, java.lang.String type)
        throws java.io.IOException, MediaException;
  public static Player createPlayer(DataSource source)
    throws java.io.IOException, MediaException;
  public static java.lang.String[] getSupportedContentTypes(
    java.lang.String protocol);
  public static java.lang.String[] getSupportedProtocols(
    java.lang.String content_type);
  public static TimeBase getSystemTimeBase();
  public static void playTone(int note, int duration, int volume)
    throws MediaException;
}
```

Class MediaException

A MediaException indicates an unexpected error condition in a method.

```
public class MediaException extends java.lang.Exception {
  // Constructors
  public MediaException();
  public MediaException(java.lang.String reason);
}
```

Interface Player

Player controls the rendering of time-based media data.

```
public interface Player extends Controllable {
  // Constants
  public static final int CLOSED;
  public static final int PREFETCHED;
  public static final int REALIZED;
  public static final int STARTED;
  public static final long TIME_UNKNOWN;
  public static final int UNREALIZED;
```

```
  // Methods
  public void addPlayerListener(PlayerListener playerListener);
  public void close();
  public void deallocate();
  public java.lang.String getContentType();
  public long getDuration();
  public long getMediaTime();
  public int getState();
  public TimeBase getTimeBase();
  public void prefetch() throws MediaException;
  public void realize() throws MediaException;
  public void removePlayerListener(PlayerListener playerListener);
  public void setLoopCount(int count);
  public long setMediaTime(long now) throws MediaException;
  public void setTimeBase(TimeBase master) throws MediaException;
  public void start() throws MediaException;
  public void stop() throws MediaException;
}
```

Interface PlayerListener

PlayerListener is the interface for receiving asynchronous events generated by Player instances.

```
public interface PlayerListener {
  // Constants
  public static final java.lang.String BUFFERING_STARTED;
  public static final java.lang.String BUFFERING_STOPPED;
  public static final java.lang.String CLOSED;
  public static final java.lang.String DEVICE_AVAILABLE;
  public static final java.lang.String DEVICE_UNAVAILABLE;
  public static final java.lang.String DURATION_UPDATED;
  public static final java.lang.String END_OF_MEDIA;
  public static final java.lang.String ERROR;
  public static final java.lang.String RECORD_ERROR;
  public static final java.lang.String RECORD_STARTED;
  public static final java.lang.String RECORD_STOPPED;
  public static final java.lang.String SIZE_CHANGED;
  public static final java.lang.String STARTED;
  public static final java.lang.String STOPPED;
  public static final java.lang.String STOPPED_AT_TIME;
  public static final java.lang.String VOLUME_CHANGED;

  // Methods
  public void playerUpdate(Player player, java.lang.String event,
                                          java.lang.Object eventData);
}
```

Interface TimeBase

A TimeBase is a constantly ticking source of time.

```
public interface TimeBase {
  // Methods
  public long getTime();
}
```

Package javax.microedition.media.control

Interface FramePositioningControl

The FramePositioningControl is the interface to control precise positioning of a video frame for Player instances.

```
public interface FramePositioningControl extends Control {
  // Methods
  public long mapFrameToTime(int frameNumber);
  public int mapTimeToFrame(long mediaTime);
  public int seek(int frameNumber);
  public int skip(int framesToSkip);
}
```

Interface GUIControl

GUIControl extends Control and is defined for controls that provide GUI functionalities.

```
public interface GUIControl extends Control {
  // Constants
  public static final int USE_GUI_PRIMITIVE;

  // Methods
  public java.lang.Object initDisplayMode(int mode, java.lang.Object arg);
}
```

Interface MetaDataControl

MetaDataControl is used to retrieve metadata information included within the media streams.

```
public interface MetaDataControl extends Control {
  // Constants
  public static final java.lang.String AUTHOR_KEY;
  public static final java.lang.String COPYRIGHT_KEY;
  public static final java.lang.String DATE_KEY;
  public static final java.lang.String TITLE_KEY;
```

```
  // Methods
  public java.lang.String[] getKeys();
  public java.lang.String getKeyValue(java.lang.String key);
}
```

Interface MIDIControl

`MIDIControl` provides access to MIDI rendering and transmitting devices.

```
public interface MIDIControl extends Control {
  // Constants
  public static final int CONTROL_CHANGE;
  public static final int NOTE_ON;

  // Methods
  public int[] getBankList(boolean custom) throws MediaException;
  public int getChannelVolume(int channel);
  public java.lang.String getKeyName(int bank, int prog, int key)
    throws MediaException;
  public int[] getProgram(int channel) throws MediaException;
  public int[] getProgramList(int bank) throws MediaException;
  public java.lang.String getProgramName(int bank, int prog) throws MediaException;
  public boolean isBankQuerySupported();
  public int longMidiEvent(byte[] data, int offset, int length);
  public void setChannelVolume(int channel, int volume);
  public void setProgram(int channel, int bank, int program);
  public void shortMidiEvent(int type, int data1, int data2);
}
```

Interface PitchControl

`PitchControl` raises or lowers the playback pitch of audio without changing the playback speed.

```
public interface PitchControl extends Control {
  // Methods
  public int getMaxPitch();
  public int getMinPitch();
  public int getPitch();
  public int setPitch(int millisemitones);
}
```

Interface RateControl

`RateControl` controls the playback rate of a `Player` instance.

```
public interface RateControl extends Control {
  // Methods
  public int getMaxRate();
  public int getMinRate();
```

```
  public int getRate();
  public int setRate(int millirate);
}
```

Interface RecordControl

RecordControl controls the recording of media from a Player instance.

```
public interface RecordControl extends Control {
  // Methods
  public void commit() throws java.io.IOException;
  public java.lang.String getContentType();
  public void reset() throws java.io.IOException;
  public void setRecordLocation(java.lang.String locator)
    throws java.io.IOException, MediaException;
  public int setRecordSizeLimit(int size) throws MediaException;
  public void setRecordStream(java.io.OutputStream stream);
  public void startRecord();
  public void stopRecord();
}
```

Interface StopTimeControl

StopTimeControl allows one to specify a preset stop time for a Player instance.

```
public interface StopTimeControl extends Control {
  // Constants
  public static final long RESET;

  // Methods
  public long getStopTime();
  public void setStopTime(long stopTime);
}
```

Interface TempoControl

TempoControl controls the tempo, in musical terms, of a song.

```
public interface TempoControl extends RateControl {
  // Methods
  public int getTempo();
  public int setTempo(int millitempo);
}
```

Interface ToneControl

ToneControl is the interface to enable playback of a user-defined monotonic tone sequence.

```
public interface ToneControl extends Control {
  // Constants
  public static final byte BLOCK_END;
  public static final byte BLOCK_START;
  public static final byte C4;
  public static final byte PLAY_BLOCK;
  public static final byte REPEAT;
  public static final byte RESOLUTION;
  public static final byte SET_VOLUME;
  public static final byte SILENCE;
  public static final byte TEMPO;
  public static final byte VERSION;

  // Methods
  public void setSequence(byte[] sequence);
}
```

Interface VideoControl

VideoControl controls the display of video.

```
public interface VideoControl extends GUIControl {
  // Constants
  public static final int USE_DIRECT_VIDEO;

  // Methods
  public int getDisplayHeight();
  public int getDisplayWidth();
  public int getDisplayX();
  public int getDisplayY();
  public byte[] getSnapshot(java.lang.String imageType) throws MediaException;
  public int getSourceHeight();
  public int getSourceWidth();
  public java.lang.Object initDisplayMode(int mode, java.lang.Object arg);
  public void setDisplayFullScreen(boolean fullScreenMode) throws MediaException;
  public void setDisplayLocation(int x, int y);
  public void setDisplaySize(int width, int height) throws MediaException;
  public void setVisible(boolean visible);
}
```

Interface VolumeControl

VolumeControl is an interface for manipulating the audio volume of a Player instance.

```
public interface VolumeControl extends Control {
  // Methods
  public int getLevel();
  public boolean isMuted();
  public int setLevel(int level);
  public void setMute(boolean mute);
}
```

Package javax.microedition.media.protocol

Class ContentDescriptor

A ContentDescriptor identifies media data containers.

```
public class ContentDescriptor {
  // Constructors
  public ContentDescriptor(java.lang.String contentType);

  // Methods
  public java.lang.String getContentType();
}
```

Class DataSource

A DataSource is an abstraction for media protocol handlers.

```
public abstract class DataSource implements Controllable {
  // Constructors
  public DataSource(java.lang.String locator);

  // Methods
  public abstract void connect() throws java.io.IOException;
  public abstract void disconnect();
  public abstract java.lang.String getContentType();
  public java.lang.String getLocator();
  public abstract SourceStream[] getStreams();
  public abstract void start() throws java.io.IOException;
  public abstract void stop() throws java.io.IOException;
}
```

Interface SourceStream

Abstracts a single stream of media data.

```
public interface SourceStream extends Controllable {
  // Constants
  public static final int NOT_SEEKABLE;
  public static final int RANDOM_ACCESSIBLE;
  public static final int SEEKABLE_TO_START;

  // Methods
  public ContentDescriptor getContentDescriptor();
  public long getContentLength();
  public int getSeekType();
  public int getTransferSize();
  public int read(byte[] b, int off, int len) throws java.io.IOException;
  public long seek(long where) throws java.io.IOException;
  public long tell();
}
```

APPENDIX B

URI Syntax for Media Locators

The Uniform Resource Identifier (URI) syntax is described using a Request For Comment (RFC) paper as a universal means of describing the location of different types and kinds of resources. The RFC in question is 2396 and its full text can be accessed at *http://www.ietf.org/rfc/rfc2396.txt*.

Essentially, this RFC defines a way for providing a uniform and consistent way of describing the location of different types of resources, wherever they may be located. This is important to us in MMAPI, because MMAPI, being protocol and format agnostic, requires consistent means to access resources.

URI defines two parts to each identifier string: the scheme part and the scheme specific part separated by a `':'` as shown here:

```
<scheme>:<scheme-specific-part>
```

As it applies to MMAPI, the scheme part is the protocol over which the resource is being referenced, whereas the scheme-specific part is a hierarchical, location-specific string, which tells the system the exact physical location of the resource.

Not surprisingly, the most common example of this is when resources are accessed over the Internet using HTTP. As an example, *http://www.ietf.org/rfc/rfc2396.txt* consists of the scheme "http" and the scheme-specific part of "//www.ietf.org/rfc/rfc2396.txt". The hierarchies in the scheme-specific parts are separated by the "/" character. Thus, `rfc2396.txt` is a physical document located in the `rfc` folder on the `www.ietf.org` server.

Of course, with MMAPI, the scheme part can be an entire range of options. As you have seen in this book, the scheme part can be any one of `capture`, `rtp`, `file`, `resource`, and, of course, `http` strings.

With each scheme part, different options for the scheme-specific part can be set. For capture scheme, you have used the `audio` and `video` scheme-specific parts. These can be further qualified to specify attributes, for example: `capture://audio?encoding=pcm` would give you a specific URI for capturing WAV audio files.

APPENDIX C

Advanced Multimedia Supplements—JSR 234

The Java Community Process (JCP) at *http://www.jcp.org* defines new technology for the Java technology using a community process, whereby new specifications are released for public overview and debated on. Once approved, the specs are introduced in the Java language. One of the most prolific areas of technology development is Java ME, and new APIs are being constantly created and released to target this area of Java development.

Specifications are released with a Java Specification Request (JSR) number. MMAPI was released as JSR 135 (*http://www.jcp.org/en/jsr/detail?id=135*). However, this specification is now more than two years old, and newer advances in technology have necessitated an update. JSR 234 (*http://www.jcp.org/en/jsr/detail?id=234*), titled Advanced Multimedia Supplements, is a step in updating the MMAPI for new technology devices. The final release of this specification was in June 2005.

However, note that JSR 234 is a supplement to JSR 135. Thus, it doesn't replace MMAPI nor is it used on its own, but provides supplementary implementations for newer technology devices. This appendix gives you an overview of the new JSR.

Introduction to JSR 234

JSR 234 was initiated by a Nokia request to create an API that could provide richer experiences to users of mobile devices. Mobile devices are increasing in their processing power capacity, so this enables sophisticated media processing functionalities available to MIDlet developers and distributors. Specifically, better controls for camera, radio and audio, and sophisticated MIDlets created based on them is the target aim of this specification.

The specification creates a new package, `javax.microedition.amms`, where `amms` stands for Advanced Multimedia supplements. The specification mostly defines new controls that are derived from the `javax.microedition.media.control.Control` interface, thus making these controls compatible with MMAPI (as you would expect, as JSR 234 is a supplement to JSR 135). It also defines four new concepts in the main `javax.microedition.amms` package, `GlobalManager`, `Spectator`, `Module`, and `MediaProcessor`.

GlobalManager

GlobalManager is like a Manager class for JSR 234. It provides methods to retrieve the specialized objects present in this specification. However, it doesn't replace or extend the Manager class, and you still use the Manager class for creating and managing Player instances.

Spectator

The Spectator class represents a virtual listener. It provides acoustic controls that can help create MIDlet applications that mimic sound coming from different locations and areas. You can create a Spectator class by using the getSpectator() static method in the GlobalManager class. This class implements the Controllable interface, which allows it to provide implementation of the getControl() and the getControls() methods.

Module

The Module interface is a logical grouping of multiple Player instances and/or MIDI channels. This functionality was missing from MMAPI, where you can treat a group of such instances as one entity. This interface is extended by two subinterfaces, EffectsModule and SoundsSource3D, which represent different types of groupings. EffectsModule represents Player instances and/or MIDI channels, to which a common effect can be applied, whereas SoundsSource3D represents this group in a virtual acoustical space.

Modules can be fetched from the GlobalManager class using the createEffectModule() or the createSoundSource3D() methods. Note that the Module interface also implements the Controllable interface.

MediaProcessor

MediaProcessor is an interface for postprocessing of media data. A MediaProcessor works very much like a Player interface and defines various states that mimic it as well. A MediaProcessor instance can be in one of UNREALIZED, REALIZED, STARTED, or STOPPED states.

You can retrieve an instance of MediaProcessor by using the GlobalManager class's static method createMediaProcessor(String type), passing to it the MIME type of target processor.

This interface also extends the Controllable interface.

Controls

The rest of the interfaces in this API are various controls and are divided in various packages depending on the type of functionality that they provide.

Package javax.microedition.amms.control

There are two main control interfaces in this package that impact the rest of the packages as well.

FormatControl is used for specifying the format of the various media types. This interface is implemented by four different types of media formats using their own interfaces: AudioFormatControl, ContainerFormatControl, ImageFormatControl, and VideoFormatControl.

EffectControl is used to preset a filter on some media data to provide different types of effects. This interface provides a method, setEnabled(boolean enable), to turn the effects on or off. This interface is supported with the EffectOrderControl interface, which controls the order in which multiple effects are applied.

Finally, this package contains the interface PanControl, which controls the panning of audio and video media data, and PriorityControl, which allows the manipulation of the priority given to various Player instances in a group situation.

Packages javax.microedition.amms.control.imageeffect and javax.microedition.amms.control.audioeffect

All of the interfaces in these two packages extend the EffectControl interface and provide various effects that can be applied to audio and image media data.

Package javax.microedition.amms.control.audio3d

All of the interfaces in this package provide controls for manipulation of audio in a 3D environment. The controls are retrieved from either the SoundSource3D or Spectator class, as the case may be.

Package javax.microedition.amms.control.camera

The controls in this package are retrieved from a Player instance that is created by using the Manager.createPlayer("capture://camera") method. These controls provide control over the exposure, the flash, focus, zoom, and burst shooting of snapshots (as opposed to single snapshots using the getSnapshot() method of the VideoControl interface provided in MMAPI). A CameraControl control provides further control over the camera by providing methods for shutter control, camera rotation, and so on.

Package javax.microedition.amms.control.tuner

This package contains two control interfaces for radio tuning. RDSControl is used for Radio Data System (RDS) tuning and provides methods to manage that. TunerControl isn't specifically targeted for radio tuning, but it can be used to tune into any Player instance that supports tuning, however unlikely.

JSR 234 Implementations

At this point, being a relatively new API, there are no known implementations on any devices, and neither is there any known emulator support. However, Nokia provides a reference implementation with some examples, which can be downloaded at *http://forum.nokia.com/java/jsr234*.

Index

T

U